The Drama of History

The Drama of History

Ibsen, Hegel, Nietzsche

KRISTIN GJESDAL

OXFORD
UNIVERSITY PRESS

OXFORD
UNIVERSITY PRESS

Oxford University Press is a department of the University of Oxford. It furthers the University's objective of excellence in research, scholarship, and education by publishing worldwide. Oxford is a registered trade mark of Oxford University Press in the UK and certain other countries.

Published in the United States of America by Oxford University Press 198 Madison Avenue, New York, NY 10016, United States of America.

Library of Congress Cataloging-in-Publication Data
Names: Gjesdal, Kristin, author.
Title: The drama of history : Ibsen, Hegel, Nietzsche / by Kristin Gjesdal.
Description: New York : Oxford University Press, 2021. |
Includes bibliographical references and index.
Identifiers: LCCN 2020018268 (print) | LCCN 2020018269 (ebook) |
ISBN 9780190070762 (hardback) | ISBN 9780190070786 (epub)
Subjects: LCSH: Ibsen, Henrik, 1828–1906—Criticism and interpretation. |
Hegel, Georg Wilhelm Friedrich, 1770–1831—Philosophy. |
Nietzsche, Friedrich Wilhelm, 1844–1900—Philosophy. | Theater—Philosophy. |
Drama—19th century—History and criticism.
Classification: LCC PT8895 .G54 2020 (print) | LCC PT8895 (ebook) |
DDC 193—dc23
LC record available at https://lccn.loc.gov/2020018268
LC ebook record available at https://lccn.loc.gov/2020018269

1 3 5 7 9 8 6 4 2

Printed by Integrated Books International, United States of America

Contents

Illustrations

Plate 1   Erik Werenskiold, *Portrait of the Poet Henrik Ibsen*. 1895. Painting; oil on
Canvas. 121.5 × 71.5 cm. The National Museum of Art, Architecture and
Design (Inventory no.: NG.M.04206). Photographer: Børre Høstland.
Copyright Nasjonalmuseet for kunst, arkitektur og design.

Plate 2   Edvard Munch. *The Sun*. 1911. Oil on canvas. 455 × 780 cm.
The University of Oslo. Photo © Munchmuseet.

Plate 3   Hans Gude and Adolph Tidemand. *Bridal Procession on the Hardanger Fjord*.
1848. Painting; oil on Canvas. 93.5 × 130.1 × 2.9 cm. The National Museum
of Art, Architecture and Design (Inventory no: NG.M.00467). Photo: Børre
Høstland. Copyright: Nasjonalmuseet for kunst, arkitektur og design.

Plate 4   Werner Rehm as Peer Gynt. From Peter Stein's production of *Peer Gynt* (1971).
Schaubühne, Berlin. Photographer: Abisag Tüllmann. Copyright:
Theatermuseum München.

Plate 5   Anne Tismer as Nora. From Thomas Ostermeier's production of *Nora* (2003).
Photographer: Arno Declair. Copyright: Schaubühne, Berlin.

Plate 6   Edvard Munch. Set Design for Henrik Ibsen's *Ghosts*. 1906. Oil on cardboard.
47.5 × 68 cm. Munchmuseet Photo © Munchmuseet.

Plate 7   Tessman (Lars Eidinger) and Julle (Lore Stefanek). From Thomas Ostermeier's
production of *Hedda Gabler* (2006). Photographer: Gianmarco Bresadola.
Copyright: Shaubühne, Berlin.

Plate 8   Edvard Munch. *Hedda Gabler*. 1906–07. Watercolour and pencil. 660 × 487 mm
Munchmuseet, Oslo Photo © Munchmuseet.

Illustrations

Preface

"Prose style is for ideas," wrote Henrik Ibsen, the great Norwegian playwright, at the outset of the 1870s (rhyme letter to J. L. Heiberg, April 15, 1871; HIS XII 493). In the second half of the Nineteenth Century, Ibsen played a significant role in the larger, European movement to reinvent drama. His towering presence—in drama and cultural life more broadly—is nicely captured in Erik Werenskiold's 1895 portrait of the poet (see color plate 1).

Ibsen and his peers sought to develop a drama for modernity. Creating a drama for modernity, they also reflected on past dramatic forms—and on the relationship between drama and historical consciousness, more broadly. The intersection between modern drama and history had been at the center of modern philosophy of theater as it developed in the late Enlightenment and *Sturm und Drang* period. Later, these discussions of tragedy and drama would fundamentally shape the works of Georg Wilhelm Friedrich Hegel and Friedrich Nietzsche. Playwrights, directors, and critics, on their side, would turn to philosophy for intellectual nourishment. Throughout the Nineteenth Century, philosophy and drama engage in an ongoing process of mutual trade and exchange.

The present study investigates this exchange between philosophy and drama. By placing Ibsen's dramatic engagement with history, tradition, and the challenges of modern life and art within a broader intellectual context, it offers a philosophical interpretation of Ibsen's work and discusses the contributions of nineteenth-century philosophy from the point of view of modern drama. Focusing on the intersection between historical consciousness and modern drama, it shows not only how Ibsen's work reverberates with philosophical insights but also how philosophers in this period had made their work artistically relevant through a discussion of drama and related issues. The point is not to determine a set of fixed philosophical ideas and movements that inspired Ibsen and other poets of his time, but to highlight, discuss, and analyze the productive interchange between drama and philosophy that characterizes the second half of the Nineteenth Century. In this way, the goal is to deepen and actualize the relationship between philosophy and drama—not by suggesting that either philosophy or drama should have the upper hand, but by indicating how a dialogue between them can bring out the best in both.

Acknowledgments

Since I started teaching philosophy, Henrik Ibsen's drama has served as a reminder that philosophical thought can take many forms—some of which transcend the boundaries of philosophy as an academic discipline. I thank my colleagues and students at Temple University for providing a scholarly context that is conducive to interdisciplinary work.

Ibsen's work has given me a way to stay in touch with my Norwegian background. I am grateful to my family and friends for making sure that Oslo is—and will continue to be—a place I consider home. In particular, I want to thank my parents and my brothers, Ola and Grunde. I also thank my colleagues at IFIKK, the University of Oslo, for offering me a four-year Professorial Fellowship in philosophy (2014–2018). I thank the Ibsen Centre at the University of Oslo for welcoming me as a frequent visitor and collaborator.

Some of the present material has been explored in a series of workshops on Ibsen and philosophy at the Ibsen Centre at the University of Oslo, the Center for Humanities at Johns Hopkins University, and Temple University. I thank my co-organizers, Frode Helland and Leonardo Lisi, and the speakers who have contributed to the success of these events. Special thanks go to Frode Helland, former Director of the Ibsen Centre, who read and offered feedback on the manuscript for this book. A warm thank you, also, to Paul Kottman and Kristin Boyce for their comments on an earlier version of this manuscript.

Among much-appreciated colleagues and friends, I especially thank Lydia Moland for her insightful and detailed comments on my manuscript and for constructive exchanges on nineteenth-century philosophy and drama. I thank Lior Levy and Tom Stern for rewarding conversations on Ibsen. I thank Andrew Huddleston and Joshua Billings for interchanges on Hegel, Nietzsche, and tragedy. My thanks, also, to Dalia Nassar for a long-standing friendship and discussions, across time-zones and continents, of nineteenth-century philosophy in its many permutations.

I am grateful to the Ibsen Centre in Oslo for organizing a workshop on my book manuscript as I was preparing for final submission to the press. In particular, I thank Giuliano D'Amico, Ellen Rees, Christian Janss, Tore Rem, Svein Henrik Nyhus, Marit Grøtta, and Tone Selboe for perceptive comments and suggestions. I thank Martin Puchner for his comments to my reading of *A Doll's House*.

Lucy Randall at Oxford University Press deserves a heartfelt thank you; she has been an important source of support in this and other projects. I thank Jon-Ove Steihaug, Karen Lerheim, and the Munch Museum in Oslo for the rights to reproduce the Munch images included in this study. I thank Schaubühne, especially the photographers Arno Declair and Gianmarco Bresadola, for allowing me to use images from Thomas Ostermeier's production of *Nora* and *Hedda Gabler*. Finally, I thank Rudolf Mast, at the Archiv Darstellende Kunst at the Akademie der Künste, Berlin, for his help with archive photos from Peter Stein's production of *Peer Gynt*.

Meryl Lumba and Raciel Cuevas have competently assisted the final preparation of my manuscript. Fred Rowland, Temple University's philosophy librarian, has offered invaluable assistance. Likewise has Kristin Kosberg, the librarian at the Centre for Ibsen Studies, been a generous source of information.

Most of all, though, I thank my family: Stella, Mathias, and Espen. Stella and Mathias have endured (and, I hope, occasionally enjoyed!) what may seem like an inappropriate amount of Ibsen performances across Europe and the United States. Espen is not only my husband and favorite philosophical interlocutor, but he has also read and commented on my drafts for the present study. I thank him for that and for much else.

I have presented my work on Ibsen at the University of Chicago, the Egyptian Ministry of Culture, the University of Pennsylvania, the Open University of Hong Kong, Swarthmore College, the Munch Museum in Oslo, the University of Oslo, and the University of Haifa. My work on nineteenth-century philosophy has been presented at the University of Oregon, Fordham University, the University of Sydney, the University of Copenhagen, the University of Toronto, University College Dublin, Princeton University, the University of Vienna, Humboldt-Universität zu Berlin, Södertörn University (Stockholm), the University of Bonn, the University of Chicago, the University of Jena, the London Aesthetics Forum, SUNY Buffalo, CUNY's Graduate Center, Boston University, the Vietnam National University, the University of Århus, Freie Universität Berlin, the University of Pittsburgh, the University of Trondheim, and the University of Bremen. I have benefited from exchanges with colleagues and students in each of these places.

Parts of the material included in this book have been published in "Ibsen on History and Life: *Hedda Gabler* in a Nietzschean Light," and "Philosophizing with Ibsen," my introduction to *Ibsen's Hedda Gabler: Philosophical Perspectives* (Oxford: Oxford University Press, 2018); "Nietzschean Variations: Politics, Interest, and Education in Ibsen's *An Enemy of the People*," *Ibsen Studies*, vol. 14, no. 2 (2014), 109–135; "Tragedy and Tradition: Ibsen and Nietzsche on the Ghosts of the Greeks," *The Graduate Faculty Journal of Philosophy*, vol. 34, no. 2 (2013), 391–413; "Self-Knowledge and Aesthetic Consciousness in Ibsen and Hegel," in Terry Yip and K.K. Tam (eds.), *Ibsen and the Modern Self* (Hong Kong: Open University of Hong Kong Press, 2010), 1–17; "Ibsen on Hegel, Egypt, and the Beginning of Great Art," *The Bulletin of the Hegel Society of Great Britain*, vol. 55/56, no. 1–2 (2007), 67–86. I thank the editors and publishing houses for allowing me to use and expand on this material.

Abbreviations

Works by Henrik Ibsen

HIS *Henrik Ibsens skrifter*. Edited by Vigdis Ystad et al. Oslo: Aschehoug/Universitetet i Oslo, 2008–2010. References to the accompanying commentary volumes are marked by volume number/B.

HU *Hundreårsutgaven*. 21 vols. Edited by Francis Bull, Halvdan Koht, and Didrik Arup Seip. Oslo: Gyldendal forlag, 1928–1957.

OI *The Oxford Ibsen*. 8 vols. Edited by James Walter McFarlane. Oxford: Oxford University Press, 1961.

P *Ibsen's Poems*. Edited and translated John Northam. Oslo: Norwegian University Press, 1986.

PG *Peer Gynt: A Dramatic* Poem. Translated by John Northam. Oslo: Scandinavian University Press, 1993.

PI *The New Penguin Ibsen*. General editorship by Tore Rem. London: Penguin, 2015–.

SV *Samlede Værker*. København: Gyldendalske Boghandels forlag, 1898.

Works by G. F. W. Hegel

HW *Werke in 20 Bänden*. Edited by Eva Moldenhauer and Karl Markus Michel. Frankfurt am Main: Suhrkamp Verlag, 1970.

LFA *Lectures on Fine Art*. 2 vols. Translated by T. M. Knox. Oxford: Clarendon Press, 1975.

LHP *Lectures on the History of Philosophy*. 3 vols. Translated by E. S. Haldane and Frances H. Simson. Lincoln: University of Nebraska Press, 1995.

PS *Phenomenology of Spirit*. Translated by A. V. Miller. Oxford: Oxford University Press, 1977.

Works by Friedrich Nietzsche

BT *The Birth of Tragedy and Other Writings*. Edited by Raymond Geuss and Ronald Speirs. Translated by Ronald Speirs. Cambridge: Cambridge University Press, 1999.

KSA *Kritische Studienausgabe*. Edited by Giorgio Colli and Mazzino Montinari. Vols. 1–15. Berlin: DeGruyter, 2012.

UM *Untimely Meditations*. Edited by Daniel Breazeale. Translated by R. J. Hollingdale. Cambridge: Cambridge University Press, 1997.

Timeline of Ibsen's Published Drama

Catiline (1850)

The Burial Mound (written in 1850, revised version published in 1854)

Norma (1851)

St. John's Night (written in 1852, published in 1909)

Lady Inger of Ostrat (written in 1854, published in 1857)

The Feast at Solhaug (1856)

Olaf Liljekrans (written in 1856, published in 1902)

The Vikings at Helgeland (1858)

Love's Comedy (1862)

The Pretenders (1863)

Brand (1866)

Peer Gynt (1867)

The League of Youth (1869)

Poems (1871)

Emperor and Galilean (1873)

Pillars of Society (1877)

A Doll's House (1879)

Ghosts (1881)

An Enemy of the People (1882)

The Wild Duck (1884)

Rosmersholm (1886)

The Lady from the Sea (1888)

Hedda Gabler (1890)

The Master Builder (1892)

Little Eyolf (1894)

John Gabriel Borkman (1896)

When We Dead Awaken (1899)

Introduction

Among Edvard Munch's portraits of Henrik Ibsen, an oil sketch from 1909 stands out (see the book cover). It is large in format and with Munch's characteristic palette of rough-hewn gray, blue, green, and yellow. Munch's sketch shows Ibsen, who had died three years earlier, in the company of Socrates and Nietzsche. Ibsen is barely recognizable, save for his eyebrows and sideburns—both of some nineteenth-century magnitude. He is placed slightly to the side but is still the dominant figure. Nietzsche is at the center, but he is smaller in shape and with a less monumental presence. Then there is Socrates: old, frail, and pushed even further back. He is supported by two vaguely distinct figures, and it is unclear exactly where Socrates ends and his helpers begin. It seems that Socrates—and, with him, the ideals of the classical world—is about to fade, and Nietzsche and Ibsen, champions of a new era in philosophy and drama, are prepared to take over.[1]

Munch pays homage to Ibsen's drama through several hundred illustrations, prints, and sketches, many of which were commissioned for theaters in Oslo, Berlin, and Paris.[2] The 1909 sketch is part of Munch's commission for the Great Festive Hall at the University of Oslo. In the end, Munch decided to leave out Socrates, Ibsen, and Nietzsche—at least this is the case as far as direct portraiture is concerned. Instead, we get the famous sun, Oswald's sun, as Munch called it, with reference to the dying male protagonist of Ibsen's *Ghosts* (see color plate 2).[3]

---

[1] See Joan Templeton, *Munch's Ibsen: A Painter's Visions of a Playwright* (Seattle: University of Washington Press, 2008), 37.

[2] See Templeton, *Munch's Ibsen*, 37. Munch's work with the theater is covered in Carla Lathe, "Edvard Munch's Dramatic Images 1892–1909," *Journal of the Warburg and Courtauld Institutes*, vol. 46 (1983): 191–206.

[3] References to the sun figure prominently in Ibsen's work. For Munch's remark, see *Munch med egne ord*, ed. Poul Erik Tøjner (Oslo: Press Forlag, 2003), 169 (no. 45). Munch had been commissioned to design the stage for Max Reinhardt's 1906 production of *Ghosts* in Berlin. See Erika Fischer-Lichte, "*Ibsen's Ghosts*—A Play for All Theatre Concepts?" *Ibsen-Studies* vol. 7, no. 1 (2007): 61–83, and Hans Midbøe, *Max Reinhardts iscenesettelse av Ibsens Gespenster i Kammerspiele des deutschen Theaters Berlin 1906–Dekor Edvard Munch*, Det Kgl. norske videnskapers selbskaps skrifter 1969, nr. 4 (Trondheim: F. Brun, 1969).

The Drama of History. Kristin Gjesdal, Oxford University Press (2021). © Oxford University Press. DOI: 10.1093/oso/9780190070762.001.0001.

Yet, the initial sketch makes it clear that, in the period following Ibsen's death, Munch found it appropriate to portray the Norwegian dramatist in the company of central European philosophers—indeed, the whole span of the European philosophical tradition, from its early beginnings in the classical world to its most controversial spokesman in the late 1800s. Tellingly, Munch decided to call his sketch *The Geniuses*.

Like many other artists of the time, Munch was an avid reader of Nietzsche.[4] From this point of view, his painting of the old and new geniuses is not without an agenda of its own. For even though later scholars have identified a Socratic element in Nietzsche's philosophy,[5] Nietzsche himself was often critical of Socrates, or, rather, of the Socratic spirit that he takes to have saturated Western philosophy and culture more broadly. Munch, who had painted his famous Nietzsche portraits in Weimar and Bad Elgersburg, must have been aware of Nietzsche's criticism.[6] In Nietzsche's view, tragedy and the great era of Greek culture died when the Socratic spirit took center stage.[7] In Munch's painting, the Socratic period, which Nietzsche had taken to represent the destruction of tragedy by optimism (BT 60; KSA I 83), is definitely over. Nietzsche's philosophy now provides a more adequate companionship for a modern playwright. Further, with the diminishing influence of the classical ideals, Munch's sketch indicates how Ibsen was viewed as an artist who left behind the ideals of the ancients—or, at the very least, what was seen as a naïve and uncritical espousal of these ideals. His is, emphatically, a drama of and about the Nineteenth Century.

Yet, as far as the Nineteenth Century goes, Ibsen's philosophical company—indeed, the philosophical milieu of his native Norway—includes figures beyond Nietzsche. For in addition (and somewhat prior) to Nietzsche's breakthrough in Scandinavia, intellectuals, critics, and theater directors had

---

[4] For a discussion of Munch's reading of Nietzsche, see Ingeborg Winderen Owesen, "Friedrich Nietzsches innflytelse og betydning for Edvard Munch," *Agora*, no. 3–4 (1995): 94–111, and "Edvard Munch: Between Gender, Love, and Women's Rights," in *Munch 1863–1944*, ed. Mai Britt Guleng, Jon-Ove Steihaug, and Ingebjørg Ydstie (Milan: Skira Editore, 2013), 296–305.

[5] This line of thought is pursued, for example, in Alexander Nehamas, *Nietzsche: Life as Literature* (Cambridge, MA: Harvard University Press, 1987).

[6] Munch's Nietzsche portraits are housed, respectively, in the Munch Museum in Oslo and the Thielska Galleriet in Stockholm. The paintings were commissioned by the Swedish Banker Ernest Thiel, who was in contact with Nietzsche's sister. Munch was already familiar with her work on Nietzsche and would later visit her. For Munch's visit, see http://www.emunch.no/HYBRIDNo-MM_N0134.xhtml#ENo-MM_N0134-00-01r (Accessed October 2019).

[7] It is unclear if, in Nietzsche's view, this is because of Socrates or if Socrates simply consolidates the increasingly reflective spirit that Nietzsche finds in late tragedy, especially the work of Euripides. See BT 65–75; KSA I 82–102. In either case, it applies that, in Nietzsche's view, Socrates' position is facilitated by larger, rationalist currents that also influenced tragedy (ibid., 66–67, 90–91).

been inspired by the late Enlightenment and *Sturm und Drang* movements and the work of philosophers and literary critics such as Gotthold Ephraim Lessing and Johann Gottfried Herder.[8] What attracted the young Ibsen's generation to this movement was, among other things, its discussion of drama as an artform of particular relevance to the modern age. Subsequently, the worlds of theater and Hegelianism were curiously intertwined, with theater directors and critics in Copenhagen and Christiania (later Kristiania, now Oslo) formulating a largely Hegelian program. In the latter half of the century, artists and writers took a particular interest in Nietzsche's writings. As unapologetic defenders of art—dramatic art in particular—philosophers like Hegel and Nietzsche would influence Scandinavian theater and drama. From this point of view, it should not surprise us that we find points of dialogue— of spoken and unspoken exchanges—between Ibsen, on the one hand, and the philosophers of the long Nineteenth Century, on the other.

Through the lens of Ibsen, Hegel, and Nietzsche—as read against the background of the *Sturm und Drang* movement and its interest in theater—the present study seeks to map the relationship between drama and philosophy in the Nineteenth Century. It aims to trace some of the ways in which Scandinavian nineteenth-century culture reverberated with philosophical ideas and show how a close analysis of these ideas can help us appreciate the poetical and intellectual commitments of Ibsen's work. I also hope that my focus on Ibsen's work can help highlight aspects of nineteenth-century philosophy that have not received the attention they deserve. The point, in other words, is not primarily to identify what philosophical ideas might have influenced Ibsen's drama, but, rather, to ask what hermeneutic-artistic possibilities were disclosed by the philosophical contributions at the time and how Ibsen, as an artist, makes use of and often goes beyond them.

At the center of my discussion is the dramatic and philosophical response to the experience of history as a formative condition of modern life.[9] My claim, obviously, is not that previous periods lacked a sense of history. Rather,

---

[8] J. E. Schlegel spent a period of time in Denmark, as did Klopstock and Gerstenberg. Further, there was Knud Lyne Rahbek, whose activities spanned drama, criticism, and academic discourse. For an overview of German culture in Denmark in this period, see J. W. Eaton, *The German Influence in Danish Literature in the Eighteenth Century: The German Circle in Copenhagen 1750–1770* (Cambridge: Cambridge University Press, 1929).

[9] For a discussion of Ibsen in the context of the Nineteenth Century—its industry, law, capital, national and international conflicts—see Helge Rønning, *Den umulige friheten. Henrik Ibsen og moderniteten* (Oslo: Gyldendal, 2006). Rønning discusses Ibsen's relationship to history in Chapter 4. A more recent source is Narve Fulsås and Tore Rem, *Ibsen, Scandinavia and the Making of a World Drama* (Cambridge: Cambridge University Press, 2018).

it is that as we approach the long Nineteenth Century, the world is thought to change at a new pace and the very question of how to relate to the past—one's own past and that of one's culture—was foregrounded by philosophers and artists. Philosophers explored this question in a systematic and discursive manner. Artists, dramatic poets included, searched for other ways to deal with historical material and forms. Many of Ibsen's protagonists embody, realize, and, often when life takes a turn for the worse, question the central philosophical tenets of the Nineteenth Century. While his *métier* was certainly not that of systematic philosophy, Ibsen realized, on stage and in text, the lived dimensions of nineteenth-century thought: its credence as a set of concrete experiences and not just intellectually conceived positions.

Hence, to the extent that philosophical topics resonate in Ibsen's work, they resonate *as* drama—and explicitly so. Ibsen picked and chose what he needed, acted it out on stage and in book-form, thereby bringing to life, criticizing, amplifying, and developing the leading ideas of the Nineteenth Century. As such, his work came to fascinate readers and audiences of a philosophical disposition, including Sigmund Freud, Henry James, James Joyce, Lou Andreas-Salomé, Georg Lukàcs, Theodor W. Adorno, Jean-Paul Sartre, and Simone de Beauvoir.

Today, Ibsen is best known for his contribution to dramatic realism and naturalism. In his own time, however, he was first recognized as the author of historical plays. During the first twenty-five years of his production, the bulk of his work was classified as historical drama. In different guises and manifestations, an interest in history and historicity runs through Ibsen's entire work. Even Ibsen's contemporary plays—*Hedda Gabler*, for example, or *Ghosts, The Wild Duck, Rosmersholm, The Lady from the Sea*, and practically all the later symbolic plays—explore the power of the past and the growing despair in the face of crumbling traditions and values. Ibsen would return to the early historical plays in his later years. It is not unfair to suggest that Ibsen never left behind his ambition to explore history and historical consciousness. Nor did he take leave of his ambition of doing so through a dissection of individual characters that grapple with what it means to lead lives that are marked by history. But even his early drama explores history from within the point of view of Ibsen's own period. Many, but not all, of his famous characters are historically out of tune: they appear to be either stuck in the past or ahead of their time. Ibsen's historical drama and his later interest in the conditions of bourgeois life are two ways in which he responds to, and reflects on, the modern period.

The culture in which Ibsen grew up was still struggling to ascertain its own identity after centuries of Danish hegemony. From this point of view, it should not be a surprise that Ibsen and his peers took a particular interest in history and historical culture.[10] Ibsen's circles included poets, composers, painters, historians, and philosophers. Some, like Edvard Grieg, are well known beyond Norway. Others today are less so (Bjørnstjerne Bjørnson, Camilla Collett, J.C. Dahl, Marcus Jacob Monrad, Ernst Sars), though some (like Bjørnson) spent a considerable amount of time outside of Norway and were internationally recognized in their time.[11]

In the mid-Nineteenth Century, early feminist thought got a hold in Norwegian avant-garde culture and we see the surfacing of a generation of strong women writers and thinkers. Many of Ibsen's central characters are women—existential heroines, as Lou Andreas-Salomé would see them.[12] They navigate the uncertain terrain between the old and the new. This experience is obviously not exclusive to women. However, the new position of women emblematically captured the drama of time passing and new values breaking through while old values linger. Ibsen's respect for, and fascination with, women's life and psychology is one of the areas in which he certainly stands out from the most well-known philosophers of the period, Hegel and Nietzsche included.[13] However, the Nineteenth Century is also a period in

[10] In Denmark, poets like Adam Gottlob Oehlenschläger had already turned to historical material, and the philosopher Henrik Steffens had helped increase the interest in German-language philosophy, including philosophy of history.

[11] Bjørnson's work was well known in Germany, later also in the United States and elsewhere. When the Norwegian classicist Ludvig Ludvigsen Daae visited Lübeck in 1875, he was surprised to hear that Bjørnson was read but Ibsen remained unknown. See Narve Fulsås, "Innledning til brev," http://ibsen.uio.no/BRINNL_brevInnledning_7 1.xhtml. See also Wolfgang Pasche, *Skandinavische Dramatik in Deutschland. Bjørnstjerne Bjørnson, Henrik Ibsen, August Strindberg auf der deutschen Bühne 1867–1932* (Basel: Helbing & Lichtenhahn Verlag, 1979), 32–163.

[12] Lou Andreas-Salomé, *Henrik Ibsens Frauen-Gestalten. Psychologische Bilder nach seinen sechs Familiendramen*, ed. Cornelia Pechota (Taching am See: Medien Edition, Welsch, 2012); *Ibsen's Heroines*, trans. Siegfried Mandel (Redding Ridge, CT: Black Swan Books, 1985). Salomé's work was translated into Norwegian in Ibsen's lifetime. See *Henrik Ibsens Kvindeskikkelser*, trans. Hulda Garborg (Oslo: Alb. Cammermeyer forlag, 1893).

[13] In an even more radical spirit, Bjørnson wrote home from Boston (1880) with the following note: "In the afternoon, I was in the 'Women's Congress,' which is held every year in Boston. Here we find the most famous followers of the case, since no outstanding scientist or literary person is present who does not fully share the work of women's liberation and equal rights. Here are also the most excellent women who lead the movement; here their journals come out, I have read a number of issues. Their meetings have been overcrowded. And I want to say that I think the hours I spent here were the most beautiful in my life; for I sat as in the future and I had a hard time controlling my emotions. America's best women—with an education that matches that of the best men: well-traveled and educated, many of them with university exams, like Doctors, etc.—got up, one after another, so as, with a skill, truthfulness, and breathtaking conviction, to elaborate their views of the present case." Published in *Dagbladet* November 16, 1889, under the heading "Bjørnstjerne Bjørnson." See https://

which women were publishing philosophical works, some of which reverberate in Ibsen's work and Scandinavia more broadly.

Ibsen himself does not say much about what he reads and whose work inspires him. This goes for drama and literature in general, but also for philosophy. Yet Ibsen's interest in philosophical questions appears to have been prompted in his early years as a theater director in Bergen. Later, he spent twenty-seven years in Italy and Germany. In Italy, he was part of the Scandinavian circles of academics, artists, and intellectuals. In Germany, he encountered a culture in which theater and drama had already been topics of intense philosophical discussion for a good century. This debate had originated in a situation not unlike that of Ibsen's Norway. In a German-language area that was not yet politically unified, there was a widespread interest in cultural and linguistic identity and in understanding the complex dialectics between old and new artistic forms. The aesthetic-ideological underpinnings of Francophile classicism were being questioned, and Shakespeare's drama, especially his historical work, was taken to offer an alternative artistic model. During this period, we see an upsurge not only in historical art and drama, but also, with the contributions of Lessing, Herder, and others, a discussion of human history and historicity *and* of the role drama can play in exploring both the past, the present, and, above all, the relationship between them. These topics fundamentally shape the works of later philosophers such as Hegel and Nietzsche.

Hegel and Nietzsche are two figures whose names are not usually mentioned together. Hegel, who died in 1831, was a thinker of an unbending, idealist disposition. Nietzsche is viewed as an outspoken anti-idealist. Born thirteen years after Hegel's death, Nietzsche lived until 1900. As such, he was indeed Ibsen's contemporary (Ibsen was born in 1828 and died in 1906). Nietzsche did not have many compliments for Ibsen.[14] Nor, for that matter, did he have much patience with Hegel. Down to the very form of his philosophizing—was there ever a starker protest against philosophical system-building?—Nietzsche sought to break free of traditional idealism. Moreover, when it comes to tragedy, Hegel saw this artform, at least in its

www.nb.no/items/67314750e99f13a310fc26dd394f1f1f?page=0, my trans. I thank Marit Grøtta for this reference.

[14] For a discussion of Nietzsche's comments on Ibsen, see Matthias Straßner, *Flöte und Pistole. Anmerkungen zum Verhältnis von Nietzsche und Ibsen* (Würzburg: Königshausen & Neumann, 2003). See also Thomas F. Van Laan, "Ibsen and Nietzsche," *Scandinavian Studies*, vol. 78, no. 3 (2006): 255–302.

ancient articulation, as playing out the conflict between various worldviews incarnated by the tragic characters and their actions.[15] Nietzsche, by contrast, focused on how the tragic chorus (rather than the tragic characters) lent expression to a deeper, metaphysical truth that transcends the individual character or spectator. It is hard to deny that Nietzsche sought to overcome the very premises of Hegelian thought. When it comes to the fundamental role of human history, for example, Hegel, in his *Logic*, downplays the vicissitudes of history in favor of a set of transhistorical (philosophical) forms while Nietzsche remains open to the fact of historical contingency. Yet the very philosophy of art, culture, and education that we find in Nietzsche's work was made possible by the turn to drama, art, culture, and history in the philosophical lineage from Lessing and Herder to Hegel.

Hegel and Nietzsche were both critics of ahistorical thinking and traditional forms of metaphysics.[16] Further, they both rejected the aestheticizing of art and the reduction of art to pleasing entertainment and idealized representations of human life. Both Hegel and Nietzsche traced great art back to a fundamental kind of human truth and self-understanding and saw this self-understanding as historically mediated. They both took art and philosophy to be closely related. And, finally, for all their differences in style and orientation, both Hegel and Nietzsche insisted that art as well as philosophy are profoundly and essentially historical.[17]

In pursuing a study of the synergy between philosophy and drama in the long Nineteenth Century, I do not intend to make any conclusive, systematic claims about the overall contributions of Hegel and Nietzsche. Instead, I seek to highlight, through the lens of drama, their responses to history and reflections on the modern world, especially the position of art in modernity. Further, I do not intend to suggest that Hegel and Nietzsche are the only philosophers whose insights reverberate in Ibsen's work. The work of John Stuart Mill and the liberal tradition could be mentioned too. The influence of Søren Kierkegaard's thought would deserve a separate examination.[18] There

[15] A helpful retrieval of this point can be found in Stephen Houlgate, "Hegel's Theory of Tragedy," in *Hegel and the Arts*, ed. Stephen Houlgate (Evanston: Northwestern University Press, 2007), 173n.
[16] For this point, see Stephen Houlgate's *Hegel, Nietzsche and the Criticism of Metaphysics* (Cambridge: Cambridge University Press, 1986), 1–24.
[17] Nonetheless, Nietzsche writes that even if there were no Hegel, the Germans would still be Hegelians. He traces this back to an orientation toward becoming (over against that which is) and also to what he calls their sixth sense—that of history. See Nietzsche, *The Gay Science*, ed. Bernard Williams, trans. Josefine Nauckhoff (Cambridge: Cambridge University Press, 2001), 218–219; KSA III 599.
[18] Leonardo Lisi and others have done important work in this respect. See, for example, Lisi's *Marginal Modernity: The Aesthetics of Dependency from Kierkegaard to Joyce* (New York: Fordham

is also the Darwinian tradition, broadly conceived.[19] However, what has been of interest for my project is, first and foremost, how Ibsen connects with, and makes creative use of, a line of thought in which drama and philosophy join forces in exploring the fundamental experience of history and human historicity, especially in its modern forms. Here the works of Hegel and Nietzsche, as they emerge against the background of the earlier thinking about history and drama, prove particularly significant.

Ibsen, though, was never willing to take on the solemnity of the philosophers. He tackles philosophical claims and positions with humor, playfulness, and ironical distance. In his work, he draws on philosophical insights, but never commits himself, in a deeper sense, to a theoretical standpoint. Hence, when we study the exchange between drama and philosophy in the Nineteenth Century, we need not see Ibsen as either a representative of the *Sturm und Drang* movement or as a critic of it, either a Hegelian or an anti-Hegelian, either a Nietzschean or a critic of Nietzsche's thought. Instead, we can trace the way his work, in a complex dramatic weave, borrows from *and* goes beyond the philosophers of his time. As philosophers, we can learn from this exchange.

Previous studies of Ibsen's relationship to Hegel and Nietzsche—I have scholars like Harald Beyer, Ole Koppang, Asbjørn Aarseth, Thomas F. Van Laan, Brian Johnston, and Matthias Straßner in mind—have been Ibsen-heavy, but lighter on philosophical content and detail. Moreover, some of these studies, while pathbreaking in their time, are outdated in terms of their philosophical approaches. The focus has often been on tracing ideas that have influenced Ibsen rather than untangling these ideas and asking how Ibsen responds to them. In wanting to take seriously the complexity of the issues at stake, I have sought to combine attentiveness to recent philosophical scholarship, a commitment to the historical context of Ibsen's work and intellectual environment, and close readings of philosophical and dramatic texts.

With a focus on the decades between 1858 and 1890—the dramatic arc from *The Vikings at Helgeland* to *Hedda Gabler*—my discussion is organized

---

University Press, 2013) and "Endelighedens æstetik: Modernismens problematik hos Kierkegaard og Ibsen," in *Kierkegaard, Ibsen og det moderne*, ed. Vigdis Ystad et al. (Oslo: Universitetsforlaget, 2010), 99–116.

[19] See Kirsten Shepherd-Barr, *Theatre and Evolution from Ibsen to Beckett* (New York: Columbia University Press, 2015). Shepherd-Barr discusses Darwin (and Ernst Haeckel) in the context of naturalist theater and beyond. Less attention is paid, in her work, to the importance of the early historical turn in German philosophy and its interrelation with developmentalist approaches.

through seven chapters, each of which revolves around a particular play (albeit with references to Ibsen's larger oeuvre). Chapter 1 shows how the *Vikings at Helgeland* draws on, but also further develops, the interplay between history and a modern mindset that had motivated mid-eighteenth-century philosophers of drama. Throughout the 1860s, we see a transition in Scandinavia from *Sturm und Drang* to Hegelianism. This transition is at the heart of Chapter 2. Through his portrait of the charming, yet thoroughly self-centered character of Peer Gynt, Ibsen interrogates, with humor and irony, the relationship between self and other. By having Peer encounter a Hegelian philosopher in Egypt, Ibsen also sheds light on Hegel's problematic treatment of non-European cultures. A few years later, Ibsen publishes what he calls "a world historical drama." Along Hegelian lines, *Emperor and Galilean*, which is the focus of Chapter 3, grippingly displays the price of the rising Christian mindset as it is prone to overlooking earthly beauty and joy. Chapter 4 continues this line of thought and shows how *A Doll's House* investigates the costs of ahistorical and aestheticizing mindsets, thus bringing out the relevance of Hegel's critique of naïvely romanticizing attitudes. However, with his determination to develop drama beyond its late romantic instantiations, Ibsen, with *A Doll's House*, also points beyond the limitations of Hegel's understanding of art.

Toward the late 1870s, Nietzsche's work gradually gained traction among Scandinavian intellectuals and poets. Ibsen is no exception. Borrowing from classical tragedy, *Ghosts*, at the center of Chapter 5, explores the possibility of breaking with the past and presents a modern family tragedy that is both tangential to and critical of Nietzsche's call for a return to classical, tragic culture. Chapter 6 turns to *An Enemy of the People*, a play that brings to life the tension between a sole truth-teller and his community—a tension that is only resolved in the main character's commitment to break with the traditions of the town and, in a Nietzschean spirit, embrace a future-oriented educational project. Finally, in Chapter 7, we see how Ibsen, with *Hedda Gabler*, scrutinizes the disconnect between the past and the prosaic reality of the new and educated middle classes. For Ibsen, though, it seems that it is the task of the artist, rather than just the historians and philosophers, to mend, or at least articulate, this gap. I conclude by offering some brief reflections on Ibsen's symbolic drama and the way in which his treatment of historicity, tradition, and drama is brought to a close in his late works.

In order to preserve the flow of the presentation, I have sought to avoid an extended apparatus of names, historical details, and philosophical references in the main text. As a result, more detailed discussions of philosophical arguments and references to Norwegian culture and historical material that will be of interest primarily to scholars in these respective fields have been allocated to footnotes. I have mainly used the Oxford translation of Ibsen's work. I have also consulted the new Penguin translation. Translations of sundry material are my own (though in cases of interest mostly to Ibsen scholars, the original is left untranslated). In order to avoid confusion, it must also be mentioned that Ibsen's Copenhagen publisher, Frederik Vilhelm Hegel, should not be mixed up with his almost-namesake among the philosophers.

1

Losing Time (*The Vikings at Helgeland*)

The first twenty-five years of Ibsen's production, the period between *Catiline* and *Emperor and Galilean*, his two Roman plays, were mostly (but not exclusively) spent on historical drama and mostly (again not exclusively) on historical material that derived from Ibsen's own culture. It is in this period that we see the publication of *Lady Inger of Ostrat, The Feast at Solhaug, The Vikings at Helgeland*, and *The Pretenders*—plays that are often characterized as products of the *Sturm und Drang* or the closely related movement of Scandinavian romanticism.[1]

The *Sturm und Drang* movement—and its Norwegian offshoot, *nasjonalromantikken* (national romanticism)—is typically traced back to a German context and, in particular, Johann Gottfried Herder.[2] From the mid-Eighteenth Century onward, Herder collected, translated, disseminated, and wrote about non-canonical literature, songs, and folklore. He recognizes the power and importance of history, but also praises the potential of modern art and thought. Indeed, it is his claim that we moderns can only grasp our position in history—our position as modern—in and through an understanding of past forms and expressions. In developing this position, Herder draws on Kant, his former mentor, but also on Hume, Diderot, Lessing, and other Enlightenment philosophers for whom drama and theater were the objects of a renewed philosophical interest. A similar trend can be found in Scandinavia. In Denmark, Knud Lyne Rahbek, director of the Royal Theater in Copenhagen and the founder of the country's first drama school, testified to a modified Lessingian view on art and, in this spirit, had translated Diderot's dramatic work.[3] His brother-in-law, Adam Gottlob Oehlenschläger, contributed to the broadly conceived attempt, spanning dramatists, historians, and

---

[1] See for instance Introduction in HIS XVI/B 50.

[2] Herder's influence is emphasized in the Introduction to vol. XVI of HIS (HIS XVI 50–55). See also Bjørn Hemmer, *Ibsen og Bjørnson. Essays og analyser* (Oslo: Aschehoug, 1978), 44–45.

[3] Denis Diderot, *Herren af Diderot's Theatralske Verker, tilligemed en Samtale over den dramatiske Digtekunst*, trans. Knud Lyne Rahbek (Kjøbenhavn: Johan Rudolf Thiele, 1779). See also Knud Lyne Rahbek, *Om Ludvig Holberg som lystspildigter og om hans lystspil*, 3 vols. (Kjøbenhavn: Brødrene Thiele, 1815–1817).

The Drama of History. Kristin Gjesdal, Oxford University Press (2021). © Oxford University Press.
DOI: 10.1093/oso/9780190070762.001.0001.

translators, at returning to and exploring the artistic resources of the past. With a culture that was steeped in Danish influence, Norway saw the rise of similar movements, now with a focus on retrieving what was perceived as a distinctively Norwegian heritage. As a consequence, the intellectual milieu of the mid-1800s is characterized by a new appreciation of vernacular poetry and a general orientation toward historical literatures, folk art, and drama, especially Shakespeare, whose work was taken to disclose an artistic space that pointed beyond classicism. It is out of this era—with its combination of European impulses and a new sense of Norwegian history and culture—that Ibsen's work emerges.[4]

As periodic-stylistic labels, "*Sturm und Drang*" and "romanticism" have often been associated with a heedless celebration of feelings and an unmediated longing for the past. Such associations also color the reception of Ibsen's early work. While a massively popular piece in Ibsen's lifetime, a play such as *The Vikings at Helgeland*—Ibsen's *Sturm und Drang* drama above any—has been dismissed by later critics.[5] We find examples of this in Halvdan Koht's observation that the play no longer has a grip on us,[6] Michael Meyer's description of *The Vikings at Helgeland* as a mere pastiche, and Bjørn Hemmer's suggestion that the play is unsophisticated in its engagement with past literature and styles.[7] Further, when the play is recognized, it is often because its main character, Hjørdis, is taken to anticipate the later, realist works, especially *Hedda Gabler*.[8] That is, to the extent that *The Vikings at Helgeland* is appreciated, it is for the way in which it *transcends* the historical drama of the *Sturm und Drang* and points to Ibsen's later realism.

---

[4] I thus deviate from Toril Moi's claim that Ibsen, in his early work, does not relate to European culture. In Moi's view, it is only with *Emperor and Galilean* that "Ibsen breaks with Norwegian nationalism and defines himself as a European." As I see it, by contrast, Ibsen, even in his early historical works, is a European precisely *in* his turn to a more local material. For Moi's claim, see *Henrik Ibsen and the Birth of Modernism: Art, Theater, Philosophy* (Oxford: Oxford University Press, 2006), 188.

[5] For a discussion of the popularity of the play, see Michael Meyer, *Ibsen: A Biography* (Harmondsworth: Penguin, 1985), 165. See also the introduction, covering Ibsen's sources and the reception of the play, in HIS III/B, 177–209.

[6] I quote from Koht, *Henrik Ibsen, Eit Diktarliv*, two vols., 2nd edition (Oslo: Aschehoug, 1954), vol. I, 134. *The Life of Henrik Ibsen*, trans. Ruth Lima McMahon and Hanna Astrup Larsen, two vols. (New York: W. W. Norton, 1931) does not cover later amendments and additions.

[7] Hemmer, *Ibsen og Bjørnson*, 20. Hemmer's point is later repeated in *Ibsen. Kunstnerens vei* (Bergen: Vigmostad & Bjørke, 2003), 193–195.

[8] As Meyer puts it, "buried in the impossible form of this pastiche, [we find] the kernel of what, thirty years later, in a very different setting, was to become one of his greatest plays." Meyer, *Henrik Ibsen*, 163.

In the philosophical literature, however, the movements of *Sturm und Drang* and early romanticism have been subject to reevaluation. While previously viewed as opposed to the progressive Enlightenment movement, they are now seen as a deepening—indeed an enlightening—of the Enlightenment itself, granting it cultural depth and credence. As such, the *Sturm und Drang* movement marks the point at which the Enlightenment proceeds from an abstract defense of ideals such as freedom, tolerance, and cultural diversity to an attempt at demonstrating commitment to these ideals through hermeneutic, historical, and artistic work.[9]

Understood in this way, the *Sturm und Drang* movement does not represent a sentimental evocation of the past for the past's own sake. Nor does it limit itself to an appropriation of history as a topic of naïve artistic longing. Instead, it is the *experience* of the past—more often than not, the experience of the past as irrevocably gone—that is being articulated. While this experience is certainly not exclusive to the modern mindset, it is still of an unparalleled centrality to it. This modernity is explored in the *Sturm und Drang* circles' new dramatic works, its theaters, and, relatedly, its rich philosophical discussions of drama and theater.

The present chapter asks to what extent this broader, philosophical *Sturm und Drang* movement carries over into Ibsen's *The Vikings at Helgeland*. Viewing the *Sturm und Drang* movement and its historical interests as expressive of a modern mindset, I suggest that while the young Ibsen is, indeed, a playwright of the *Sturm und Drang* era, we do ourselves a disservice if we think that this, per se, makes the early historical plays less relevant and interesting. Further, by placing Ibsen's turn to Norwegian history within the wider context of German-language art and philosophy,[10] I propose that we leave behind the categorical distinction between his early and late work and realize how his historical drama develops a set of concerns that reverberate in his turn to contemporary material (but whose significance cannot be reduced to its merely anticipating the later plays). While Hjørdis, in my view, is indeed a character who points toward Hedda Gabler, this is not

---

[9] See for example Michael L. Frazer, *The Enlightenment of Sympathy: Justice and the Moral Sentiments in the Eighteenth Century and Today* (Oxford: Oxford University Press, 2010), and Sankar Muthu, *Enlightenment against Empire* (Princeton: Princeton University Press, 2003). Michael Mack's *Spinoza and the Specters of Modernity: The Hidden Enlightenment of Diversity from Spinoza to Freud* (New York: Continuum, 2010) focuses on the literature and aesthetics of this period.

[10] My emphasis on the *Sturm und Drang* movement does not imply a devaluation or rejection of the significance of French philosophy of theater (Voltaire, Rousseau, d'Alembert, Diderot, and others). However, it is only with Lessing, Herder, and the German-language tradition that we see the joint contemplation of drama, history, and historicity that later resounds in Ibsen's work.

because she transcends the *Sturm und Drang* horizon out of which she was born, but because she is a character who lives through, grapples with, and acts out the internal dramatic tensions of the movement. With the relatively late emergence of the *Sturm and Drang* in Scandinavia, Ibsen's early work demonstrates how the *leitmotifs* of this movement, once taken up in modern drama, necessitate a notion of subjectivity that, eventually, points beyond its philosophical-artistic forms.

Introducing Ibsen's Early Work

Ibsen's productive decade of the 1850s includes *Catiline, The Burial Mound, Lady Inger of Ostrat, The Feast at Solhaug*, and *The Vikings at Helgeland. The Vikings at Helgeland* was first performed in 1858, a year after Ibsen's move from Bergen to Christiania.[11] The premier night saw an unexpected turnout and the success was immediate (HIS III/B 204–208). No other Ibsen play was performed more frequently in Christiania before 1900, and no other early (pre-1864) play was performed as frequently in Ibsen's lifetime (HIS III/B 209).

In *The Vikings at Helgeland*, the characters are fairly simple, each embodying a fundamental trait, virtue, or outlook on life. There are only eight named characters in the play. There is Hjørdis, her foster sister Dagny, and their abductors *cum* husbands, Gunnar and Sigurd. Hjørdis and Gunnar have a four-year-old son. Their lowly neighbor, Kaare, features as a catalyst of feuds and bad blood. We also encounter Ørnulf, Dagny's father and Hjørdis's foster father, and his son Torolf. The action is precipitated by Ørnulf, who has come to Helgeland to claim compensation for Sigurd and Gunnar's abduction of his daughters from Iceland.

As the play opens, we are presented with figures whose clothing and jewelry situate them in the Tenth Century. The scenery is rather spectacular. In Ibsen's directions:

> *A rocky coast, which in the background drops steeply away to the sea. Left, a boat-house; right, hills and forest. The mast of two Viking ships can be seen*

---

[11] Ibsen had announced his plans for this work early on, but then put it aside to complete *The Feast at Solhaug*.

down in the bay; far out to the right, reefs and skerries; the sea is running high;
it is winter, with driving snow and wind. (OI II 31; HIS III 353)

Against this sublimely inhospitable landscape, a drama of love, intrigue, and belated recognition is played out. At its center is the proud and unforgiving Hjørdis, who not only fails to come to terms with her own history, but also (and relatedly) refuses to recognize that the honor code of the old world is dying and a milder, Christian mindset is gaining ground.

The Vikings at Helgeland borrows heavily from the newly translated Saga literature (including the Volsung saga, which was translated into Danish in 1829). As scholars have pointed out, Ibsen presents this material as un-problematically Norwegian rather than Icelandic.[12] When the play was later rejected at the Royal Danish Theater, this was partly due to its national orientation, but also to genre-related concerns about the use of the old epic material in drama form. Heiberg, the Hegelian director, concluded that Ibsen's experiment would probably not contribute much to the formation of a Norwegian theater. The project, as he saw it, was a mere misunderstanding—no dramatic tour de force, but an artistic cul-de-sac. It was, in short, too rash and unsophisticated an expression of *Sturm und Drang* sentiments.[13]

German Prelude

In Ibsen's own circles, his fellow poet Bjørnstjerne Bjørnson was reluctant in his response to the *Vikings at Helgeland*. Bjørnson's argument, though, differs from Heiberg's. In this period, Bjørnson was an unapologetic defender of the new Norwegian literature and drama. His work, too, had been turned down by the stage in Copenhagen.[14] Even though he was sympathetic to the *Sturm und Drang* movement,[15] Bjørnson was not convinced by the dramatic characters of *The Vikings at Helgeland*. In a letter to a mutual friend, Bjørnson worries that by turning the sagas, the poetry of the people, into material for

[12] See Merrill Kaplan, "Hedda and Hjørdis: Saga and Scandal in *Hedda Gabler* and *The Vikings at Helgeland*," *Ibsen Studies*, vol. 4, no.1 (2004): 18–29. See also HIS III/B 183–188. The HIS editors also mention possible influences from Shakespeare.

[13] Johan Ludvig Heiberg, *Prosaiske Skrifter*, eleven vols. (Kjøbenhavn: C.A. Reitzel, 1861–62), vol. VII, 401.

[14] The work in question is *Halte-Hulda* (1858).

[15] In his letters, Bjørnson repeatedly affiliates himself with Goethe, whose interest in Shakespeare and drama was mediated by Herder. See for instance Bjørnson, *Gro-tid*, 24–26.

dramatic poetry, Ibsen makes the characters too polished and their lines too perfect. He transforms the people into gods and the poetry of the people into artful poetry (*Kunstpoesi*). In Bjørnson's judgment, Ibsen's approach is therefore not properly historical. As such, it represents a failed romanticism.[16]

In Ibsen's circles, the term "romanticism" was used in a comprehensive sense; it also covered what we today speak of as the *Sturm und Drang* movement. Hence, in order to understand the responses—then and now—to Ibsen's play, we need to turn to the *Sturm und Drang* movement in its larger European form and ask how it views the relationship between history and drama. In this context, the works of Lessing and Herder stand out as particularly important.[17]

The *Sturm und Drang* movement assumed a close connection between philosophy and drama, but also acknowledged the broader political and educational aspects of the performative arts. Lessing's *Hamburg Dramaturgy* was written soon after the author had taken over as the artistic director at the theater in Hamburg, a city that had just gained (relative) independence from its erstwhile Danish rule.[18] A new, impressive theater, it seems, made for a fitting expression of the newly won autonomy of the Hansa city.[19] However, to properly utilize the new national stage, playwrights and dramaturgs needed to overcome the long-standing dominance of classicist drama—whether in the French variety or in its Francophile, German offspring. Hence, Lessing's criticism of classicist drama is not presented as a matter of personal aesthetic preference. Nor is it a matter of pragmatic considerations concerning

[16] It is an example of *romantikens Vildfarelser*. Bjørnstjerne Bjørnson, letter to Clemens Petersen, Nov. 1857, in *Brev, Brev fra årene 1857–1879*, ed. Halvdan Koht (Kristiania and Kjøbenhavn: Gyldendal, 1912), *Gro-tid*, vol. I, 52–55. Bjørnson and Ibsen had a turbulent friendship, partly due to different poetic orientations, partly to political differences. See Fulsås and Rem, *Ibsen, Scandinavia, and the Making of a World Drama*, 77–79.

[17] As Georg Brandes would argue, it was "Lessing who laid the foundations of the intellectual life of modern Germany" and this intellectual life, in turn, was decisive for the literary developments in Scandinavia. Georg Brandes, *Hovedstrømninger i det 19de Aarhundredes Litteratur*, vol. II, *Den Romantiske Skole i Tyskland*, 29, in *Main Currents in Nineteenth Century Literature*, trans. not listed (London: Heinemann, 1923), 19. Later, Ibsen briefly refers to Lessing in his correspondence. See letter to Jakob Løkke, Nov. 23, 1873 (HIS XIII 161) and letter to Erik af Edholm, May 23, 1878 (HIS XIII 440). In Italy, Ibsen borrowed Lessing's *Laocoon* from the Scandinavian Library. See Øyvind Anker, "Ibsen og den skandinaviske Forening i Roma," *Edda*, vol. 56 (1956): 161–178, 174.

[18] Prior to *Hamburg Dramaturgy*, Lessing had discussed drama in a number of contexts, including his *Beyträge zur Historie und Aufnahme des Theaters* (1750), *Theatralische Bibliothek* (1754–1758), "Briefwechsel über das Trauerspiel mit Nicolai und Mendelssohn" (1756–1757), and *Briefe, die neueste Literatur betreffend* (1759–1765). See Peter Höyng, "Lessing's Drama Theory," in *A Companion to the Works of Gotthold Ephraim Lessing*, ed. Barbara Fischer and Thomas C. Fox (Rochester, NY: Camden House, 2005), 211–229.

[19] See H. B. Nisbet, *Gotthold Ephraim Lessing: His Life, Works, and Thought* (Oxford: Oxford University Press, 2013), 360.

the repertoire. At stake is nothing short of the future of German drama and theater *überhaupt*. Lessing defends the view that a culture develops through a conceptual articulation of its taste. By way of some hundred short review essays, he surveys the opening season of the theater so as to better assess the achievements of the new stage and the artistic challenges that were still ahead.[20]

Lessing's campaign for a new theater went hand in hand with his interest in Shakespeare, whose works had first taken France and then Germany by storm.[21] More than anything, the part of Shakespeare's work that had caught Lessing's attention was his historical drama.[22] Lessing argued that Shakespeare, in his historical drama, enters into a dialogue with the ancient tragedians. They, too, had sourced dramatic material from a historical and mythological past. However, Shakespeare lives in a different time period and relates to an altogether different historical past. And, what is more, he approaches it in an altogether different manner: *his* relationship to history and tradition is profoundly different from the ancients' relationship to *their* past. In their call for a return to Greek and Roman art, the classicists fail to realize that modern art must take into account its status as modern—and thus, by implication, the deep and profound historicity that saturates the fields of art and culture.

Lessing targets Corneille and Voltaire. He is critical of their dramatic works, but even more critical of their German acolytes. In a sweeping generalization (that downplays his own appreciation of Diderot's drama and Voltaire's philosophy of history), he suggests that the French completely misunderstand the ancients.[23] And the Germans, in turn, misunderstand the French, which makes them guilty of a double misunderstanding. Lessing is particularly worried about Corneille's treatment of historical topics. Corneille's drama, as

---

[20] See Gotthold Ephraim Lessing, *Hamburg Dramaturgy*, trans. Helen Zimmern (New York: Dover, 1962); *Hamburgische Dramaturgie, Werke und Briefe in zwölf Bänden*, ed. Wilfried Barner et al., vol. VI (Frankfurt am Main: Deutscher Klassiker Verlag, 1985), Preface.

[21] Yet, Lessing himself was not ready to stage Shakespeare in Hamburg. For a discussion of Lessing's repertoire, see Nisbet, *Gotthold Ephraim Lessing*, 370. For the absence of Shakespeare in Hamburg and on the German stage, see Roger Paulin, *The Critical Reception of Shakespeare in Germany 1682–1914: Native Literature and Foreign Genius* (Hildesheim: Georg Olms, 2003), 92 and John G. Robertson, *Lessing's Dramatic Theory: Being an Introduction to and Commentary on His Hamburgische Dramaturgie* (New York: Benjamin Bloom, 1965), 245.

[22] However, Lessing also discusses other aspects of Shakespeare's drama, including his (or rather Hamlet's) advice on acting, which Lessing presents as "a golden rule for all actors who care for sensible approbation." See *Hamburg Dramaturgy; Hamburgische Dramaturgie*, no. 5.

[23] According to Lessing, "[n]o nation has more misapprehended the rules of ancient drama than the French." *Hamburg Dramaturgy; Hamburgische Dramaturgie*, no. 104.

Lessing views it, does not relate to history in a historically adequate manner. This, Lessing fears, makes it untrue. The truth in question, though, is not a matter of correspondence between work and (historical) facts or reality,[24] but of *artistic truthfulness*: of the artist approaching the material in a historically sound and sensitive manner.[25] At the end of the day, this is what makes the historical material come alive to a modern audience.

Being a modern playwright, Corneille is, in principle, free to treat the historical material as he pleases. However, as Lessing sees it, Corneille, in making use of his artistic freedom, fails to realize that the material must be presented so that a modern audience will care about it. It cannot be presented in a way that appears antiquarian or plainly outdated. For Lessing, this is, ultimately, a matter of making the audiences relive the past and see *its* values and preferences as values and preferences to which they could adhere—the experiences presented as experiences that could have been their own.[26] Going beyond the context of Corneille, Lessing illustrates his point through a comparison of Voltaire's and Shakespeare's drama. In *Semiramis*, for example, Voltaire produces a ghost that his Enlightenment audience cannot possibly believe in—it is "only a disguised actor," as Lessing polemically puts it.[27] Shakespeare, by contrast, heeded the historical position of his audience. In *Hamlet,* he presents us not first and foremost with a ghost, but with Hamlet's fear upon his encounter with it. And, unlike the outdated spectral apparitions Lessing finds in *Semiramis*, fear is an emotion with which modern audiences can identify.[28] Lessing's argument is cleverly worked out. For even though Voltaire had brought Shakespeare to Paris, he himself had been rather cool in his reception of the bard.[29]

As Lessing sees it, Voltaire had failed to learn from Shakespeare. Shakespeare successfully brings history on stage. He stages historical plays, and he does so in a historically sensitive manner. In Lessing's words, "even

---

[24] Similarly, we find Ibsen insist, in an 1857 comment on Andreas Munch's historical tragedy, *Lord William Russell*, that we cannot expect historical facts from a true tragedy, yet it should convey historical thoughts and possibilities.

[25] Thus, Lessing writes of Corneille: "It is true that everything with him breathes of heroism, even that which should not be capable of it and is not capable it, namely vice. The Monstrous, the Gigantic they should call him, not the Great. For nothing is great that is not true." *Hamburg Dramaturgy; Hamburgische Dramaturgie*, no. 30.

[26] *Hamburg Dramaturgy; Hamburgische Dramaturgie*, no. 32.

[27] *Hamburg Dramaturgy; Hamburgische Dramaturgie*, no. 11.

[28] *Hamburg Dramaturgy; Hamburgische Dramaturgie*, no. 11.

[29] For an overview of Voltaire's changing approaches to Shakespeare, see Michèle Willems, "Voltaire," in *Great Shakespeareans*, eighteen vols., ed. Peter Holland and Adrian Poole, vol. III, *Voltaire, Goethe, Schlegel, Coleridge*, ed. Roger Paulin (London: Continuum, 2010), 5–43.

the smallest portions of [Shakespeare's plays] are cut according to the great measures of his historical plays, and these stand to the tragedies of French taste much as a large fresco stands to a miniature painting intended to adorn a ring."[30] Shakespeare breathes life into history; he presents the past with energy and vibrancy, and he does so with an awareness of his own position in history. Understood in this way, the success of historical drama is not simply a matter of what material is chosen (i.e., what historical events or sources the playwright draws on). *How* a given material is presented is equally important. With its emphasis on ahistorical rules and harmony, modern French drama, Lessing finds, falls prey to an obsolete formalism that prevents it from adopting the historical material to a modern context: It lacks sensitivity to the uniqueness of the material staged, the historical context into which it is brought to life, *and* the interplay between these historical horizons.

While we can, obviously, question Lessing's nation- and language-based generalization and his aesthetic criteria—it could, for example, easily be argued that we can enjoy a play even if we would have acted and chosen differently than the characters on stage—two points are worth stressing. First, Lessing approaches both Greek and Shakespearean tragedy as examples of historical drama. Second, with his reference to Shakespeare, he argues that a modern dramatist, in turning to history, should present the material in a manner that makes it relevant to a modern audience. As far as theater goes, historical material should not only be about the past, but also about our modern *experience* of it. By critiquing a paradigm that views classical art as a trans-historical ideal and elevates a historical period to an extra-historical paragon, Lessing's discussion of French classicism marks an important turn in modern philosophy of art.

Placing drama at the center of historical culture—and history at the center of drama—Lessing breaks new ground in eighteenth-century aesthetics. Yet he does, by and large, follow the classicists in that he still adheres to the normative grip of Aristotle's *Poetics*. Because of this, he ultimately fails to redeem his own insistence on the modern condition. This, at least, is Herder's assessment as he seeks to further expand the horizon disclosed by Lessing's philosophy of drama.

Herder was Lessing's acquaintance and, in many a context, philosophical defender. Yet he argues that Lessing, in his writing on drama, cannot fully redeem his philosophical insights. In writing on theater and art, Lessing, in

---

[30] *Hamburg Dramaturgy; Hamburgische Dramaturgie*, no. 73.

Herder's view, fails to purge the last relics of ahistorical thought from philosophy of drama. Lessing, to be sure, sees the need for a historical drama
and takes note of the historical perspective of the audience. In this way, he
conducts a shift from ahistorical aesthetic norms to an attempt to develop
a drama that also reflects the modern era. Lessing senses, furthermore, that
Shakespeare's historical drama reveals richer dramatic possibilities than
the classicism of the Francophile kind *and* that this has to do with its reflection of modern life within the framework of modern theater (even though
the dramatic material may well be pre-modern). Yet, in Herder's mind,
Lessing fails to realize that a drama that reflects the cultural awareness and
self-understanding of the modern world cannot be justified by reference
to Aristotle and classical tragedy. Without dismissing classical tragedy—
nothing would be farther from Herder's mind!—he insists that a new drama
calls for a new poetics: a poetics for *its* time and place.

In an early version of his influential essay on Shakespeare—later to
provide the basis for the protagonist's reflections on theater in Goethe's
Wilhelm Meister—Herder likens the possibilities of modern drama with
the reflections of light in a drop of water: compared to the classical unity
of time, place, and character background, modern drama is colorful,
multi-faceted, and oftentimes surprising.[31] This, for Herder, is what makes
Shakespeare's work both important and importantly ours. The point is not
that we moderns should imitate Shakespeare, but that we should approach
the drama of our time with a boldness of the kind that characterizes his
work.[32] Just as Shakespeare made a drama for his time—and a drama that,
precisely *because* of this, is still experienced as relevant—later playwrights
also need to find forms of expression that respond to their time. In this way,
Herder redirects the focus in philosophy of drama from a question of simply
conveying historical content and form, to human historicity and, as a consequence, the historicity of art and taste.[33]

In a language colored by metaphors and images—often of the organic
kind—Herder advocates free, dynamical expression over ahistorical

[31] Herder, *Werke*, II, 532.

[32] See Johann Gottfried Herder, *Shakespeare*, trans. Gregory Moore (Princeton: Princeton
University Press, 2008), 53; *Werke*, II, 517.

[33] As Herder puts it, "Shakespeare had no chorus before him; but he did have historical dramas and
puppet plays—well then! So from these historical dramas and puppet plays, from this inferior clay,
he fashioned the glorious creation that stands before us and lives! He found nothing comparable to
the simple character of the Greek people and their polity, but rather a rich variety of different estates,
ways of life, convictions, peoples, and idioms—any nostalgia for the simplicity of former times would
have been in vain." *Shakespeare*, 29; *Werke*, II, 508.

formalism. He calls for a reassessment of the arts of the Middle Ages and seeks to reevaluate folk art and other artforms that had not been recognized by the classicists, including the ballad. If the artistic poetry of the upper classes had dominated the stage across the French and German-speaking lands, it was now time to rescue the broader culture that, as a result, had been sidelined. For Herder, humanity, when fully realized, is diverse and varied. Each culture and subculture, further, should be appreciated in light of its own aspirations, symbolic resources, and measures of aesthetic success and failure. No historical culture (e.g., that of the ancient Greeks or Romans) should be held up as an ahistorical ideal; no single culture, period, or form (in the singular) should determine the criteria by which we assess cultures, periods, and arts (in the plural).[34] This, for Herder, is not simply an aesthetic, but also a political matter. A staunch critic of colonialism and slavery,[35] Herder not only defends an abstract notion of respect and tolerance, but also propagates a democratic right to human prospering across cultures, languages, classes, aesthetic media, and forms. Hence, it is no matter of coincidence that his philosophy went hand in hand with his literary criticism.[36] Nor is it a matter of coincidence that this period also saw a budding interest in indigenous arts, including Sami songs and poetry.[37]

Herder's philosophy of drama grows out of his early work on poetry. In Herder's view, poetry emerges out of song.[38] Later, in *Ideas for the Philosophy of History of Humankind*, he even suggests that the "songs of a people are

[34] This, as we will see, is why Herder rejects aesthetic imitation and insists that the modern use of historical material must remain, precisely, modern (and therefore reflect its own time).

[35] Herder is concerned that even if Europe has officially abandoned slavery, we still continue "to *use* as slaves, to *trade, to exile* into silver mines and sugar mills, three parts of the world." Johann Gottfried Herder, *Philosophical Writings*, ed. and trans. Michael N. Forster (Cambridge: Cambridge University Press, 2002), 328; *Werke in zehn Bänden*, ed. Martin Bollacher et al. (Frankfurt am Main: Deutscher Klassiker Verlag, 1985–1998), vol. II, 73–74. As it is, Herder also criticizes the anti-slavery movements in Europe. Their motivation, as he sees it, is not that slavery is ethically wrong, but that "it has been calculated how much more these slaves would cost, and how much less they would bring in than free people" (*Philosophical Writings*, 328; *Werke*, IV, 74). Hence the real problem is not only slavery, but, even more comprehensively, a failing to recognize humanity beyond the continent of Europe. I return to this point in Chapter 2.

[36] Herder not only moves between philosophy and literary criticism, but he is also, as René Wellek sees it, the very first philosopher of literature. For this point, see René Wellek, *A History of Modern Criticism, 1750–1950*, 4 vols., vol. I, *The Later Eighteenth Century* (London: Jonathan Cape, 1966), 176. Although not mentioned by Wellek, it is significant that Herder's early philosophy of literature centers on drama in particular.

[37] Andreas F. Kelletat also traces the radical translations and mistranslations of such literatures in his *Herder und die Weltliteratur. Zur Geschichte des Übersetzens im 18. Jahrhundert* (Frankfurt am Main: Peter Lang, 1984), 127–185.

[38] Herder, *Philosophical Writings*, 103–104; *Werke*, I, 740–741.

the best testimonies of their peculiar feelings, propensities, and modes of viewing things; they form a faithful commentary on their way of thinking and feeling, expressed with openness of heart."[39] Song, as he sees it, gives a most fundamental articulation of human spirituality and concretely expresses its sensuous aspect. Poetry, further, is deeply historical; it has gone through different phases of development and varies across cultures and subcultures. While ancient poetry is free and immediate, modern poetry has lost that immediacy. Now poetry tends to be reflective: it has, as it were, become philosophical (this point later resonates not only in Hegel, to whose end of art thesis I return in Chapter 3, but also in Nietzsche's philosophy of tragedy, which will be discussed in the second half of this study).[40] Thus, an adequate philosophy of (dramatic) poetry ought to reflect on the history of the genre and acknowledge that a return to past forms must involve reflection on how we relate to the past and to our historical being. For this, we cannot passively rely on old dramatic forms, but must instead explore new possibilities such as the hybrid *Schauspiel*.[41]

In this way, Herder proposes that in modernity, accepting the historicity of drama is not simply a matter of returning to the form and material of the tradition in a historically responsible way, but also, and equally important, about exploring our own position as moderns. With this philosophical-poetical tableau in mind, we return to Ibsen.

Scandinavian Reverberations

When Ibsen established himself as a playwright, the theaters in Norway were dominated by Danish culture and taste. This was also true of the Christiania Theater. The repertoire at the theater was reflective of a Danish taste: the theater had a Danish director, and it was predominantly staffed by

---

[39] *Philosophical Writings*, 216; *Werke*, VI, 323–324.

[40] See Gottfried Herder, *Selected Early Works, 1764–1767*, ed. Ernest A. Menze and Karl Menges, trans. Ernest A. Menze with Michael Palma (University Park: Pennsylvania State University Press, 1992), 81; *Sämmtliche Werke*, ed. Bernhard Ludwig Suphan et al. (Berlin: Weidmannsche Verlag, 1877–), vol. XXXII, 101. See also my *Herder's Hermeneutics: History, Poetry, Enlightenment* (Cambridge: Cambridge University Press, 2017), Chapter 3.

[41] The philosophical discussion of drama as a hybrid form thus predates Hegel's lectures on art, to which it is often traced back.

Danish-speaking actors. Indeed, the theater was sometimes spoken of as the Christiania Danish Theater or simply the Danish Theater.[42]

It was at the Christiania Theater that Ibsen's *The Burial Mound*, the first play by Ibsen to be staged, would premiere in 1850. Shortly after, Ibsen was hired at the Norwegian Theater in Bergen.[43] The theater in Bergen was committed to developing a Norwegian-language repertoire and a distinctly Norwegian acting style.[44] During his tenure in Bergen, Ibsen took an active part in stage-production. When Ibsen, in 1857, transitioned from Bergen to Christiania—and his position in Bergen was taken over by Bjørnson—he was appointed at the newly established Norwegian Theater there. During the years in Bergen and Christiania, Ibsen was exposed to the practical aspects of stagecraft. Once he left Norway, he would be farther away from the daily life of the theater.[45]

Just as in the case of Lessing and Herder, Ibsen—first in Bergen, then in Christiania—faced a reality in which the theater served as a cultural and linguistic laboratory. And just as had been the case when Lessing tried to free himself of the hegemony of Francophone taste, the new theaters in Norway faced the question of how Norwegian language and culture could develop an identity independently of Danish hegemony. Could Norwegian be spoken on stage at all? Could Norwegian culture be presented in drama form? The young Ibsen takes a clear stance on these issues. He collects folk tales and writes folk-inspired poems and historical drama.[46] Like Herder before him,

---

[42] See for example Ann Schmiesing, *Norway's Christiania Theatre, 1827–1867: From Danish Showhouse to National Stage* (Madison: Farleigh Dickinson University Press, 2006).

[43] Ibsen was hired by Ole Bull, the violin virtuoso, composer, and cultural entrepreneur, who was also a cofounder of the theater in Bergen.

[44] Johannes and Louise Brun and Louise Wolf are names worth mentioning in this context. Ibsen would first travel abroad, to Copenhagen and then Dresden, with the Bruns. Moreover, Marcus Jacob Monrad, a Hegelian philosopher and critic (to whose influence I return in Chapter 2), had worked for an independent Norwegian stage. The year Ibsen was hired in Bergen, Monrad had published a series of three articles promoting Norwegian pronunciation in the theater (albeit, mostly of Danish texts). The essays were published under the title "Om norsk Udtale" in *Den norske Rigstidende*. In 1854, Monrad also published *Om Theater og Nationalitet og om en norsk dramatisk Skole* in *Norsk Tidsskrift for Videnskab og Litteratur*. See http://urn.nb.no/URN:NBN:no-nb_digibok_2008042812002 (Accessed May 2019).

[45] For a discussion of Ibsen's years at the theaters in Bergen and Christiania, see P. F. D. Tennant, "Ibsen as a Stage Craftsman," *The Modern Language Review*, 34, no. 4 (1939): 557–568. See also Frederick J. Marker and Lise-Lone Marker, *Ibsen's Lively Art: A Performance Study of the Major Plays* (Cambridge: Cambridge University Press, 1989), especially the introduction. More recent sources include Jan Olav Gatland, "Repertoiret ved det Norske Theater 1850–1863" (Bergen: Universitets-biblioteket i Bergen, 2000), and Ellen Karoline Gjervan, "Ibsen Staging Ibsen: Henrik Ibsen's Culturally Embedded Staging Practice in Bergen," *Ibsen Studies*, vol. 11, no. 2 (2011): 117–144.

[46] Supported by an academic scholarship, Ibsen had traveled across the country in order to collect folk stories and fairy tales for publication. The journey took him through Gudbrandsdalen and over to Sogn and the Western coast of Norway. The planned collection was not published. For Ibsen's collection of folk tales, see HIS V/B 550.

Ibsen addresses the stylistic resources of a popular form such as the ballad, which he would draw from in *The Feast at Solhaug* and *Olaf Liljekrans*. He turns to sagas, folk tales, and orally transmitted songs and stories (in *Peer Gynt*, for example). Ibsen, in short, has all the credentials of a *Sturm und Drang*er.

In a Norwegian context, the *Sturm und Drang* movement extends well beyond Ibsen and his circle of poet-friends. The paintings of J. C. Dahl, for example, clearly express a *Sturm und Drang* sensibility. Dahl was a colleague of Caspar David Friedrich and a professor at the Academy in Dresden and thus served as a bridge between German and Scandinavian art.[47] During his first visit to Dresden, Ibsen, a talented painter himself, socialized with the Norwegian circle of artists.[48] Another important name in this context is Adolph Tidemand, whose most famous work, *Bridal Procession on the Hardangerfjord*, was produced in tandem with Hans Gude.[49] Now prominently displayed at the National Gallery in Oslo, this work was originally produced as a tableau for Christiania Theater (see color plate 3). Among these painters, we see a desire to explore Norwegian nature, culture, history, and art. Yet this project is itself mediated by larger movements in European culture. This is also the case with Ibsen—a point that becomes particularly evident if we take into account his writings on drama and theater.

In the period around *The Vikings at Helgeland*, Ibsen published a two-part essay on the heroic ballad (*Kjæmpevisen*).[50] Ibsen deals specifically with folk song—a kind of poetry that, in his view, is not sung *for* but *by* and *of* the people (HIS XVI 140). He assumes a Herderian connection between song

---

[47] Toril Moi even airs the proposition that Ibsen, in *The Vikings at Helgeland*, "follows in Dahl's footsteps." It is, she writes, "as if Dahl urges Norwegians to go on to produce new heroic deeds in remembrance of their past greatness." Moi, *Henrik Ibsen and the Birth of Modernism*, 47.

[48] After his initial visit, Ibsen would reside in Dresden between 1868 and 1875; Dahl, though, died in 1857. See Koht, *Henrik Ibsen. Eit Diktarliv*, vol. I 97; *The Life of Ibsen*, vol. I, 79–80. Ibsen offers sustained impressions and reflections on painting in a lengthy poem from this period, "In the Picture Gallery."

[49] J. C. Dahl and Tidemand both had a background in more popular, decorating arts. Much later, when Munch was sketching stage images for Hermann Bahr's 1906 production of *Hedda Gabler* in Berlin, he was encouraged to draw on the more decorative arts and crafts movement. See Templeton, *Munch's Ibsen*, 56–57. Munch also made a series of works based on Ibsen's early, historical drama, especially *The Pretenders*.

[50] The article addresses the resuscitation of historical, especially Scandinavian material, with which Ibsen had been occupied since his reading of Niels Matthias Petersen's translation of the Icelandic sagas. Petersen's efforts comprised not only translations and a comprehensive history of Scandinavian literature, but also more political work with respect to Scandinavian identity, including his making the case for old Norse to replace Latin in the gymnasium.

and poetry. Song and poetry, he suggests, grow out of a surplus of energy.[51] Ibsen also advocates a reassessment of Medieval poetry and sees the return to Medieval literature as a particularly romantic gesture (HIS XVI 146). These points, too, had been made by Herder. Two further considerations link Ibsen's position to Herder: his insistence on the importance of the historicity of art and his interest in Shakespeare.

According to Ibsen, the element of song is drained from modern art. Modern poetry is reflective of, and driven by, a quest for knowledge (HIS XVI 142). Thus, to present contemporary art as sung would be to ignore history. Just as Herder compares the classicist approach with an attempt to bring back to life dead flowers,[52] Ibsen, when discussing a return to past artforms, suggests the image of cut flowers that can no longer grow roots (HIS XVI 142). He emphasizes that in turning to historical material and forms we need an awareness that they, in a modern context, cannot be brought to life in their original appearance. In addressing the saga literature as material for contemporary drama, Ibsen thus speaks of a need to synthesize the epic and the lyrical—a synthesis that he, like Herder (and, as we will see in Chapter 2, Hegel follows suit), locates at the heart of modern drama (HIS XVI 144). With this gesture, the historical material is turned into something new. The production of a new, synthetic artform is indeed the very point of this historical maneuver; the goal is not to breathe life into an old form but to present the saga material with a form that matches the awareness of its historicity. As Ibsen polemically reminds his readers, a sculpture does not grow ears and eyes just because it is created in a material evoking the color(s) of human skin (HIS XVI 144).[53]

Like the philosophers before him, Ibsen connects the spirit of *Sturm und Drang* movement with a new interest in Shakespearean drama.[54] Ibsen had been familiar with Shakespeare at least since his first trip to Copenhagen.[55] In

---

[51] In Ibsen's words: "det synger kun naar det i sit Indre bærer paa mere end det kan raade med, mere end det tiltrænger til dagligt Behov" (HIS XVI 142). The Herderian notion of a surplus of energy being required for art echoes, in different forms, in Hegel and Nietzsche.

[52] Herder, *Werke*, II, 531.

[53] It is worth noting that the reference to sculpture (a medium that is central to Lessing's and Herder's aesthetics) also features in *Peer Gynt, Emperor and Galilean*, and *When We Dead Awaken*. I return to this point later on.

[54] Similarly, we find Bjørnson, in a 1858 letter, report that he has spent the summer reading nothing but Shakespeare, romances, and Oehlenschläger—"what joy!," he exclaims. See Bjørnstjerne Bjørnson, *Gro-tid*, vol. 1, 71.

[55] While in Copenhagen, Ibsen saw four Shakespeare performances, including *Hamlet*. See letter of May 16, 1852 (HIS XII 49). According to Meyer, the other Shakespeare plays he saw were *King Lear, Romeo and Juliet*, and *As You Like It*. Meyer, *Ibsen*, 114. Heiberg, the director of the theater, had met with Ibsen and showed him around the theater. Even though he was a philosopher of a

an earlier newspaper note, Ibsen draws attention to a reading (performance) of *Hamlet*. The performance, as he sees it, not only offers the Norwegian audience a chance to familiarize itself with Elizabethan drama, but also realizes "the massive importance Shakespeare has had for Scandinavian art" (HIS XVI 138, my trans.). One can only wonder what art Ibsen had in mind and whether his own work would qualify.[56] Ibsen also speaks of the need to cultivate a taste for Shakespearean poetry in Norway (HIS XVI 138, my trans.). Seeking to facilitate such cultivation, Ibsen not only integrates Shakespearean elements into his historical drama, but also gives a lecture on Shakespeare, though the manuscript for this lecture is lost.[57] Ibsen's interest

Hegelian disposition (I return to this point in Chapter 2), he did not share Hegel's fascination with Shakespeare on stage. Yet, Heiberg valued Shakespeare's work as literature and used lines from *Hamlet* in the introduction to his logic. As part of his more romantic phase, Heiberg had turned to Calderón (see Finn Hauberg Mortensen, "Heiberg and the Theater: In Oehlenschläger's Limelight," in *The Heibergs and the Theater: Between Vaudeville, Romantic Comedy and National Drama*, ed. Jon Stewart [Copenhagen: Museum Tusculanum Press, 2012], 21). In spite of Heiberg's reluctance, there had been a bit of a Shakespeare craze in Copenhagen. Following the 1813 production of *Hamlet*, there had been no fewer than 385 performances of fifteen Shakespeare plays. For Heiberg's antipathies, see András Nagy, "Either Hegel or Dialectics: Johan Ludvig Heiberg, *Homme de théâtre*," in *Johan Ludvig Heiberg: Philosopher, Littérateur, Dramaturge, and Political Thinker*, ed. Jon Stewart (Copenhagen: Museum Tusculanum Press, 2008), 366–367. For Shakespeare in Copenhagen, see Elisabete M. de Sousa, "Eugène Scribe: The Unfortunate Authorship of a Successful Author," in *Kierkegaard and the Renaissance and Modern Traditions*, vol. III: *Literature, Drama, and Music*, ed. Jon Stewart (Farnham: Ashgate, 2009), 169–185 (173 in particular). For an overview of Shakespeare in Danish translation and on stage, see Martin B. Ruud, *An Essay toward a History of Shakespeare in Denmark*, Studies in Language and Literature, no. 8 (Minneapolis: University of Minnesota, 1920).

[56] Some have argued that *The Pretenders* is a study of Shakespeare in drama form. See Francis Bull, "The Influence of Shakespeare on Wergeland, Ibsen and Bjørnson," *The Norseman*, no. 15 (1957): 88–95.

[57] As Inga-Stina Ewbank makes clear, the Shakespeare Ibsen encountered, both in Copenhagen and elsewhere, was mediated through German translations and criticism. See Inga-Stina Ewbank, "Ibsen and Shakespeare: Reading the Silence," in *Ibsen at the Centre for Advanced Study*, ed. Vigdis Ystad (Oslo: Scandinavian University Press, 1997), 89–90. Needless to say, the German reception includes Herder's work to promote Shakespearean drama and, somewhat later, the Schlegel-Tieck translation. It also includes the work of Hermann Hettner, who had argued that Shakespeare ought to serve as a model for modern drama. Hettner views Shakespeare as, among other things, an example of a historical dramatist. See *Das moderne Drama. Aesthetische Untersuchungen* (Braunschweig: F. Vieweg, 1852), 18–42. Beyond the works of German critics and philosophers, the Shakespeare centenary in 1864 would further the interest in his work. This interest did not only cover Shakespeare's drama (as text), but also the stage and its architecture. In Dresden, Ibsen was affiliated with the Shakespeare translator Wolf Graf von Baudissin, who had joined forces with Gottfried Semper to try and reconstruct the theatrical spaces of the Elizabethan era. See Introduction to *Letters*, XIII/B 59. See also Herbert A. Frenzel, *Geschichte des Theaters. Daten und Dokumente 1470–1890* (München: Deutscher Taschenbuch Verlag, 1984), 509. Later, Semper's work would influence Wilhelm Dilthey. See Wilhelm Dilthey, *Poetry and Experience, Selected Works*, vol. V, ed. Rudolf A. Makkreel and Frithjof Rodi (Princeton: Princeton University Press, 1985), 190; *Gesammelte Schriften*, twenty-six vols. (Göttingen: Vandenhoeck and Ruprecht, 1914–2005), vol. VI, 256. Ibsen and Dilthey met in Tyrol, where they both vacationed. Dilthey's wife, Katharina Dilthey describes their conversation in Gossensass in the summer of 1889. See Katharina Dilthey, "Eine Erinnerung an Henrik Ibsen," *Westermanns illustrierte deutsche Monatshefte*, Dec. 1922, pp. 362–364. See also Narve Fulsås and Gudrun Kühne-Bertram, "Ibsen and Dilthey: Evidence of a Forgotten Acquaintance," *Ibsen Studies*,

in Shakespeare was not a short-lived infatuation. While Ibsen, during his years as theater director, did not stage an original Shakespeare play—his work was only staged in Norway in 1865–66 (by Bjørnson)[58]—he retained an interest in Shakespearean drama.[59]

It is important to grasp the polemical backdrop of Ibsen's interest in Shakespeare. For Ibsen, romanticism is Shakespearean, and the new drama to which Ibsen connects is, in turn, of a romantic hue. Ibsen also conveys the Herderian (and later Hegelian) thought that the poetry of the people is its philosophy (HIS XVI 157). Further, he sees Shakespearean theater as realizing Hamlet's insight that "[t]here are more things in heaven and earth . . . than are dreamt of in your philosophy."[60] This, he further argues, is the germ of the romantic outlook on life (*den romantiske livsanskuelse*; HIS XVI 157). By turning to Shakespeare, Ibsen, in the vein of the *Sturm und Drang*'ers, could view himself as contributing to the establishment of a Norwegian literature and theater independent of Danish culture. As he makes it clear, "the nation and the Danish theater are two altogether different entities" (HIS XVI 198, my trans.). What is more, this is not simply a Norwegian, but indeed a European matter. From a European point of view, Ibsen argues, the dominance of Danish theater prevents artistic flourishing in Scandinavia; it quells the manifold of poetry and stage life (HIS XVI 210). For Ibsen, the reevaluation of Norwegian drama (vis-à-vis a Danish taste) is part of a broader appreciation of artistic manifold. As he puts it in 1861, we should realize that the stage art in Berlin will differ from that in Vienna.[61]

With this larger picture in mind, we see that while scholars are right in taking Ibsen's early work to be expressive of a deep-seated commitment to romanticism and the *Sturm und Drang* program, it is not right to see this, per

---

vol. 9, no. 1 (2009): 3–18. For a helpful study of Semper's historicism, see Mari Hvattum's *Gottfried Semper and the Problem of Historicism* (Cambridge: Cambridge University Press, 2004), especially Chapters 7 through 9.

[58] Ewbank, "Ibsen and Shakespeare: Reading the Silence," 96. Ibsen, though, staged an adapted version of *As You Like It* (*Livet i Skoven*, 1855). I thank Narve Fulsås for this point.

[59] As late as in 1896, Ibsen mentions that he has read and appreciated Brandes's work on Shakespeare: "Hele Deres store monumentale værk om Shakespeare har jeg ikke alene læst men jeg har fordybet mig deri, som neppe i nogen anden bog. Jeg synes at både Shakespeare, hans samtid og De selv med lever og ånder i denne Deres geniale digtning. Hjertelig tak for den berigelse De derigennem har skænket mig!" Letter of October 3, 1896 (HIS XV 361); see also letter of Dec. 30, 1898 (HIS XV 459).

[60] For Shakespeare, see *Hamlet*, 1.5.167–8 (Hamlet to Horatio). Ibsen lightly edits the quote, rendering it "there is more between heaven and earth than philosophers know how to say [veed af at sige]" (HIS XVI 146, my trans.).

[61] HIS XVI 230, see also 240–241 for a discussion of Danish theater at the time.

se, as a sign of regressive nostalgia or a naïve historical attitude. Instead, a full appreciation of Ibsen's *Sturm und Drang* commitment requires an appreciation of the complex relationship between drama and history that is developed in this movement. How, then, is this relationship between drama and history reflected in *The Vikings at Helgeland*? In order to answer this question, we need to ask what sense of history is conveyed in this work, most importantly through the character of Hjørdis.

Traditions Fading

As the play's main character, Hjørdis embodies the values of the saga period. She is uncompromisingly proud, and her pride is related to her willingness to stick to customs and family obligations. For her, values such as forgiveness and compassion are signs of weakness. Facing a demand for compromise, Hjørdis claims that she would rather perish than save her life through settlement (OI II 39; HIS III 369). When challenged, she brazenly threatens her foster father and relatives:

> HJØRDIS. [. . . .] As for you, Ørnulf—beware! This is where our paths divide. But I thereby swear enmity against you and all your kinsmen, whenever and wherever we may meet. You will never feel safe, either for life or limb, nor shall any of the others. (OI II 41; HIS III 372)

Hjørdis's husband, Gunnar, is her opposite. He is gentle and incorporates the promises of a future Christian era ("brave though he is, he has no taste for fighting" [OI III 42; HIS III 375]). His friend Sigurd is heroic and, in this sense, Hjørdis's equal. Yet Sigurd's actions are marked by kindness and generosity. An example of this is his effort to save Gunnar, his blood-brother, by offering the angry Ørnulf the following deal:

> Take it all, both my ships, every single thing that is mine, and let me return with you to Iceland as the poorest man in your company. What I give, I can win again. But if you march against Gunnar, I shall never know happiness again. (OI II 42; HIS III 375)

Sigurd's wife, and Hjørdis's foster sister, Dagny, is compassionate and mild-mannered but fails to understand the passions that funnel into her husband's heroic ways.

Hjørdis and Sigurd are similar in outlooks and visions of life and, it turns out, in their feelings for each other. Back in Iceland, Hjørdis was excited to hear about Sigurd's dream of finding, in his wife, a true Viking companion. She later remembers his calling word by word. As she reconstructs this episode to the tortured Dagny, who is certainly no Viking, Sigurd had made it clear that "[t]he one [he] must choose must not be content to live modestly. No distinction must seem too high for her to aspire to. She must be willing to come with [him on his] Viking raids, and wear the armor of battle; she must urge [him] to the fight, and not flinch when sword-blades flash" (OI II 72; HIS III 435). It was, moreover, Sigurd who had met Hjørdis's challenge of killing the ferocious white bear that guarded her door, only to ascribe, in a gesture of heroic friendship, this deed to Gunnar. Gunnar then went off to marry her. Sigurd married Dagny. However, with Sigurd's marriage to Dagny and his friendship with Gunnar, a true union between Sigurd and Hjørdis cannot be completed. Yet, in a certain sense, Sigurd and Hjørdis's relationship is the only true marriage in the play. When Hjørdis realizes that Sigurd has loved her the entire time, she is prepared to denounce her family and embark on a heroic quest for traditional glory:

HJØRDIS. Let Gunnar stay here. Let Dagny go back to Iceland with her father. I will follow you, in battle array, wherever you may go [SIGURD *shows agitation*]. Not as your wife will I go—for I have belonged to another, and the woman still lives who has lain by your side. No, not as your wife, Sigurd, but as a Valkyrie is how I will come—firing blood to battle and to great deeds, standing by your side as the sword-blows fall, shoulder to shoulder with your fighting men in storm and tempest. And when your funeral song is sung, it shall tell of Sigurd and Hjørdis together. (OI II 78; HIS III 447)

For Sigurd, this is not an option:

SIGURD. That used to be my fondest dream. Now it is too late. Gunnar and Dagny stand between us, and both with every right to stand where they do. I destroyed my young love for Gunnar's sake—if I am to suffer the pain of that, at least what I did must not be in vain. And then Dagny—leaving her home and her people so trustingly, putting all her faith in me. She must never suspect that every time she took me in her arms I really yearned for Hjørdis. (OI II 78; HIS III 447)

The play ends with Hjørdis killing Sigurd in the hope of an eternal union in afterlife. Upon killing him, however, she realizes that he is a Christian and that their ways must therefore part.[62]

In Ibsen's drama, Hjørdis feels more strongly and is more dedicated to her values than the other characters. Moreover, her passion is fueled by an acute awareness of inhabiting a period of transition. She senses how old values vanish before they are fully understood and appreciated. In a world of change, Hjørdis clings to the values of the past: pride, honor, and old-fashioned heroism.

What makes Hjørdis such a troubled yet fascinating character is, therefore, not simply that she stands opposed to Gunnar, her weak husband, and Sigurd, her real love. In a certain sense, she stands opposed to the entire world of which she is a part. She is pained by her humiliating position first as the foster daughter of the man who killed her father (Ørnulf), and then as the wife of a man who had, after all, not met her challenge of killing the bear. But she is also pained at the pace with which the world she knew, that of family, tradition, bravery, and pride, is eroding. Hjørdis suffers not only because she cannot have Sigurd, for whom she clearly longs, but also because the ideals she lives by no longer have a place in the world. Hence, Hjørdis's tragedy is of love lost, but also of transience and decaying values.

The Vikings at Helgeland is not merely a historical play (i.e., a play about a Norwegian-Icelandic past), but also a play about Hjørdis's attempts—or rather: failing attempts—to return to the past. Further, in the spirit of Ibsen's essay on the ballad, it is a play about a certain kind of literature: the poetry of the saga period, as it is now a thing of the past. As such, it is a play about historical experience. In The Vikings at Helgeland, Ibsen does not naïvely seek to restore the past and shape the cultural identity of the audience in its image. At stake, rather, is a work that, in line with the ambitions of the Sturm und Drang and early romantic movements, explores how pre-modern literature can be re-actualized and gain a new life in the modern era. Hjørdis's dream of

---

[62] Echoing the Sturm und Drang movement's return to Norse mythology, Hjørdis is carried away by an Aasgardsrei. Peter Nicolai Arbo, known as the illustrator of Asbjørnsen and Moe's collection of folktales, painted several pictures of the Aasgardsrei. Arbo had spent time in Düsseldorf with Tidemand and Gude.

creating a new saga, that of Hjørdis and Sigurd, was doomed to fail.[63] Ibsen, by contrast, does not create a saga, but, through his choice of the drama form, expresses an awareness of the distance between the old and the new, the time of the saga and the time of the dramatic poet.

Past and Present Histories

When Ibsen first mentions *The Vikings at Helgeland*, he describes a play that would "be rather different from [his] previous works, both in tone and content."[64] How? Ibsen does not answer this question. In his reflections on the ballad, however, he offers some clues. The saga literature, he claims, is a thing of the past. We cannot relate to it in an immediate way or read it as it was once read. Further, a dramatist wanting to draw on the sagas is bound to modify its content and poetic form. Ibsen's worry, though, is not that such a modification will distance us too much from the original pathos of the saga literature. Rather, he worries that a translation from one genre to another will bring the saga material too close and make it too familiar to us moderns. As he puts it in his 1857 essay, this would not be desirable: if "the dramatic treatment brings the saga age closer to light and shadows ... closer to reality ... this is precisely what should *not* happen" (HIS XVI 144). Ibsen, further, compares this to the situation of French classicism, which, in his view, did not succeed in bringing to life the forms of the past.[65] Finally, he dismisses classical poetical forms (especially iambic pentameter) when making use of the old, Nordic material.

While the characters of *The Vikings at Helgeland*, could, as Bjørnson points out, come across as being of an undeniably saga- or god-like stature,[66] the real

[63] This point is nicely spelled out in Kaplan's "Hedda and Hjørdis."
[64] Letter to Paul Botten-Hansen, Apr. 28, 1857 (HIS XII 96). The letter arrived only a week or so after Botten-Hansen had received the essay on the ballad, which had been properly written out after Ibsen initially presented the material in lecture form on February 2 (at the "Society of December 22," an intellectual Bergen circle).
[65] In the Norwegian original: "I Frankrig besidder man noget Lignende i den eftergjorte antike Tragedie, men som det gik med denne der, saa gik det med Skaldepoesien her; til en vis Grad fandt begge Kunstarter et Slags Udbredelse indenfor enkelte Kredse af Samfundet, men dybt og inderligt at gro ind i Folket, at indforlive sig i dettes Tænkesæt, dertil har ingen af dem været istand" (HIS XVI 151).
[66] The first exchange between Sigurd and Hjørdis's father, Ørnulf, exemplifies this point:
ØRNULF [*shouts*]. Stand away, Viking!
SIGURD [*turns, and grasps his sword.*] If I did, it would be the first time ever!
ØRNULF. You must! And you shall! My men are frozen. I need that shed as a shelter for them tonight.
SIGURD. I need it for an exhausted woman.

drama cannot be reduced to the level of plot, outer character formation, or spoken lines. The driving conflict is not the one between Sigurd and Hjørdis, nor the one that is played out in the affective quadrangle of which they are a part. What really matters, I want to propose, is the drama between old and modern times.[67] This drama is played out in terms of Hjørdis's subjective (and in this sense: modern) responses to her world and her experiences.

In my reading, *The Vikings at Helgeland* is certainly an expression of *Sturm und Drang* sentiments. However, it is not, for that reason, sentimental or backward-looking. It is a *modern* historical play. Once Ibsen, in his *Sturm und Drang* spirit, has rejected the ideal of an imitation of the past, he is free to explore the lived experience of time passing, of values changing, and of individuals failing to adjust their self-understanding to the horizon of meaning that characterizes the world in which they live. In *The Vikings at Helgeland*, Hjørdis understands herself as somebody who lives in and by the tradition. It is, paradoxically, precisely *by* this self-understanding that she proves to be out of pace with her time. The plot-based question of whether or not Hjørdis will be able, as it were, to return to the past, rewrite it, and be unified with Sigurd is of marginal interest.[68] As the audience will know far too well, such a turn of events is impossible. Nor are the characters exhausted by reference to their god-like speech (Bjørnson). Rather, the dramatic nerve of the play is related to how Hjørdis, being cut off from the tradition with which she grew up, relates to what she experiences as a loss of values. As Hjørdis puts it in her *Todeslied*:

> This place holds no happiness for me.... The White [Christian] God makes for the north. I do not wish to meet him. The old gods are no longer strong, not as they were before.... They sleep, they are almost like shades. (OI II 90; HIS III 470)

ØRNULF. My men are worth more than your women!
SIGURD. Then they must put a high price on the heads of outlaws here in Helgeland.
(OI II 31; HIS III 353–354)
   This barren, cleanly chiseled form, we must assume, is what Bjørnson had in mind.

[67] Indeed, we find similar topics in the saga literature itself, including *Njáls saga* and its portrait of the transition from a pagan to a Christian era.

[68] Nevertheless, Hjørdis's lines and actions demonstrate the aporetic status of her values in the modern (Christian) world: This contributes not only to her confusion, as a character, but also to the intrigue of Ibsen's drama: If Sigurd kills Gunnar, so as to be able to marry Hjørdis, then she, in turn, cannot marry Sigurd but needs to kill him to keep her pride and honor intact—the pride and honor that made Sigurd fall for her in the first place.

Hjørdis's torment is not just her tragic love story, but also her inability to live through change. Her world is god-forsaken, her very self, her identity and self-understanding, emerges as hollow and without anchoring in the tradition she had previously taken for granted. More than the back and forth of lost love, pride, and revenge, this is the challenge she confronts—and that she tragically fails to live up to.

I want to dwell, at this point, on how Ibsen gets this point across at the level of dramatic nuance (rather than spoken language). In Hjørdis's lines, the literal meaning of her words is often tempered down, modified, or questioned by way of stage directions. She expresses herself "*with suppressed scorn,*" she is "*controlling herself,*" and she speaks "*sharply.*" The list goes on to instruct the performance of Hjørdis's lines: "*forcefully,*" "(being in) *a wild outburst,*" "*laughing,*" "*smiling,*" and "*raising her voice.*" The Hjørdis character, further, is instructed to deliver her lines "*with a mocking smile,*" "*in a low voice quivering with anger,*" "*restraining herself,*" "*wildly,*" "*with suppressed emotion,*" "*trembling with agitation,*" "*pensively,*" "*with forced laughter,*" "*vehemently,*" "*passionately,*" "*with a scornful smile,*" "*with a quiet smile,*" "*bitterly,*" "*breathlessly,*" "*with composure,*" "*quickly,*" "*with dignity,*" "*tensely,*" "*hastily,*" "*quietly triumphant,*" "*softly and pensively,*" "*with dignity,*" "*joyfully,*" "*aghast,*" "*in despair,*" and "*quietly.*" It is through the tone of her voice and her body language—as it is acted out—that the audience gets to know Hjørdis's existential quandary. In her final, dying gesture, Hjørdis no longer speaks with force but mutters to herself in utter desperation:

> Dead! Then mine is indeed a wasted soul! [*The storm increases and she cries out wildly.*] They are coming [the forces that will carry her to the land of the dead, my addition (KG)]! My spells bring them here! No, no! I will not come with you! I will not ride without Sigurd! No good . . . they can see me! They are laughing, they are waving to me! They spur on their horses [*She rushes to the edge of the cliff in the background.*] Here they are upon me . . . and nowhere to shelter, nowhere to hide! Yes, perhaps at the bottom of the sea! [*She throws herself over*]. (OI II 91; HIS III 471–472)

Hjørdis's drama can only be fully captured in the theater or by an audience that, when reading, is attuned to dramatic cues—thus emphasizing the sense that we here encounter the saga material precisely in the context of modern performative art.

With Hjørdis's tragedy at its center—the tragedy of her demise when facing times lost, values fading, and the realization that she is a "wasted soul"—*The Vikings at Helgeland* emerges as a modern drama in Herder's meaning of the term.

Reassessing *Sturm und Drang*

In *The Vikings at Helgeland*, Ibsen actively and consciously appropriates and modifies historical material so as to present it in drama form. It is by preparing it for stage—and for a reading audience that is sensitive to dramatic cues—that this turns into a deliberately modern work. In dealing with the historical material, in preparing it *as drama*, Ibsen does not seek to imitate, but makes a thoughtful, artistically productive, and modern use of the historical material.

Ibsen's early work focuses on moments at which old worldviews are about to lose their grip, but it is still not clear what, exactly, the future will bring and what patterns of self-understanding and cultural identifications are about to emerge. He, no doubt, writes historical plays—but historical plays that, with their emphasis on individual experience and reflection, have a contemporary edge and philosophical depth. Throughout his historical drama, Ibsen develops his craft as a playwright. He also, in this period, introduces a number of powerful, female protagonists that lay the groundwork for later characters such as Nora and Hedda Gabler, but also Hedvig, Rebecca West, and Ellida Wangel.[69] Most importantly for our context, Ibsen's early historical drama develops the kinds of questions—of identity, self-understanding, of tradition making and -breaking, of the relationship between historical normativity and contemporary ideals of autonomy—that will characterize his later work. In this sense, *The Vikings at Helgeland* crucially contributes to Ibsen's oeuvre *and* serves to illuminate his interest in historical drama and historical experience more broadly.

---

[69] From this point of view, I question Toril Moi's suggestion that it is only with *Emperor and Galilean*, and with even more force and clarity, *A Doll's House*, that Ibsen makes a full-fledged turn to female characters and psychology, which, as she sees it, is closely associated with his turn to modernism. If the early plays are not works of dramatic modernism, they still explore the kind of modernity that, in turn, establishes the conditions of possibility for the modernism to come. What is more, they do so through a series of unforgettable female characters—characters that are not only staged (and thus offering acting opportunities to women actors), but that are also, within their own plays, staging the social relationships and interpersonal encounters that drive these works to their completion. For Moi's point, see *Henrik Ibsen and the Birth of Modernism*, 188–223, in particular 188–189.

Once we have grasped the philosophical complexity of the *Sturm und Drang* movement, we can see how Ibsen, as a dramatist, makes active and poetic use of it. He brings the insights of the *Sturm und Drang* philosophy of drama as far as it can possibly be taken—and then he continues, from within this very framework, beyond it. With splendid dramatic necessity, the character of Hjørdis realizes the impossibility of a return to the past. Moreover, the very moment Hjørdis realizes that her values and her tradition are gone, the focus is no longer on the values she holds and the way she holds them, but on her subjective suffering. In the final scene, Hjørdis's agonizing, her subjective response to her predicament, is all-encompassing. While growing out of the kind of experiences that were at the center of the *Sturm und Drang* movement's discussion of history, this subjective turn cannot be fully exhausted by its philosophical resources. It is as if the somewhat belated *Sturm und Drang* movement in Scandinavian art and letters enables Ibsen, in his early work, to dramatize how this kind of paradigm bursts its own boundaries and calls for an orientation toward selfhood and subjectivity that it itself enables but cannot fully encompass.

This gets even clearer when we, in Chapter 2, turn to *Peer Gynt*, the great, ironical epos that—pulling together *Sturm und Drang* sentiments, romantic fantasy, and a play with Hegelian-philosophical references—would fascinate not only the contemporary audiences in Ibsen's Norway, but also the avant-gardes in France and Germany.[70]

---

[70] For example, Alfred Jarry would stage *Peer Gynt* in Paris in 1896. See Jill Fell, *Alfred Jarry* (London: Reaktion Books, 2010), 80. See also Catherine Naugrette, "Patrice Chéreau's *Peer Gynt*: A Renewed Reception of Ibsen's Theater in France," in *Global Ibsen: Performing Multiple Modernities*, ed. Erika Fischer-Lichte, Barbara Gronau, and Christel Weiler (London: Routledge, 2011), 166–175, 167–169 in particular. For a discussion of Jarry's importance for later avant-garde theater, see Manuel L. Grossman, "Alfred Jarry and the Theater of His Time," *Modern Drama*, vol. 13, no. 1 (1970): 10–21.

2

History Adrift; Subjectivity Probed
(*Peer Gynt*)

With *Peer Gynt*, we transition from the second half of the 1850s to the second half of the 1860s. The Norwegian Theater in Christiania, where Ibsen had taken up the position as artistic director, struggled financially. Not long after, he left for Continental Europe. It would take almost twenty-seven years for him to return to live in Norway. Ibsen first settled in Rome, where he was exposed to a new historical, artistic, and intellectual environment.

Both in Norway and in Ibsen's circles in Rome, the *Sturm und Drang* sentiments were waning. Hegelianism was a rising intellectual star—philosophy *de rigueur*—among intellectuals, artists, critics, and stage directors. In Rome, Ibsen socialized with Lorentz Dietrichson, who had started out as a Hegelian art historian.[1] Among the influential aestheticians and critics back in Christiania was Marcus Jacob Monrad, who had produced his own version of the Hegelian system of the arts, written on theater and acting, and also reviewed Ibsen's work.[2] In Copenhagen, Johan Ludvig Heiberg, the Director of the Royal Theater, had started out as a romantic, but had later turned into a card-carrying Hegelian.[3]

---

[1] For an account of Dietrichson's intellectual development and his transition from idealism to a Hippolyte Taine–inspired, inductive notion of art history (after he got his professorship in Christiania in 1875), see Mai Britt Guleng, "Lorentz Dietrichson and the Making of Norwegian Art History," in *Towards a Science of Art History: J. J. Tikkanen and Art Historical Scholarship in Europe*, ed. Johanna Vakkari, Studies in Art History, no. 38 (Helsinki, 2009), 59–71. Dietrichson also wrote a study of poetry, claiming that the early modern period, rather than a Danish-oriented later phase, paved the way for Ibsen's breakthrough (ibid., 60–61). See also Asbjørn Aarseth, "*Peer Gynt* and Hegel's Ideas on Egyptian Art," *Scandinavian Studies*, vol. 74, no. 4 (2001): 563. For a fuller account of Ibsen's stays in Rome and travels with Dietrichson, see Per Jonas Nordhagen, *Henrik Ibsen i Roma, 1864–1868* (Oslo: Cappelen Forlag, 1981), Koth, *Henrik Ibsen*, 231–233, and Aarseth's introduction to HIS V/B 55256.

[2] For Monrad's reviews, see http://ibsen.nb.no/id/186.0. For Monrad's general aesthetic position, see M. J. Monrad, *Tolv Forelæsninger om det Skjønne* (Christiania: Det Norske Studentersamfunds forlag, 1859). Later, Monrad would publish *Tankeretninger i den nyere Tid. Et kritisk Rundskue* (Christiania: Aschehoug, 1874) and *Æsthetik. Det Skjønne og dets Forekomst i Natur og Kunst*, three vols. (Christiania: Cammermeyer, 1889–1890).

[3] Before Heiberg was introduced to Hegel in 1824, his work had leaned on Tieck and the Schlegels. Heiberg's exposure to romanticism may have been strengthened through his friendship with Ida Bruun, who had spent time with Germaine de Staël (whom, in turn, was close to A.W. Schlegel). It

The Drama of History. Kristin Gjesdal, Oxford University Press (2021). © Oxford University Press.
DOI: 10.1093/oso/9780190070762.001.0001.

Ibsen rarely engages in explicit discussion of philosophy. However, in this period, he makes an important exception when responding, in 1872, to the Danish translation of John Stuart Mill's *Utilitarianism*. While he admits that he has no professional training in philosophy, Ibsen continues to note that, insofar as "there are writers [like Mill] who lay down the law about philosophy without any knowledge of Hegel or German thought in general," it seems that "anything goes [mangt og meget kan være tilladt]" (HIS XIII 119, my trans.). For the former *Sturm und Drang*'er, to think philosophically without Hegel now appears irresponsible. From this point of view, it is no surprise that readers of Ibsen's work from this period have been struck by its Hegelian tone.

Interpreters of *Peer Gynt* have pointed out how Ibsen borrows from Hegel's *Lectures on Fine Art*, especially in Act Four.[4] The play's Act Four is partly situated in Egypt, the culture that, in Hegel's view, had established the beginning of great art. Here Ibsen has Peer encounter a character with the name of Herr Begriffenfeldt, whose overly Hegelian language is colored by a characteristic Berlin accent.[5] Further, as Asbjørn Aarseth has pointed out, Ibsen's description of Egypt, especially the Sphinx and the Colossi of Memnon, seems to borrow heavily from Hegel's lectures on fine art.

Ibsen clearly borrows from Hegel in recounting the adventures of Peer Gynt, a legendary figure in Norwegian folklore. Yet, this borrowing is neither limited to the Egypt scene nor to Hegel's philosophy of art. Instead, Ibsen, from the very beginning of *Peer Gynt*, draws on a broader set of Hegelian ideas, especially the philosophy of selfhood and the idea of intersubjective recognition. These topics had also featured prominently—albeit in a more direct historical and political way—within the *Sturm und Drang* movement with which Ibsen had been affiliated. However, even though

is also worth mentioning that, while growing up, Heiberg spent two years with Knud Lyne Rahbek, who was a friend of his father. See John Stewart, *The Cultural Crisis of the Danish Golden Age: Heiberg, Martensen, and Kierkegaard* (København: Museum Tusculanum Press, 2015), 23 and 35. See also Mortensen, "Heiberg and the Theater," 18.

[4] See for example Josef Collin, *Henrik Ibsen. Sein Werk, seine Weltanschauung, sein Leben* (Heidelberg: Carl Winters Universitätsbuchhandlung, 1910), 266–353; Arne Lindén, "Peer Gynt i Egypten," *Edda*, vol. 40 (1940): 237–265; Aarseth, "*Peer Gynt* and Hegel's Ideas on Egyptian Art." The play is only briefly discussed in Brian Johnston's Hegelian reading of Ibsen in *The Ibsen Cycle: The Design of the Plays from "Pillars of Society" to "When We Dead Awaken"* (University Park: Pennsylvania State University Press, 1992). Johnston discusses Peer Gynt in *To the Third Empire: Ibsen's Early Drama* (Minneapolis: University of Minnesota Press, 1980), 164–208.

[5] Though Hegel was from Stuttgart rather than Berlin, he had taught at the University of Berlin from 1818 until his death in 1831.

there are clear overlaps between the *Sturm und Drang* movement and that of Hegelianism, the former never shared in the metaphysical commitments of the latter. Given his affiliation with the *Sturm und Drang* movement, Ibsen is not very likely to simply adopt the grand ambitions of the Hegelian system. Rather, we see Ibsen, in *Peer Gynt*, not only drawing on a Hegelian mindset, but also going beyond it. With humor, irony, and dramatic playfulness, Ibsen makes us aware of a tension in Hegel's philosophy between, on the one hand, the analysis of the dialectical relationship between self and other and, on the other, the ambition to close the historical development of this dialectics with the idea of the end of history in absolute reason. For the dramatic poet, however, the contradictions that threaten the philosophical system are negotiated in artistically enriching ways.

Selfhood and Identity

Like *Brand*, published a year earlier, *Peer Gynt* is a dramatic poem. It contains five acts and counts as a "station drama": temporally, we encounter Peer at different life stages; geographically, the action takes place in Norway, in the Halls of the Mountain King, then in Morocco, Egypt, at sea, and again in Norway. The fourth act, in Morocco and Egypt, is by far the longest. We learn that Peer made his fortune as a slave trader in North America, though neither his time in Charleston nor his transition between regions and continents are directly represented. The play is a *Bildungs*-poem, though a rather peculiar one since Peer, the main character, seems resistant to learning from his experiences and encounters. While the stage is often crowded, Peer, in an emphatic sense, is isolated. This is even true of the opening dialogue with his mother, the subsequent wedding party, and his first encounter with Solvejg, his true love. The pattern is only broken when Peer, in the final scene, returns from his globetrotting and is reunited with Solvejg, who has been home waiting for him the entire time.

The staging of a dramatic poem brings with it a particular set of challenges. The challenges accrue if the poem's locations are as many and as spectacular as those in *Peer Gynt*. One such challenge is how to realize the scenes in Morocco and Egypt.[6] Another is how to stage the Trolls, the Bøyg, and

---

[6] In his discussion of Ingmar Bergman's two *Peer Gynt* productions, Egil Törnqvist remarks that the play today is often produced "by big companies and renowned directors; with its multitude of characters and locations, productions of it tend to be costly." See Egil Törnqvist, *The Serious*

the other mythological creatures that populate the poem. It was Bjørnson who first took the initiative to make a stage-production of *Peer Gynt*. After the 1870 guest performance of Goethe's *Faust* in Christiania—*Faust* being a dramatic poem and *Bildungsgeschichte* to which Ibsen refers in *Peer Gynt*[7]— Bjørnson must have thought the time was ripe to bring Ibsen's unwieldy work to the theater. However, it would take another six years—and the musical aid of Grieg's *Peer Gynt Suite*—until the work was first performed, now adapted to the stage by Ibsen himself.[8]

It is not, however, the extravagant scenery that sets *Peer Gynt* apart in a philosophically interesting way. What matters more is how Peer, right from the opening of the play, is both excluded from and fails to forge bonds with his own culture and, later on, with the cultures he encounters on his travels. This topic runs through and establishes a narrative arc across rapidly changing scenery and landscapes, be they exterior to or symbolically expressive of Peer's state of mind.

The first three acts are set in Gudbrandsdalen, a traditionally wealthy, beautiful, and culturally significant part of Norway. Peer's deceased father is described as a drunkard, but also as a legendary storyteller.[9] His mother is a kind but somewhat simple-minded woman. Peer's peers are portrayed as men of nondescript moral posture, paradigmatically represented by a blacksmith who appears at his most eloquent when communicating with his fists. With the exception of Solvejg, the play's redemptive Gretchen-character, the local girls do little but giggle.[10] Indeed, many of the characters we initially encounter are left nameless (1st WOMAN, 2nd WOMAN, A MAN, A BOY, A GIRL, ANOTHER, A THIRD, etc.). Against this undifferentiated social backdrop, Peer, from the very opening of the poem, is trying to find himself—or, rather, to find a way to be a self in the first place.

Game: Ingmar Bergman as Stage Director (Amsterdam: Amsterdam University Press, 2016), 129. For an overview of the production history, see Marker and Marker, *Ibsen's Lively Art*, 9–45.

[7] In *Peer Gynt*, we get the following reference to *Faust*: "To quote a famous author: / 'Daß ewig weibliche ziehet uns an!'" (OI III 349; HIS V 633). For a reference to the staging of Goethe's *Faust* in Christiania, see Aarseth, "Introduction," HIS V/B 583.

[8] For the relationship between the poet and the composer, see for example Letter to Grieg of January 23, 1874; HID XIII 175–178.

[9] As we will see in Chapters 4 through 6, the legacy of the debauched, deceased father is a recurring topic in Ibsen's work, not the least in *A Doll's House* and *Ghosts*. In Peer Gynt's rural community, however, his father's Dionysian propensity does not call for a response of the kind we later encounter in Mrs. Alving's attempt to cover up her husband's escapades with a facade of bourgeois respectability.

[10] In her study of Ibsen's heroines, Lou Andreas-Salomé leaves out Solvejg. Solvejg, for her, would probably be a too passive character. Her leaving out of Hjørdis is, in this context, more surprising. See Andreas-Salomé, *Henrik Ibsens Frauen-Gestalten; Ibsen's Heroines*.

The topic of selfhood is situated right at the center of Hegel's philosophy. For Hegel, modern selfhood entails a call to self-determination. However, this call to self-determination comes with a particular set of risks. As Hegel views it, these risks are especially evident in the movement of romanticism, which he takes to celebrate a particularly problematic version of individualism. Hegel's target is mainly the romantic group in Jena. With their turn to humor, irony, and the works of the imagination, the Jena romantics, in Hegel's opinion, had come to hypostatize an aestheticized and irresponsible idea of selfhood.

Hegel formulated his criticism of romanticism a good thirty years before Ibsen wrote *Peer Gynt*. For Hegel, the romantics, with their aestheticizing attitudes, had misunderstood the very nature of the self—and, moreover, their philosophy was itself a threat to modern selfhood. In Hegel's reading, the romantics saw the self as detached from a larger, intersubjective community and thus abandoned the call to action and engagement with the real world.[11] A self-absorbed ego cannot forge genuine bonds with others or with culture at large. Romantic subjectivity is therefore deprived of genuine interaction with others and, as such, it "signifies the lack of a steady basis" (LHP III 510; HW XX 418). This, Hegel continues, is nothing short of a pathological condition, one in which "[t]he extravagances of subjectivity constantly pass into madness" (LHP III, 510; HW XX 418). Madness—and the intertwining of subjectivism and madness—is also a topic in *Peer Gynt*.

I return to Hegel's discussion of subjectivity and madness. What matters at this point is how Hegel, for all his criticism, still admits that the romantic spirit correctly depicts an aspect of modern existence. In romantic art and philosophy, he grants, the modern individual has reached a sophisticated level of self-articulation—there is, as it were, a moment of truth in its exaggerated being. In his dense, philosophical prose, Hegel suggests that in its

---

[11] Had Hegel taken into account—as Brandes and Dilthey would later do—the importance of Herder for the romantic movement, he could have ended up with an altogether different picture of it. When Hegel addresses romanticism, it is not its historical-anthropological spirit but the (Kantian-Fichtean) emphasis on transcendental subjectivity that stands at the center of his analysis. For Brandes's view, see *Den romantiske skole i Tyskland*, 31; *The Romantic School*, 21: The romantics "owed far more to Herder. They evidence their descent from him both by their continuation of the *Sturm und Drang* period and by their capacity of understanding and reproducing the poetry of all countries. In Herder the new century germinated, as in Lessing the old had come to its close." And, further, "from Herder the romantics derive that which is most valuable in their literary criticism—the universal receptivity which finds expression in the impulse to translate and explain; from him they derive the first stimulus to a scientific study of both European and Asiatic languages; from him comes their love for what is national in both their own and foreign literature, their love of Spanish romance and of Shakespeare's plays" (ibid.).

turn toward individuality, romanticism indeed enables the later, more adequate forms of idealism: In the "elevation of the spirit *to itself* the spirit wins in itself its objectivity, which hitherto it had to seek in the external and sensuous character of existence, and in this unification with itself it senses and knows itself" (LFA 518; HW XIV128). As he argues, subjectivity is the driving principle of modernity, and modern philosophy first arises with subjectivity's reflective turn toward itself.[12] The problem with the romantics, as Hegel interprets them, is that they fail to see that, as far as (world-) historical spirit is concerned, an individualized, aestheticized notion of freedom, while certainly a particular moment in the development of modern spirit, cannot yield lasting satisfaction.[13]

Peer is a romantic-aestheticizing character in this sense: he is playful and adventuresome, but also, from the point of view of the Hegelian philosopher, irredeemably naïve. To Peer, life remains a solo performance, and even history and tradition are arenas of selfish pursuits and individual edification.

Pathologies of Selfhood

From the beginning of Ibsen's dramatic poem, the reader learns that Peer is unable to understand himself in terms of the ideals and aspirations that exist in his culture. As a result, Peer is ready to turn his back on traditional values and pursue a path of fantastic individualism. Like a Don Quixote of the North, he presents his deeds in an exaggerated and almost tragi-comical way, sprinkling his accounts with creatures and images borrowed from popular culture. If tradition no longer has a hold on him (at least not in the traditional way), then Peer is free to deploy it for his own gain and edification. Rather than being situated in a tradition, Peer bends the tradition to fit his individual purposes and projects. Every story leads back to himself. And his self, in turn, is boosted by the stories that he peddles.

An example of this can be found at the very beginning of the play. Peer returns from a hike in the mountains. His mother reproaches him for having

---

[12] In Hegel's work (just as with Schlegel, Ibsen, and others), the romantic period both designates a more narrow, contemporary movement and the entire period of modern (post-Medieval) art.

[13] In a similar way, modern art is an art of subjectivity, and the romantic genius makes this its very *raison d'être*. As Hegel puts it, the true content of romantic art "is absolute inwardness, and its corresponding form is spiritual subjectivity with its grasp of its independence and freedom" (LFA 519; HW XIV 129). This, for Hegel, is an art that is too reflective and, as such, points beyond art as a sensuous embodiment of spirit.

been away for too long, and Peer responds by telling her that he rode a reindeer over a dangerous mountain pass. His mother eventually recognizes the
barely clad traveling story. A similar episode is played out a little later when
Peer brags that he once caught the devil in a nut and is quickly scorned for
having appropriated a well-known folk tale.[14]

Asbjørnsen and Moe's Grimm-style collection of Norwegian folk tales—
featuring the story of the reindeer ride and the devil in the nut—had
been published in the mid-1840s (their work was also illustrated by Erik
Werenskiold, whose 1895 portrait of Ibsen is here included as color plate 1).[15]
Ibsen had endorsed this *Sturm und Drang* motive and even collected folk poetry. Folk poetry had also featured on the new Norwegian stages, sometimes
accompanied by romantic paintings (see Chapter 1). Ibsen's *Peer Gynt*, however, brings to light a situation in which the authority of a shared tradition is
questioned by the notoriously unreliable character's use of traditional material for individual self-dramatization.

Ibsen is not moralizing about his main character. Nor is he, like
nasjonalromantikerne are often accused of doing, suggesting a return to
naïve folk culture. Quite to the contrary, the naïve cultivation of folk culture
and nationalism are subjected to ironic treatment in *Peer Gynt*. This is particularly clear as Peer, in Act Two, emerges at the court of the Troll King. With
his appetite for life, Peer is prepared to trade his humanity for a night with the
Troll Princess.[16] In his interaction with Peer, the Troll King brags about how
his own culture offers both physical and existential sustenance. Having already gone on about his food being homemade,[17] the Troll King pronounces
that the distinction between man and troll rests with man's search for himself
as opposed to the troll's "being himself *only*":

So there is a difference, after all.
Allow me to tell you what it consists of:

---

[14] It is worth keeping in mind at this point how Ibsen's historical drama, as we saw in Chapter 1,
had not only been about historical events, but also made use of historical culture (the saga literature).
[15] Peer's reindeer venture draws on "Reensdyrjagt ved Ronderne," published in the second volume
of Asbjørnsen's *Norske Huldreeventyr og Folkesagn*, two vols. (Christiania: Fabritius forlag, 1845–
1847). Shepherd-Barr draws attention to Asbjørnsen's role as a mediator of Darwinian theory in
Norway. In effect, Asbjørnsen connects the historical interest of the *Sturm und Drang* with the new
scientific turn toward evolution. See Shepherd-Barr, *Theatre and Evolution*, 71.
[16] Trolls also feature in Ibsen's criticism of Norway and Norwegian culture in *Brand* and in
his poems.
[17] The Troll King declares that it does not matter how bad the food tastes as long as it is homemade: "Don't ask if the taste is sweet or sour; / The main thing is, and don't you forget it, / It's all homemade" (OI III 296; HIS V 550).

> Out there, under the radiant sky,
> They say "To thine own self be true."
> But here, in the world of trolls, we say
> *"To thine own self be—all-sufficient [Trold, vær dig selv—nok!]."*
> (OI III 295; HIS V 550, emphasis added)

With his untampered self-obsession, Peer is already half troll. As the Troll King puts it:

> You've a natural gift for being a troll.
> Isn't he almost a troll already? /
> And surely that's what you want?
> (OI III 299; HIS V 556)

Peer only leaves when he realizes that the union with the troll represents a point of no return: he can play with the trolls and their idea of being themselves only, but he has no desire to be a troll for good.

The confrontation with his inherent troll potential does not leave Peer more enlightened.[18] Conflating the quest for a self with a license to selfishness, he proceeds to try out the role of colonialist and opportunistic slave owner (i.e., another perversion of the idea of national superiority). Peer now wants to be the emperor of his own Gyntiana, if not of the entire world (OI III 333; HIS V 609). His ambitions are nicely summed up when he declares: "But I have to be myself *en bloc*– / Gynt of the entire globe, / Root and branch the sovereign Gynt!" (OI III 334; HIS V 611). Only as emperor of the world, it seems, can he fully be himself.[19]

The relationship between selfhood and cultural identity is further explored when we, in Act Four, encounter Peer in Morocco. In terms of dramatic effect and scenery, there is no substantive difference between the description of Norway and that of Moroccan culture.[20] Like the scenes in Jotunheimen, the Kingdom of the Trolls, the Moroccan adventure emerges as dreamy, semi-eroticized, and rich in irony. The venue is a tent in an oasis. Peer is dressed in

---

[18] Asbjørn Aarseth discusses the dialectics between animality and humanity in *Peer Gynt* in *Dyret i Mennesket. Et bidrag til tolkning av Henrik Ibsens "Peer Gynt"* (Oslo: Universitetsforlaget, 1975).

[19] In *Emperor and Galilean*, we encounter similar aspirations. I return to this point in Chapter 3.

[20] The length of Ibsen's poem, often invoking substantial cuts, has led to a concentration on Acts One through Three, as well as the final act (including more melodramatic unification with Solvejg in the final scene). An illustrious exception is Peter Stein's 1971 production of the play at the Schaubühne in Berlin.

Eastern robes, reclining on cushions, placidly smoking, while being entertained
by an enchanting dancer, Anitra, and her female friends. Against a background
of more or less conventional theater props, the interaction between Peer and
Anitra comes across as a parody (and in this sense, it mirrors Peer's relationship to the trolls). As Anitra enters, Peer's judgment is the following:

> Hey! She is exquisite, this filly.
> Her build is on the generous side,
> Not what beauty normally measures;
> But what is beauty? A pure convention,—
> Value depends on where and when. (OI III 348; HIS V 631)

Even though Peer has proven short on selfhood, he immediately seeks to im-
press Anitra by offering her a soul. Anitra, for her part, panders to his desires
but then abruptly withdraws. At the end of the day, Peer's jewelry proves a
more lasting investment than the fragile self he touts. When Anitra finally
rides off with his purse, this does not come across as betrayal of trust, but is
the logical conclusion of an encounter that is fueled by the selfishness Peer
verbally advertises and performatively presents.[21]

  The Norwegian mountains and the Moroccan desert appear as theatrical
backdrops for Peer's energetic efforts at staging himself as a legendary hero
and a seducer of global proportions. No shift of scenery can shake him out
of his romantic reveries. That is, in neither of these scenes does Peer really
manage to get beyond his state of self-obsession and engage the broader social and cultural context in which he finds himself situated. Instead, he clings
to his favorite heroic narratives, be it those of Norwegian folk tales or his
equally naïve and Orientalizing portraits of Moroccan culture. It is as if Peer's
entire existence relies upon these fantastical stories—or, more precisely, on
the ability to keep producing stories of this kind.

  Peer ventures on from Morocco to Egypt. I return to the Egypt scene later
but want to focus, first, on the final act, in which Peer's individualism—his
conflation of selfhood and selfishness—reaches its full dramatic crescendo.
We find Peer on board a ship nearing the coast of Norway. On facing his
homecoming, Peer also confronts the question of whether he really is the

---

[21] It is, in this context, interesting that Ibsen played with the idea of having "Anitra's Dance," as
Grieg had composed it, reemerging in *A Doll's House*, as part of Nora's attempt to distract Helmer
upon his receiving Krogstad's letter about her fraud. For a discussion of this point, see Nicholas
Grene, *Home on the Stage: Domestic Spaces in Modern Drama* (Cambridge: Cambridge University
Press, 2014), 26.

emperor of his own self. He realizes that the crew, too, will return home. Peer initially wants to compensate them for their work. However, upon realizing that, unlike himself, the crew will return to their families—they will have a proper homecoming—he quickly changes his mind. Peer's exchange with the Captain proceeds as follows:

> PEER. What did you say? Wives and kids?
> Are they married?
> CAPTAIN. Married? Yes, all of 'em.
> But the cook is the one most badly off;
> Black hunger is seldom out of his house.
> PEER. Married? They've someone waiting at home
> With a warm welcome? Eh?
> CAPTAIN. Why yes,
> In their simple way.
> PEER. At night, unexpected,
> What then?
> CAPTAIN. Somehow the wife would manage some special treat.
> PEER. And light a lamp? [. . .]
> And sit there snugly? Warm by the fire?
> The children with them? The room full of chatter:
> All talking at once, for the joy of the meeting?
> CAPTAIN. Very likely. And all the more so
> Because of the kind of suggestion you made
> Of a little extra—
> PEER [thumping the gunnel]. I'm damned if I do it!
> Do you think I'm mad? Do you really expect me
> To fork out for other people's kids?
> I've worked hard enough [surt nok slæbt] to earn what I've got!
> Nobody is waiting for old Peer Gynt.
> (OI III 377; HIS V 675, trans. modified)

Peer, it turns out, has not only changed his mind about giving the crew a bonus. Even worse, he wants to tempt them with brandy and actively obstruct every possibility of a happy homecoming:

> Not one of the bastards will get ashore sober.
> They shall greet their wives and children plastered,

> Cursing and hammering on the table,
> Scaring the family out of their wits!
> (OI III 378; HIS V 676).

When they encounter a group of men on a capsized boat, Peer bribes the crew to save them. The attempt fails, but Peer blames the others and continues as if nothing has happened. Finally, when his own ship goes down, he lets the cook drown, well-aware that he has a wife and children waiting at home. A bit later, we get the famous scene in which Peer, in a moment of sudden insightfulness, picks up an onion and draws a parallel between the structure of the vegetable and the structure of his self:

> You're no Emperor; you're an onion.
> Now I shall peel you, good old Peer!
> It won't help, either, to cry for mercy.
>   [*He takes the onion and peels off the layers.*]
>   [...]
> What a tremendous number of layers!
> Will the heart of it never come to light?
>   [*He pulls the whole onion to pieces.*]
> My God, no, it won't! Rift to the centre
> It is all made of layers—but smaller and smaller.
> Nature is witty [*he throws the rest away*].
> To hell with brooding! (OI III 396–97; HIS V 705)

However, just like Hegel had insisted that the romantic self, for all its shortcomings, still contains a trace of truth, so Peer's substance-less self is not without value. If Peer has not succeeded in his quest for a stable self, something is nonetheless gained along his journey. His life has become a legend. When Peer continues on his way home, he encounters a group of boys who recount the deeds of the famous Peer Gynt, thus returning Peer, the protagonist of Ibsen's play, back to the folk tale character he had originally pretended to be (OI III 392; HIS V 699).[22] Peer has let go of his social world, but he has won a story.[23]

---

[22] In Ibsen's later work, this playful gesture gets a new form in that characters from earlier plays reemerge, featuring as Ibsen's characters (from the previous plays) *and* as characters in the new play, thus gaining a literary life (or tradition) of their own.

[23] The emphasis on Peer's inability to relate to his own culture—his alienation and his questioning whether there is at all a culture in the way his peers assume—is worth taking into account when

The legend of Peer Gynt, though, needs to be inhabited. It needs a self that can own up to it. Peer finally encounters a parade of the characters he has let down, each and every one of them unwilling to attest to his character. In Ibsen's ending, only Solvejg, old and frail after all the years of waiting, is able to save him. When Peer desperately exclaims that he is lost (*fortabt*), he has Solvejg answer the riddle of where he has been all these years. In a gesture of unconditioned kindness, she finds the riddle is easy: while he has traveled all over the world, he has been present in her faith, hope, and love (OI III 421; HIS V 745). Peer's belated redemption, resounding with the words of the first Corinthian Letter 13:13, is still a worldly one.[24]

Peer is only saved when he gives up on the illusion of being the emperor of his own self. He is, it turns out, the protagonist of an overtly artistic— potentially also aestheticized—narrative, but not of his own existence. For this, it seems, he needs the acknowledgement of an other.

Self and Other

The topic of selfhood and recognition—the very idea that a self only becomes a self in and through its relation to others—is associated with Hegel. For Hegel, the aesthetic celebration of subjectivity is based on the erroneous premise of an auto-constitutive selfhood; that is, the illusion of the self as its own author. It is based on a model that fails to appreciate the dialectical relationship between self and other.

In *The Phenomenology of Spirit*, Hegel prepares his discussion of the dialectics of recognition by having us imagine an encounter between two

---

assessing how the play, popular on the National Socialist stage and screen in Germany, was fitted to the ideology of an immediate, innocent *Volk*-culture. In adaptations by Dietrich Eckart and others, the romantic idea of a homecoming features prominently. Ibsen's text, though, makes it an open question whether Peer has a home to which he can return—and to the extent that he has, whether this home is associated with a subjective love story (Solvejg) rather than community. While I will return to the question of subjective love (can it at all be a subject of tragedy?) in my discussion of *A Doll's House*, it is worth noting that the idea of a redemptive home sphere will be thoroughly shattered in Ibsen's later works. For an overview of Ibsen productions in National Socialist Germany, see Uwe Englert, *Magus und Rechenmeister. Henrik Ibsens Werk auf den Bühnen des Dritten Reiches* (Tübingen: Franke, 2007).

[24] Here, my reading differs from the interpretation we find for example in Collin's *Henrik Ibsen*, 346.

beings in an unspecified place and time.[25] Upon encountering another being of its kind, each of these beings sees in the other a creature that appears to be like itself and that demands recognition as such. As Hegel puts it, "[s]elf-consciousness is faced by another self-consciousness; it has come *out of itself*" (PS 111; HW III 146). This, he continues, has a twofold significance: first, the self, by entering into the give and take of recognition, loses itself, "for it finds itself as an *other* being" (PS 111; HW III 146); second, and equally important, "in doing so it has superseded the other, for it does not see the other as an essential being, but in the other sees its own self" (PS 111; HW III 146). In order to gain reality, however, the conception of oneself *in* the other must be confirmed *by* the other. This is the demand put forth by both of these beings.[26]

At stake in this encounter—in this drama of intersubjectivity—is the conscious recognition of oneself as a self-conscious subject. In Hegel's account, both beings are prepared to fight in order to obtain recognition. However, only one of the two is prepared to risk its life in the fight. The other pulls out and renounces the acknowledgment of its subjectivity so as to preserve its life. It thus ends up in a situation where, as Hegel puts it, it may "well be recognized as a *person*, but . . . has not attained the truth of this recognition as an independent self-consciousness" (PS 114; HW III 149). The former ends up as lord; the latter ends up in bondage and is forced to work for the lord. However, by transforming nature into culture through labor, the bondsman externalizes his self. Through work, the bondsman gradually rises to freedom. The lord, by contrast, does not shape his external surroundings in this picture. Nor is he recognized by someone whom he is able to see as his equal.

Hegel's argument has given rise to a veritable literature of interpretation. For our context, however, what we need to take into account is simply the basic thought that the self needs the recognition of an other through which it can gain self-consciousness. A self that hypostatizes its own power—be it at

[25] Or, in even better line with Ibsen's play, as John McDowell reads this passage of *The Phenomenology of Spirit*, we here encounter two different aspects of one and the same being. See John McDowell, "The Apperceptive I and the Empirical Self: Towards a Heterodox Reading of 'Lordship and Bondage' in Hegel's *Phenomenology*," in *Hegel: New Directions*, ed. Katerina Deligiorgi (Chesheim, Bucks: Acumen, 2006), 33–48. Hegel's discussion of desire, animality, and humanity is also of relevance to this part of Ibsen's *Peer Gynt*.

[26] In Hegel's words, the process "is simply the double movement of the two self-consciousnesses. Each sees the *other* do the same as it does; each does itself what it demands of the other, and therefore also does what it does only in so far as the other does the same. Action by one side only would be useless because what is to happen can only be brought about by both" (PS 112; HW III 146–47). For an analysis of Hegel's dialectics of recognition, see Robert B. Pippin, *Hegel on Self-Consciousness: Desire and Death in the "Phenomenology of Spirit"* (Princeton: Princeton University Press, 2014).

an aesthetic, ethical or epistemic level—is stuck in an illusion that cannot last. On the Hegelian scheme, it takes a we to be an I.[27] Only when an I engages in a dialectics of intersubjective recognition—only when it is recognized by an other—can it fully be a self. Furthermore, recognition can only come from others whom the "I" itself recognizes as worthy of recognition—others whose recognition *counts*. To the extent that the self, in its individual quest for independence, cuts itself off from the larger realm of intersubjectivity, it ends up, as in Hegel's image of the romantic poet and philosopher, bordering on madness.

The topic of recognition is present throughout *Peer Gynt*. I have already discussed the basic structure of Peer's failed social relationships and of Solvejg's ultimate act of redemption at his much-delayed homecoming. It is even possible to read Peer's encounter with Dovregubben, the Troll King, as a humorous version of the lordship–bondsman dialectic: Peer is seeking recognition, but the other he encounters is, at one and the same time, less than Peer (he is not human, but a troll), and yet, also more (he is, after all, the king). In order for the encounter to assume significance, in order for Peer to enter into real interaction with the trolls, he is asked to mark his eyes in a way that will permanently alter his vision, making him, too, a troll and thus, presumably, recognizing the Troll King as his regent. Similarly, in the Morocco scene, we see Peer failing to recognize Anitra (as a person with a soul), yet she is given the last word when she rides off with Peer's purse and leaves him stranded in the desert.

In *The Phenomenology of Spirit*, Hegel discusses the dialectics of recognition at a fairly abstract level. In Ibsen's work, we get Peer spanned out between his self and others in a far more concrete sense: first through his failing social relationships in Norway, then in the halls of the Troll King, and finally in Morocco. However, neither in Norway, nor in Morocco do we get an explicit reference to Hegel. This only happens when Peer arrives in Egypt. It is to this scene we now turn, though with the understanding that the reference to Hegel has been prepared for in Acts One through Three.

---

[27] I lean on Terry Pinkard's interpretation in *Hegel's Phenomenology: The Sociality of Reason* (Cambridge: Cambridge University Press, 1996).

Hegelianism in the Madhouse

When Peer, in Act Four, arrives in Egypt, he finds himself standing by the Colossus of Memnon (presented in the singular in Ibsen's play) and then moves on to the Sphinx at the outskirts of Giza. It is at this point that Herr Begriffenfeldt demands Peer's attention (OI III 363; HIS V 652). (For Peter Stein's staging of the Sphinx scene, see color plate 4). Begriffenfeldt introduces himself with the question, posed in German in Ibsen's original, "Ach, Sphinx, wer bist du?" (OI III 363; HIS V 652), before he proceeds to ask Peer, "Mein Herr, excuse me—! Eine Lebensfrage—! / What brought you here on this day of all days?" (OI III 363; HIS V 653). In response, Peer informs him that the Sphinx is an old acquaintance. When Begriffenfeldt asks what the Sphinx is, Peer promptly answers that "He is himself" (OI III 364; HIS V 653). The venue for this encounter is significant and lends philosophical weight to the exchange. Hegel discusses ancient Egyptian culture in a number of works, including *Elements of the Philosophy of Right, Lectures on the Philosophy of Religion*, and *Lectures on the History of Philosophy*. In all these writings, Egypt represents the early beginning of spirit's path to itself. It is a presupposition for, yet less mature than, spirit's later manifestations in nineteenth-century German philosophy. As a beginning, ancient Egyptian culture is granted significance and weight. Yet, it must also be surpassed by more advanced stages.

In *Elements of the Philosophy of Right*, Hegel refers to the political and legal order of the ancient Egyptians. He describes how the socio-political climate of the "Orient" (Hegel's term) hardens into a natural system of castes, or, as he puts it, a structure that is "fossilized [versteinert]."[28] In his 1827 lectures on religion, Hegel is slightly more positive and grants that the "Egyptians were the first to declare that the human soul is immortal." With the ancient Egyptians, moreover, we first "have subjectivity in the form of representation" and "exalted above the natural."[29] Yet Hegel is clear that ancient Egyptian buildings and sculptures do not qualify as art proper. In his view, "[t]his colossal diligence of an entire people was not yet in and for itself pure fine art; rather it

[28] G. W. F. Hegel, *Elements of the Philosophy of Right*, ed. Allen Wood, trans. H. B. Nisbet (Cambridge: Cambridge University Press, 1991), 377; HW VII 294, §355.

[29] G. W. F. Hegel, *Lectures on the Philosophy of Religion: The Lectures of 1827*, ed. Peter C. Hodgson, trans. R. F. Brown, P. C. Hodgson, and J. M. Stewart (Berkeley: University of California Press, 1988), 315 and 317; *Vorlesungen über die Philosophie der Religion*, ed. Walter Jaeschke, vols. 3–5 of *Vorlesungen. Ausgewählte Nachschriften und Manuskripte* (Hamburg: Felix Meiner, 1985), 520 and 522.

was the *impulsion* toward fine art."[30] Fine art involves free subjectivity. The ancient Egyptians stand at the brink of freedom, yet they do not possess it.[31] Their social organization—in which only one person, the Pharaoh, is allowed to be free—does not accommodate for a developed idea of freedom.[32]

It is, however, in the *Lectures on Fine Art*, the center of the Hegel reception at the Copenhagen stage and the most popular course he ever taught,[33] that Hegel fully develops his thesis about the beginning of great art in ancient Egyptian culture. Addressing ancient Egyptian culture under the rubric of symbolic art, he states that "[t]he symbol, in the meaning of the word used here, constitutes the beginning of art . . . and is therefore to be considered only, as it were, as the threshold of art. It belongs especially to the East and only after all sorts of transitions, metamorphoses, and intermediaries does it carry us over into the genuine actuality of the Ideal as the classical form of art" (LFA 303; HW XIII 393). As it marks the beginning of art, an understanding of Egyptian culture is a necessary step on the way to a true, philosophical concept of great art.

Being a systematic philosopher, Hegel wishes to explain what defines art *qua* art (i.e., regardless of the period and culture in which it was

---

[30] *Lectures on the Philosophy of Religion*, 322; *Vorlesungen über die Philosophie der Religion*, 528, emphasis added.

[31] With his interest in freedom—his reading of the history of human spirit as a history of increasing freedom—Hegel stands forth as a Kantian (albeit a defender of a Kantianism that is mediated through Fichte's philosophy). It follows from this position that, as Hegel puts it in a manifestly non-Kantian gesture, aesthetics should exclude the beauty of nature: "By adopting this expression [aesthetics] we at once exclude the beauty of nature." For, he continues, when considered formally "the beauty of art is *higher* than nature" and "even a useless notion that enters a man's head is higher than any product of nature, because in such a notion spirituality and freedom are always present" (LFA 1–2; HW XIII 14). While the focus on art (as different from a focus on taste and/or natural form) already had a long history in German aesthetics, the focus on freedom is given a special consideration in Hegel's lectures. In order for us to speak of art, claims Hegel, spirit "must have become free from desire, free from natural life generally, from subjugation by inner and outer nature . . . it must have the need to know itself as free, and to be free, as the object of its own consciousness." Hegel, *Lectures on the Philosophy of Religion*, 322; *Vorlesungen über die Philosophie der Religion*, 528.

[32] Only with the Greeks, their religion and their political system, does Hegel locate genuine freedom and, with it, an art that is fully realized. Classical Greek sculpture, for Hegel, is the epitome of art. In classical sculpture, spirit, as free, obtains an entirely adequate expression in a sensuous form. In the language of the aesthetics lectures, ancient sculpture "comprises the miracle of spirit's giving itself an image of itself in something purely material" (LFA 710; HW XIV 362). We here encounter a realm in which spiritual content is such that it can and must reach an external expression and this external expression, in turn, is seen as adequate to the idea. As mentioned in Chapter 1, we encounter references to sculpture in *Emperor and Galilean*—first in the form of sculptures that are taken down and turned over, then, with Julian's rise to power, of sculpture reestablished—but also, more prominently, in *When We Dead Awaken*. For Ibsen's interest in sculpture, see Robert Ferguson, *Henrik Ibsen: A New Biography* (New York: Dorset Press, 1996), 262. Faaland, on his side, quotes Dietrichson's claim that Ibsen was a *plastiker*. See Josef Faaland, *Henrik Ibsen og antikken* (Oslo: Johan Grundt Tanum, 1943), 134.

[33] See Terry Pinkard, *Hegel: A Biography* (Cambridge: Cambridge University Press, 2000), 593.

produced)—the "universal moments of the Idea of beauty," as he puts it (LFA 90; HW XIII 124). Yet he is critical of how earlier philosophers, in particular Kant, had overlooked the historical conditions of beauty and thus he also seeks to take into account the development of art through history. Hegel's aim is to arrive at a definition that captures the essence of art as such, and yet this definition has to be capacious enough to make sense of cultural variation and historical change. It is no small challenge that Hegel sets for himself. He responds to it by suggesting that, as beautiful, great art represents the way in which a given culture symbolizes its ethical and religious thought. Art is spirit made sensuous (LFA 39; HW XIII 61). Since spirit is essentially temporal, so is art.

With its position as an early beginning, Egyptian art anticipates what art substantially will become. Hegel is particularly attentive to how ancient Egyptian architecture expresses the ethical, political, and religious values of its society. These buildings, he argues, serve no pragmatic end, such as providing shelter and safety (they were, as Ibsen had claimed with respect to poetry, expressions that humans had more than they needed [HIS XVI 142]). Hegel deems this a significant step in the history of mankind: the step from nature to culture in and through the expression of humanity *for its own sake*.

Egyptian art is greatly admired by Hegel. Yet, in his view, this art belongs to a stage that must be surpassed by more "advanced" cultures (represented by classical and romantic art). When we "first enter the world of the old-Persian, Indian, Egyptian shapes and productions," Hegel claims, "our footing is not really secure; we feel that we are wandering amongst *problems* [Aufgaben]; in themselves alone these productions say nothing to us; they do not please us or satisfy us by their immediate appearance, but by themselves they encourage us to advance beyond them to their meaning which is something wider and deeper than they are" (LFA 308; HW XIII 400). For Hegel, the "immaturity" of Egyptian art is reflected in its lack of writing—what Hegel calls its muteness.[34]

The parallels between Ibsen's and Hegel's descriptions of Egypt are undeniable. Hegel observes that "[e]specially remarkable are those colossal statues of Memnon which, resting in themselves, motionless, the arms glued to the body, the feet firmly fixed together, numb, stiff, and lifeless, are set up

---

[34] Hegel adds another point to this. He claims that the ancient Egyptians did not create art to externalize the representation of the divine in inner life but to worship the divine in animals such as bulls and cats. However, he finds it repugnant to "see animals, dogs, and cats, instead of what is truly spiritual, regarded as sacred" (LFA 357; HW XIII 460).

facing the sun in order to await its ray to touch them and give them soul and sound" (LFA 358; HW XIII 462). Likewise, on arriving in Egypt, Ibsen's Peer Gynt is captivated by the Colossus of Memnon and its lifeless appearance. Furthermore, Hegel reports that the "statues of Memnon gave a sound automatically at sunrise" (LFA 358; HW XIII 462).[35] Ibsen, too, centers on the "stony voice" of the sculptures as they recite the "music of the past" (OI III 362; HIS V 650).

The image of an ancient culture that is "fossilized," "stony," and "petrified" lingers throughout Ibsen's description of Egypt. Indeed, Ibsen had already presented such an image of ancient Egypt in his poems from the late 1850s.[36] And even after Ibsen visited Egypt, two years after finishing *Peer Gynt*, this image was retained. In the "Balloon Letter," a poem Ibsen wrote to thank the Swedish king for his invitation to the opening of the Suez Canal, the image of ancient Egyptian civilization remained that of a culture that speaks to us in an inhuman way. The voice of the Colossus of Memnon is characterized as "frozen."[37] Ibsen notes how organic nature is unified with death in the vast open fields of the desert (P 104; HIS XI 570–571), and he describes Egyptian culture as a world of graves (P 105; HIS XI 571). In Ibsen's characterization, this seems to be what distinguishes ancient Egyptian culture from that of the ancient Greeks.[38]

As Aarseth and others have argued, Ibsen's sources here emerge as Hegelian (or at least strikingly coherent with a Hegelian position). However, only if we take into account the previous focus on selfhood and recognition can we see the full, dramatic significance of this point. Gesturing toward Hegel's aesthetics, Ibsen, at one and the same time, connects with the Hegelianism of the Scandinavian world of books and letters *and* takes *Peer Gynt* to a new dramatic level. He does this by ushering the poem's protagonist *from* the cognitive and existential cul-de-sac of aestheticizing romanticism *to* a project of self-realization through conceptual comprehension. It is no accident that

---

[35] Hegel is mistakenly quoting Herodotus where he should have instead referred to Tacitus. In Hegel's understanding, Memnon's song reflects the general soullessness of Egyptian art: "[T]hese colossi . . . do not have the spiritual soul freely in themselves and therefore, instead of being able to draw animation from within, from what bears proportion and beauty in itself, they require for it light from without which alone liberates the note of the soul from them . . . the inner life of the human form is still dumb in Egypt and in its animation it is only a natural factor that is kept in view" (LFA 358; HW XIII 462).

[36] See for example, "Prolog. Fremsagt den 17de Mai [1855] i Det norske Theater," in HIS XI 203–205, and "Sendebrev til H. Ø. Blom," in HIS XI 349–354.

[37] HIS XI 568 or, in Northam's translation: "chilly" (102).

[38] For this point, see Faaland, *Henrik Ibsen og antikken*, 160.

Peer, at this point, is equipped with pen, notebook, and a scholarly identity. Along the lines of the Hegelian science, Peer seeks to "record the progress of the human race! / . . . float like a feather on the stream of history" (OI III 359; HIS V 647). Only thus, he reckons, will he, like the Hegelian philosopher, be "the Emperor of human experience" and have "the absolute key to the past" (OI III 360; HIS V 648). By recapitulating "history's inner workings" (OI III 359; HIS V 647), Peer hopes to win self-realization at an intellectual level.

Peer's efforts, though, are destabilized by the presence of Begriffenfeldt and the quasi-Hegelian props by which he is surrounded. In spite of (or due to?) his Hegelian name, Begriffenfeldt is no ordinary philosopher, but the director of the madhouse. For all his scholarly ambitions, Peer is entering the land of the mad. That is, whereas Hegel had linked exaggerated romantic selfhood and art with a condition of madness, Ibsen has Peer approach madness not in the form of the romantic self, but as a Hegelian philosopher. At this point, however, he also reflects, in a parody on Hegelian philosophizing, on the nature of madness and the distinction between the mad and the presumably sane.

Initially, Peer had assumed that the difference between himself and the mad is that he is himself in every respect, whereas in the madhouse "it's all / A matter of being beside yourself" (OI III 368; HIS V 660). However, Peer is swiftly proved wrong. Madness, he learns, is not simply about being beside oneself. Rather, the mad are "[h]ermetically sealed with the bung of self" (OI III 368; HIS V 660). This is a condition in which "[n]o one has tears for other men's pain; / No one accepts other men's notions" (OI III 368; HIS V 660). The mad are full of themselves, described as being themselves in every syllable, which ultimately amounts to not being themselves at all (OI III 370; HIS V 663). When the mad, in their pathological self-obsession, are ready to choose their emperor, the self-possessed Peer is an obvious candidate:

> BEGRIFFENFELDT. (. . .) We're ourselves here, thought, word and deed,
> Ourselves right to the edge of the diving-board—,
> And so, now we come to elect an Emperor,
> You are obviously the perfect man. (OI III 368; HIS V 660)

Peer's self-centeredness makes him eminently qualified to be the spiritual leader of those who, in their madness, are completely self-absorbed.

Even though Ibsen, as Aarseth points out, evidently references Hegel, he does not only draw on Hegelian thinking, but also ridicules the philosopher and his world-historical ambitions.

Beyond Hegelianism

Ibsen's ridicule of the Hegelian director of the madhouse should not surprise. For as Hegelianism became increasingly influential in Scandinavia—and, with Monrad, Heiberg, and others, rose to prominence in the world of theater and drama[39]—it became *en vogue* to mock Hegel and the Hegelians on and off stage. We see this, for instance, in H. C. Andersen's *Comedy in the Open Air*, which features a hairdresser steeped in Hegelian philosophy and language.[40] This wider context sheds light on Ibsen's choice to have Peer Gynt encounter a proto-Hegelian director of the madhouse. Yet there are other questions that cannot be explained with reference to such general anti-Hegelian sentiments. How, for a start, can we explain the shift *from* the exploration, in drama form, of a set of Hegelian ideas about exaggerated (romantic) subjectivity and madness *to* a merciless mocking of Hegelianism? How can we square the previous centering in on recognition (or lack of such) with this parody of the madhouse Hegelian? And, further, is there a way of making sense of the fact that this encounter is pitched, of all places, in Egypt?

Even though Hegel typically gets the credit for having developed the famous master–bondsman dialectics, we find a powerful version of this argument in *Sturm und Drang* philosophy.[41] In Herder's work—which Hegel would have known[42]—this argument is shaped in much less abstract terms

[39] See for example Nagy, "Either Hegel or Dialectics: Johan Ludvig Heiberg, *Homme de théâtre*," 379–380.

[40] In Andersen's vaudeville, the hairdresser speaks in convoluted, arch-Hegelian, and non-sensical ways. H. C. Andersen, *En Comedie i det Grønne*, in *Samlede Skrifter*, vol. IX (Copenhagen: C. A. Reitzels Forlag, 1978), 408–409. It has been suggested that Ibsen, in *Peer Gynt*, draws on Andersen's "Snedronningen." See HIS V/B 562. One can only imagine how gestures like Andersen's would inspire Kierkegaard's biting critique of Hegel and all things Hegelian. For a study of Kierkegaard in Norway, see Harald Beyer's *Søren Kierkegaard og Norge* (Kristiania: Aschehoug, 1924). For Beyer's discussion of Ibsen, see ibid., 114–190. For explicitly Kierkegaardian readings of *Peer Gynt*, see Valborg Erichsen, "Søren Kierkegaards betydning for norsk aandsliv," *Edda*, vol. 19 (1923): 252–269; Lisi, *Marginal Modernity: The Aesthetics of Dependency from Kierkegaard to Joyce*, 87–117; Bruce Shapiro, *Divine Madness and the Absurd Paradox: Ibsen's "Peer Gynt" and the Philosophy of Kierkegaard* (Westport, CT: Greenwood Press, 1990). However, the emphasis on national identity, tradition, history, and history-making is a point at which Ibsen clearly goes beyond a Kierkegaardian framework.

[41] I discuss this in *Herder's Hermeneutics: History, Poetry, Enlightenment*, 119, 126, 158.

[42] Hegel refers to Herder's later *Ideen* in, among other places, the "Heidelberger Niederschrift." See Hegel, *Introduction to the Lectures on the History of Philosophy*, trans. T. M. Knox and A. V.

and is part of his reflections on the relationship between Europe and other parts of the world. In particular, Herder discusses the relationship between a sense of cultural superiority and the justification of slavery, colonialism, and other exploitative practices.[43] Herder, further, is a philosopher who had been particularly critical of the way in which classicist-minded art historians, most prominently Winckelmann, had looked down on Egypt.[44] Hegel's reading of ancient Egypt as "underdeveloped" resounds with such prejudices.

Given Ibsen's background in the *Sturm und Drang* movement (see Chapter 1), we cannot expect him to be a straightforward Hegelian. As far as Ibsen's philosophical ballast goes, it makes sense to assume that he will draw on the wider background that includes Hegel's thought, but he is in no way limited to it. Having made his fortune as a slave trader, Ibsen's Peer Gynt is directly linked to the concrete, historical framework of slavery and misrecognition that feature centrally in Herder (but not, in the standard readings, in Hegel).[45] In Ibsen's work, Peer's slave trade is only anecdotally brought up. The same applies to his past as a plantation owner. Yet both of these facts highlight the uncertain status of the man who has claimed superiority over others. He engages key elements of Hegel's philosophy, but also presents, in a *Sturm und Drang* spirit, a more concrete dialectic between self and other. This, in my view, contributes to the dramatic-philosophical depth of *Peer Gynt*.

Greeting Peer, the European adventurer, as "a human being!" (OI III 363; HIS V 652), Begriffenfeldt declares it nothing short of a revolution when Peer

Miller (Oxford: Clarendon Press, 1995), 10, and *Einleitung in die Geschichte der Philosophie*, ed. Johannes Hoffmeister (Hamburg: Felix Meiner, 1940), 13. For an interpretation that acknowledges the philosophical importance of Hegel's borrowing from Herder, see Charles Taylor, *Hegel* (Cambridge: Cambridge University Press, 1975).

[43] In fact, this argument was rapidly taken up by Germaine de Staël (particularly, her novella *Mirza*). Staël's work was brought into a Scandinavian context by Adam Oehlenschläger. (Staël hosted Oehlenschläger during his stay in Switzerland in the fall and winter of 1808.) Staël also featured centrally in Brandes's magisterial *Main Currents in Nineteenth-Century Literature* lectures in the early 1870s. Brandes's lectures were later published and translated into a number of languages. In the first volume, *The Emigrant Literature*, Staël's 1807 novel *Corinne* is prominently displayed. Staël's novel was translated into Danish in the 1820s. The Ibsens borrowed *Corinne* from the Scandinavian Library in Rome in 1864. See Anker, "Ibsen og den skandinaviske Forening i Roma," 172. According to Daniel Haakonsen, motifs from Staël's work resound in *Ghosts*. See Daniel Haakonsen, *Henrik Ibsen. Mennesket og kunstneren* (Oslo: Aschehoug, 2003), 86 and 145–150.

[44] See my discussion of this point in *Herder's Hermeneutics*, 154–158.

[45] A non-standard reading that emphasizes the importance of the slave revolt in Haiti for Hegel's thought in the *Phenomenology* can be found in Susan Buck-Morss, *Hegel, Haiti, and Universal History* (Pittsburgh: University of Pittsburgh Press, 2009). Buck-Morss does not discuss the fact that a discourse of slavery and recognition was already established with Herder and others.

"solves" the riddle of the Sphinx by suggesting, in the vein of the Hegelian spirit of Acts One through Three, that he is himself (OI III 364; HIS V 653). Peer is immediately hailed "Revelation's Emperor—enthroned on Self" (OI III 365; HIS V 655)[46] and celebrated as the master of the philosophical system, apparently Hegel's own. However, in this parodied version, the insistence on absolute reason is uncovered as an act of absolute *un*reason. A reason that has left out its other and no longer stands in a dialectical relationship of recognition is but a version of the falsely sovereign subjectivity that Hegel himself had criticized. As a Hegelian, Begriffenfeldt faces a world in which not only history, but also reason has reached its end: "Absolute Reason / Dropped dead [Den absolute Fornuft / afgik ved Døden i aftes Kl. 11]" (OI III 366; HIS V 657). With regard to absolute reason, Begriffenfeldt rushes to elaborate, by "dropped dead" he means that reason is being "besides himself. Jumped out of his skin," just like "Münchhausen's fox" (OI III 366; HIS V 657). Absolute reason is, it seems, beyond the rescuable: it has slid into sheer lunacy.

For Begriffenfeldt, the inevitable consequence of reason's having gone beyond itself—"the Von-Sich-Gehen (of reason)," as Ibsen puts it, with the German inserted in the original—is the "complete revolution on land and sea." In this state, "[t]he individuals once called mad / In fact became normal" (OI III 367; HIS V 658). These are the words of a man whom Peer, only a few lines earlier, has deemed "wonderfully gifted" just by virtue of the fact that almost all that he says is "incomprehensible [gaar over ens Forstand]" (OI III 365; HIS V 655). By mocking Hegelian philosophy in this way—by turning Hegel's own critique of the madness of an "I" that poses its own sovereignty against Hegel himself—Ibsen, by the same token, questions the idea that philosophy is able to exhaust every aspect of reality.

In *Peer Gynt*, the character of Begriffenfeldt is not simply a reference to Hegel, but also to a certain understanding of reason and its mandate. With his alienating German phrases, the presence of Begriffenfeldt indicates that the Egypt Ibsen stages is *not* real, but a European projection. It is the Egypt of the philosophers and playwrights.[47] From this point of view, not only

---

[46] A more precise translation here would be "the emperor of interpreters—founded on the self."

[47] It is worth bearing in mind that the late Eighteenth Century is the period when the first museums opened in Europe. In terms of timelines and exhibition politics, Egyptian art was being staged as the beginning of the Western tradition. For a description of the political dimension of the institution of the museum, see Tony Bennett, *The Birth of the Museum: History, Theory, Politics* (London: Routledge, 1995).

the encounter with Begriffenfeldt, but the entire Egypt scene emerges as a parody—one that is facilitated by the dramatic gesture of using Hegel against himself.

Whereas Hegel sets out to portray ancient Egyptian culture as it emphatically and essentially is—to grasp what is rational and lasting in it, and to show how it represents the beginning of Western art—Ibsen's characters do not embody a speculative truth about ancient Egypt or anything else. The Egypt that is presented, rather, is Egypt as portrayed by the European philosopher. And, as indicated by the spectacle of the madhouse, this portrayal does indeed prove worthy of criticism.

Placing Peer Gynt in Egypt, Ibsen takes the interplay between self and culture, explored through Acts Two and Three, to a new level and invites a critical view on the dominant portrayal of non-Western culture, his own exposition of Morocco included. From this point of view, the Egypt and Morocco scenes are not, as contemporaneous critics had worried, dramatically superficial, but significantly contribute to the play.[48] At stake is not only Peer's relationship to his own culture, but also his dealing, as a European explorer *cum* scholar, with cultural alterity. It is, in this sense, a continuation of the critique of nationalism that we encountered in the earlier acts.[49]

Systematic Lunacy

Ibsen only visited Egypt after he wrote *Peer Gynt*. Hegel did not set foot beyond Europe. In his discussion of non-Western art and history, Hegel relied mostly on written sources. Some of these sources were ancient: The Bible and Herodotus. Others were modern, such as the works of Aloys Hirt, the

[48] The Morocco scenes were deemed superficial and, simply, as an inverted image of Norwegian culture. See Edmund Gosse, "A Norwegian Drama," in *Ibsen: The Critical Heritage*, ed. Michael Egan (London: Routledge, 1972), 45–50, and Brandes, *Henrik Ibsen* (København: Gyldendalske Boghandel, 1916), 43.

[49] As Elisabeth Oxfeldt has pointed out, the very same year Ibsen finished *Peer Gynt*, the Exposition Universelle in Paris was widely covered by Scandinavian newspapers. The Swedish-Norwegian lot was close to several exhibits from Arab countries, with their display of local customs, religious texts, and even native people. The Arabic cultures, most notably those of Morocco and Turkey, were immediately branded as unhygienic and lowly by the Scandinavian press. Ibsen has Peer display similar prejudices when he remarks on Anitra's dirty feet (OI III 348; HIS V 631). See Elisabeth Oxfeldt, *Nordic Orientalism: Paris and the Cosmopolitan Imagination, 1800–1900* (Copenhagen: Museum Tusculanum Press, 2005). See also Frode Helland, "Empire and Culture in Ibsen: Some Notes on the Dangers and Ambiguities of Interculturalism," *Ibsen Studies*, vol. 9, no. 2 (2009): 136–159.

historian of architecture,[50] or the Hellenic accounts of the kind we find in Winckelmann's work. Yet Hegel eagerly followed the archaeological discoveries in Egypt and was particularly fascinated by the work of Thomas Young and Jean-François Champollion.[51]

In spite of his reliance on ongoing empirical Egyptology, and in spite of ever-new evidence being (literally) unearthed year by year, Hegel does not keep open the possibility that his views on ancient Egypt could later require improvement and revision. To be sure, Hegel celebrates Egyptian culture as the beginning of great art. Yet, there is little room within his system to consider how his view of Egyptian art is both Eurocentric and tailored to satisfy a systematic need in his aesthetics—namely the transition from nature to culture, and hence the birth of free and man-made beauty, as it culminates in romantic art and literature.

At this point, one could rush to Hegel's defense and suggest, as has been done, that a certain Eurocentricity seems to have been part and parcel of late eighteenth- and nineteenth-century culture. This, we have seen, is not entirely true. Before Hegel, philosophers such as Herder had developed a more nuanced and respectful approach to ancient Egyptian art and culture and explicitly criticized the kind of philhellenic projections we find in Winckelmann and, later, Hegel. In a larger, German-language context, Herder's writings on India, A. W. Schlegel's studies of ancient Sanskrit texts, and Alexander von Humboldt's journals from his travels to Mexico, Latin America, Siberia, and Asian-Russia expressed more liberal, sympathetic, and respectful attitudes to non-European cultures.[52] In fact, in some cases, such as in his review of Humboldt's edition of the *Bhagavad-Gita*, Hegel himself insists on the need for a historically and culturally sensitive approach to other cultures, be they temporally or geographically distant from that of the interpreter.[53]

In his lectures on fine art, Hegel, for internal, systematic reasons, needs a certain image of Egyptian art as being short on spirit and reflection (hence its "static" appearance). He needs a starting point, historically and systematically, for his narrative about spirit's progress toward post-revolutionary

---

[50] See Aloys Hirt, *Die Geschichte der Baukunst bei den Alten*, vol. I (G. Reimer: Berlin, 1821). Hegel refers to Hirt in the opening of the *Aesthetics* (LFA 17; HW XIII 33) and on a number of occasions throughout the lectures.

[51] See HW XII 245–274, in particular 247. See also Helmut Schneider, "Hegel und die ägyptischen Götter. Ein Exzerpt," *Hegel-Studien*, vol. 16 (1981): 56–68.

[52] For a balanced study of the German turn to eastern cultures in this period, see, again, Marchand, *German Orientalism*.

[53] See Hegel, "Über die unter dem Namen Bhagavad-Gita bekannte Episode des Mahabharata von Wilhelm von Humboldt (1827)," HW XI 131–204.

Europe. And if his system encompasses, ultimately, not just an account of the essence of art, but the complete recapitulation of world history as a progressive enterprise, then this implies that ancient Egyptian art will necessarily emerge as lacking in spirit. Ibsen questions this attitude by having Peer enter Egypt as a scholar but ending his stay there as the emperor of the mad.[54]

However, when staging Peer's appearance in Egypt as the ultimate victory of madness, Ibsen, as we have seen, does not leave behind the resources of Hegel's philosophy. Rather, from within the format of his dramatic poetry, he facilitates an immanent critique of the Hegelian picture of ancient Egyptian culture and the progressive path toward Hegel's own Europe. With his roots in the *Sturm und Drang* movement, Ibsen directs a version of Hegel's dialectics of self and other against Hegel himself. If the self of the Western philosopher (or artist) can allow for no other, save the one that fits into a narrative of its own teleological development, then it too turns out to inhabit a space that is uncomfortably close to madness. In *Peer Gynt*, Ibsen dramatically deploys the critique of solipsistic romanticism and the dialectics of self and other that was explored in Acts One through Three to undermine the kind of assumptions that undergird Hegel's approach to Egyptian art. The fact that Ibsen, in this way, appears to draw on Hegel in order to mock Hegel only gives his approach a more earnest ring.

No matter how much Ibsen might have reflected on the fallacies of cultural pride and self-centeredness, he himself does not steer clear of Orientalism in his descriptions of Morocco and Egypt.[55] He duplicates the Hegelian picture of Egyptian art and culture as static or dead. He, too, needs this—albeit for dramatic and not philosophical reasons. Yet, with his background from a marginalized culture recently empowered by the orientations of the *Sturm und Drang* movement, Ibsen modifies his orientalist impulses in a way that Hegel rarely did. First, he introduces the character of Begriffenfeldt, thereby making it clear that Peer's reactions are not really reflecting Egyptian culture,

---

[54] Ibsen makes an explicit point out of Peer's intellectual debts. Upon being confronted with his Norwegian heritage, Ibsen has Peer exclaim: Norwegian, yes, "by birth / but a world-citizen by nature," only to elaborate that if he owes his wealth to America, he owes his education to his "well-stocked library / To the younger school of German writers" (OI III 332; HIS V 607).

[55] As Elisabeth Oxfeldt demonstrates, Orientalist prejudices were rampant in Ibsen's Scandinavia. Oehlenschläger had published, in Danish, his dramatized version of Antoine Galland's French adaptation of *Aladdin*, and the play triggered what has later been called "the Aladdin Era" in Scandinavian literature. See, again, Oxfeldt, *Nordic Orientalism*. These tendencies did not escape the attention of Brandes, who discusses Oehlenschläger's *Aladdin* in "Adam Oehlenschläger: Aladdin," *Samlede skrifter*, vol. 1 (København: Gyldendalske Boghandel, 1889), 215–266. As we will see in Chapter 4, Brandes ultimately views romantic aestheticism as an attempt to create what he, in a gesture of blatant Orientalism, calls an "inner India" in European literature.

but, rather, a set of European prejudices and projections. Second, through Peer's scientific efforts, Ibsen ridicules a certain kind of trust in the power of grand teleological explanation in history.

It is interesting to note that both of these modifications seem to prevail after Ibsen returned from Egypt. Ibsen's later texts reflect his (Hegelian) regret that ancient Egyptian culture lacked a written aspect enabling historical mediation within modern time.[56] In "Balloon Letter," he refers to Peer Gynt (the character), but also reminds his readers that his judgments on Egypt are passed by a man who cannot, in his own words, tell a dromedary from an ostrich and whose education is from the circles of "German masters of empty speech [Svære tyske floskelhelte]" (P 100; HIS XI 566–567, trans. modified).

With *Peer Gynt*, Ibsen makes us consider the fallacies of individual and cultural narratives of self-sufficiency and supremacy. Hegel is a particularly interesting reference point in this context because he, following Herder, is a philosopher who thematizes what it is to have a culture, what it is for a self to be embedded in culture, and how this embeddedness is historically changing and modified. These are topics that Ibsen had already explored in his early drama *and* that can help us understand the transition from the early historical works to *Peer Gynt*, as well as that from *Peer Gynt* to *Emperor and Galilean*, another play showcasing the rise and fall of a sole and lonely regent.

---

[56] In Ibsen's "Balloon Letter": "Where is Horus? / Where is Hator? / nought of substance, nought of story; / not a fragment in their glory" (P 106; HIS XI 573), and, a little later, "So lies ancient Egypt humble, / four millennia of sameness, / like a crypted carcase, nameless" (P 107; HIS XI 574). For a relevant discussion of Hegel on Egypt, see Jay Lampert, "Hegel and Ancient Egypt: History and Becoming," *International Philosophical Quarterly*, vol. 35, no. 1 (1995): 50. However, Lampert does not address Hegel's claim that the ancient Egyptians' interest in numbers signifies their capacity for abstraction. See for example LFA 351–352; HW XIII 453–455. This aspect of Hegel's conception of Egypt is also mirrored in Ibsen: "Yes, but Egypt's godheads solemn? / Numbers ranged by mass and column [Men hvad var Egyptens guder? / Tal i rækker og i ruder]" (P 107; HIS XI 574).

3

Ruins of Antiquity (*Emperor and Galilean*)

With *Emperor and Galilean*, Ibsen published another philosophically grand and historically wide-ranging drama. *Emperor and Galilean* represents a return to a historical plot—indeed, a return to the ancient Roman material with which Ibsen, twenty-three years earlier, had launched his career as a playwright. No work took Ibsen longer to finish than *Emperor and Galilean*, and no work, for that matter, is more voluminous. While Ibsen, for most of his career, wrote a play more or less every other year, *Emperor and Galilean* is published four years after *The League of Youth*, and it would take another four years until he published *Pillars of Society*.[1] How does *Emperor and Galilean* fit in between these two plays? And why did Ibsen, after he had worked on material from Norwegian history for nearly two decades, return to Roman antiquity? Further, how can we make sense of the transition from the humorous, dreamlike, and burlesque *Peer Gynt* to a play of the bleakest sort, presenting the perishing Roman world, and, under the young Emperor Julian's reign, the change from an early Christian politics of tolerance to a rule of terror and persecution? Then there is the subtitle—not, as in *Peer Gynt*, A Dramatic Poem, but A World-Historical Drama[2]—indicating that Ibsen not only wants to portray a particular period or culture, but also pursues the idea of an all-encompassing (Hegelian) narrative, i.e., the kind of undertaking that had been ridiculed in *Peer Gynt*. If *Peer Gynt* had spanned the geographical and cultural distance from Norwegian valleys to Morocco and Egypt, and moved from traditional Norwegian folk tale motifs to the mysterious song

---

[1] PI translates Ibsen's title as *Pillars of the Community*. See Henrik Ibsen, *A Doll's House and Other Plays. With Pillars of the Community, Ghosts and An Enemy of the People*, trans. Deborah Dawkin and Erik Skuggevik (London: Penguin, 2016). This translation—which is, in some ways, truer to the content (but perhaps not the title) of Ibsen's play—has been circulating since Eleanor Marx's translation and is also used in Inga-Stina Ewbank, "Ibsen's Language: Literary Text and Theatrical Context," *The Yearbook for English Studies*, vol. 9 (1979): 102–115.

[2] In a letter to Frederik Hegel, his publisher (February 6, 1873), Ibsen mentions the subtitle "A World Drama" and adds that Hegel should not be surprised: the title, he emphasizes, is but another variety of folk drama, family drama, national drama, etc. However, as a world drama, it addresses both heaven and earth ("mit stykke handler om både himmel og jord," HIS XIII 102). Two weeks later, in a letter to Gosse, we find him characterize the work as "a world historical drama" (HIS XIII 104).

The Drama of History. Kristin Gjesdal, Oxford University Press (2021). © Oxford University Press.
DOI: 10.1093/oso/9780190070762.001.0001.

of the Memnon sculpture, then *Emperor and Galilean* evokes reflection on the canvas against which the vast majority of Ibsen's plays had so far been staged: that of human history at large. *Emperor and Galilean* is a philosophical drama in more than one sense of the word.[3]

Emperor and Galilean was initially conceived of in Rome around 1864.[4] The play was finished nine years later in Germany. While Ibsen was secretive about sources of influence,[5] he grants that *Emperor and Galilean* is colored by the period and culture in which it was written. While Ibsen wanted to stay true to the historical sources, he admits, in a letter to Georg Brandes, that contemporary impulses had influenced his work: "The movements here abroad [i.e., in Germany] have made this poem more influenced by the times [*mere tidsmæssigt*] than I had initially planned" (October 16, 1873, HIS XIII 154, my trans.).[6] In Germany, the year 1870 saw the centenary celebration of Hegel's birth and a stream of publications about his life and work. Given the reference to world history in the title, scholars, seeking to make sense of the play that Ibsen himself would characterize as his main work, have pointed to Hegel. The Hegelian reading is further supported by Julian's dream of a "Third Empire" that synthesizes the ancient culture of beauty and the Christian culture of faith. Ibsen, in other words, has the young Julian testify to some version of historical dialectics.

[3] As Lisbeth Wærp puts it, "*Emperor and Galilean* is regarded as an important play in Ibsen's oeuvre, and this is above all because of its philosophy." Lisbeth P. Wærp, "Ibsen's Third Empire Reconsidered," in *Ibsens "Kaiser und Galiläer." Quellen—Interpretationen—Rezeptionen*, ed. Richard Faber and Helge Høibraaten (Würzburg: Königshausen & Neumann, 2011), 106. See also her *Overgangens figurasjoner. En studie i Henrik Ibsens "Kejser og Galilæer" og "Når vi døde vågner"* (Tromsø: Det humanistiske fakultet, 2000 [dissertation]), 30–38.

[4] See Faaland, *Henrik Ibsen og antikken*, 164. For a more detailed exposition, see HIS VI/B227–228 and 233–248.

[5] Ibsen's fear of influence is so strong that at one point, when writing the introduction to *The Feast at Solhaug* for his 1898 collected works, he goes to extensive lengths to demonstrate that his early historical drama was not influenced by Henrik Hertz or Heinrich von Kleist. As he concludes: "[my drama] is written, by the necessity of nature, out of my life at a given point. It emerged from within and is not created by way of any external force or influence [er et naturnødvendigt udslag ad min livsgang på et bestemt punkt. Det er opstået indenfra og ikke formedelst noget ydre påvirkning eller inflydelse]." Showing no fear of self-contradiction, Ibsen, in this text, has just emphasized how the material did indeed draw on the saga literature. It seems he was alright wrestling with historical (collective) influences; it is contemporary (and individual) influence he zealously denies. See SV I 125–135, the quote is from 135 (my trans.).

[6] In a letter to Jakob Løkke (November 23, 1873), Ibsen makes it clear that because Winckelmann, Lessing, Goethe, and Schiller have generated a general goodwill on behalf of (ancient) paganism, Christianity has suffered in their expositions. Thus Ibsen, in turning to the figure of Julian, needs to return to the sources (HIS XIII 161). He wishes to stay true—in a way that reflects the ethos of a Herder or a Hettner—to the historical material while nonetheless granting that his choice of topic is relevant to his own time.

More than any other work by Ibsen, *Emperor and Galilean* is indeed a Hegelian play. Yet recent scholarship has questioned the Hegelian interpretations. Toril Moi, for example, reads *Emperor and Galilean* as a proto-modernist drama and Ibsen's modernism, in turn, as expressive of anti-Hegelian sentiments.[7] I sympathize with Moi's worry that a focus on Hegel's dialectics alone may leave us with an unacceptably narrow framework of interpretation, thus reducing the play to a philosophical treatise of sorts. As Ibsen puts it in a letter to Brandes, he does not want to give us the "moral" of the story. Yet Ibsen continues to indicate that the moral of the story should be distinguished from the philosophy of the time, which, in turn, is taken up and transformed as dramatic poetry.[8]

In my reading of *Peer Gynt*, I proposed that Ibsen's work, as it develops against the background of the European *Sturm und Drang*, allows us to view his engagement with Hegel through a mix of appropriation, parody, and critique. Does *Emperor and Galilean* invite a similar approach? This question will guide my interpretation.[9] I suggest that *Emperor and Galilean* indeed engages elements from Hegel's philosophy.[10] However, I do not see it as a teleological or metaphysical play. Rather than reducing the Hegelian resonance to a matter of philosophical doctrine, I focus on Hegel's understanding of the early Christian religion as a precondition for the modern mindset. Hegel's understanding of that mindset, in turn, anticipates the modern literary movements in Scandinavia. With this approach, we transcend the either-or that governs both the Hegelian readings of Ibsen and their anti-Hegelian counterparts.[11]

---

[7] Moi, *Henrik Ibsen and the Birth of Modernism*, 188–191, also 242–247 (with a reference to *A Doll's House*).

[8] In Ibsen's original: "[J]eg ser på karaktererne, på de krydsende planer, på *historien*, og giver mig ikke af med 'moralen' af det hele—forutsat at De [Brandes] ikke under historiens moral vil forstå dens filosofi; thi at en sådan kommer til at skinne frem som den endelige dom over det kæmpende og sejrende, er en selvfølge. Dog alt dette kan kun anskueliggjøres praktisk" (letter to Brandes, September 24, 1871, HIS XIII 19).

[9] My approach thus differs from the interpretations pursued in John C. Pearce, "Hegelian Ideas in Three Tragedies by Ibsen," *Scandinavian Studies*, vol. 34, no. 4 (1962): 245–257 and from Koppang's reading in *Hegelianismen i Norge* (Oslo: Aschehoug, 1943), 180–185. Similarly, Johnston claims that it is a dialectical play. See *The Ibsen Cycle*, 66–69.

[10] I do not, for this reason, deny the existence of other aspects of the work (e.g., the psychological dimensions of Julian's agonizing or of his response to the loss of his parents). Nor do I deny the Shakespearean reverberations of the play, the significance of Ibsen's use of ancient history, or the possibility that the work could be meaningfully situated in other philosophical contexts (Platonic philosophy is briefly discussed later).

[11] In positioning Ibsen's modernism as a particularly anti-Hegelian gesture, Moi goes to some length to establish *Emperor and Galilean* as a Nietzschean work. She emphasizes the Dionysian parades that Julian organizes and suggests that Ibsen might have read (or been exposed to) Nietzsche's *The Birth of Tragedy* in between his finishing Part One and Part Two (*Henrik Ibsen and the Birth of Modernism*, 196–197). Yet Moi proposes, without acknowledging the importance of Hegel (especially, but not exclusively, for Marx) that "[o]nly in Marx and Nietzsche do we find equally radical

Historical-Philosophical Preamble

In Ibsen's circles, the expectations for *Emperor and Galilean* were high. After all, it had been known for nine years that Ibsen was working on a drama about Julian. The two parts of *Emperor and Galilean* span a total of ten acts and twelve years of Julian's life. Part One, *Caesar's Apostasy*, centers on Julian and his religious agonizing before he becomes emperor (AD 351–361). In this period, his cousin, Constantius, is in power. Part Two, *The Emperor Julian*, covers Julian's years on the throne (AD 361–363). While Part One takes place in Constantinople, Athens, Ephesus, Lutetia, and Vienna, Part Two is set in Constantinople, Antioquia, and the Tigris area. As the contemporary critics were quick to point out, Part One, with its focus on Julian's quest for religious and existential truth, is dramatically more stringent. Part Two, by contrast, is meandering. *Emperor and Galilean* received an overall positive reception in Norway, and Ibsen, satisfied with the reviews, notes that none of his early works had caused such commotion (Letter to Frederik Hegel, Nov. 13, 1873; HIS XIII 260).

According to Ibsen, *Emperor and Galilean* is written in close consultation with scholarly sources on Julian the Apostate, the emperor whose rejection of Christianity had made him a hero of the Enlightenment.[12] In the work of

---

diagnoses of European modernity. In their great hymn to the power of capitalism, *The Communist Manifesto*, Marx and Engels also famously describe a culture in the throes of cataclysmic social and historical change" (ibid., 195). As it will be clear in this chapter, I find an awareness of such a cultural demise in Hegel's work too. In fact, Hegel, in my view, emerges as one of the first philosophers to systematically chronicle the genealogy of modernity—its victories, but also its fatal shortcomings, as they would later find (artistic) expression in European realism and modernism. It is also worth mentioning that if one, like Moi, pursues a feminist reading of Ibsen's work, Nietzsche's philosophical contribution seems no less problematic than Hegel's.

[12] For *Emperor and Galilean*, Ibsen probably drew on the German translation of Ammianus Marcellinus's work and additional, historical sources (see Faaland, *Henrik Ibsen og antikken*, 168, and Wærp, *Overgangens figurasjoner*, 38–41). Ibsen recounts his faithfulness to the sources in letters from February 1873 (to Hegel and Gosse, see HIS XIII 102, 104). While commentators (see for example William Archer's introduction; *The Collected Works of Henrik Ibsen* [New York: Charles Scribner's Sons, 1914], vol. V, xvii–xviii) sometimes emphasize this as a feature that sets *Emperor and Galilean* apart, Ibsen, in his 1898 introduction to *The Feast at Solhaug*, describes his early historical work as generally aspiring to relive a past historical period: "I tried, to the extent possible, to bring to life the customs and practices of past times, the emotional life of people, their ways of thinking and speaking [tænkesæt og utdryksmåde]." Ibsen, "Introduction to *The Feast at Solhaug*," SV I 132, my trans. Others, such as Adalbert von Hanstein, have cast doubt on Ibsen's objectivity in his engagement with the historical material. See his *Ibsen als Idealist. Vorträge über Henrik Ibsens Dramen* (Leipzig: G. Freund Verlag, 1897), 74. It is important, though, to note that Ibsen himself does not describe his historical reconstruction as objectivizing, but as a commitment to present everything as he himself "had seen it." He speaks of this as a mark of the work being "realistic" (HIS XIII 104 and 108).

Voltaire, for example, Julian is celebrated as a beacon of secularity.[13] In Ibsen's own time, David Friedrich Strauß had published a study of Julian, although his approach is more ambivalent than Voltaire's. The interest in Emperor Julian and his era had also surged in a Scandinavian context. There was Viktor Rydberg's 1859 *Den siste athenaren* and, seven years later, Carsten Hauch's *Julian den Frafaldne*. It is clear that in the second half of the 1800s, Emperor Julian's struggle with his faith was considered to be particularly timely. For Ibsen, Julian's religious agonizing thus provided material that demanded historical accuracy *and* served as a lens through which he could approach his own time. However, in his treatment of his historical sources, Ibsen has ambitions beyond the actual periods at stake (that of Emperor Julian and the Fourth Century and that of Ibsen, as the nineteenth-century author of the play). *Emperor and Galilean*, we learn, also stages "a battle between two irreconcilable forces in world history that will repeat themselves infinitely."[14] In this manner, three layers run through and shape the work: that of Roman antiquity, that of Ibsen's own time, *and* that of the world-historical forces of conflict and redemption that encompass them both. At stake, in other words, is an approach that is historicizing, actualizing, *and* philosophizing.

Like *Peer Gynt*, *Emperor and Galilean* represents a massive dramaturgical challenge.[15] *Peer Gynt* had been too long for an ordinary evening performance and, in the tradition of melodrama, called for Norwegian valleys, mountains, and special effects such as deserts, pyramids, trolls, and other supernatural creatures.[16] *Emperor and Galilean*, too, requires spectacular decorations and a massively populated stage. Again, Ibsen blatantly defies the classicist demand for high-born characters and well-ordered plots, and he features peddlers, beggars, parades, and more unspecified effects such as "visions and voices" (OI IV 200; HIS VI 262).[17] The opening scene alone displays soldiers, churchgoers, pagan spectators, and servants, in addition to a host of named characters. A young man of nineteen, Julian first appears against a mass gathering outside a church and the audience is presented with

---

[13] Later, Voltaire's thought would be the subject of Georg Brandes's two-volume *François de Voltaire* (Kjøbenhavn: Gyldendal, 1916–1917).

[14] Letter to Daae February 23, 1873 (HIS XIII 108). Ibsen speaks of this repetition as a *universality* (ibid.).

[15] Parallels with *Peer Gynt* are disclosed as Julian pines for the vast solitude of Egypt (OI IV 205; HIS VI 271), i.e., the landscape Peer Gynt had traversed in his quest for a genuine self.

[16] For a discussion of melodrama and stage sets, especially with respect to representations of nature, see Shepherd-Barr, *Theatre and Evolution*, Chapter 1.

[17] Supranatural forces had been a part of the early plays, including *Lady Inger, The Vikings at Helgeland*, and *Peer Gynt*.

the Christians' worries about a recent upswing of paganism. Yet, the line between Christianity and paganism is blurred: Even the Christians practice idolatry and rely on oracles. This, the audience immediately realizes, is a world in which the normal rules have been suspended.

For Julian, history serves as a battleground for two different value-systems: pagan celebration of immanence and Christian longing for transcendence. As the play unfolds, we follow his negotiation of these value-systems. Throughout the entire play—the existential-individual Part One as well as the historical-panoramic Part Two—Ibsen focuses on Julian's struggle to gain a historical-existential footing and understand the foundations of his own existence. In this struggle, the old and the new stand starkly opposed. Christian ideals, such as piety and redemption of the soul, are in conflict with the ancient cultivation of beauty and the good life. The promise of God's (future) kingdom is in conflict with the turn to the past as a source of normativity. The emphasis on individual salvation stands opposed to the pagan celebration of traditional communities.

Julian's pensive disposition had been stressed by Voltaire and Strauß.[18] Similarly, Ibsen has the young Julian approach the world with a bookish inclination and a host of teachers who strive to get a purchase on his soul.[19] His intellectualism is emphasized not only as he starts to doubt his Christian faith, but also after he returns to the ancient gods and is hailed as emperor. While Julian, as emperor, is initially committed to religious freedom, he soon emerges as a dictator representing a brutality otherwise unknown in Ibsen.[20] Yet he finds no peace—neither in his books nor in his rituals. The books seem lifeless; the rituals remain empty. In Maximus the Mystic, Julian finds a solution to his torment: his idea of a Third Empire, a synthesis of pre-Christian beauty and Christian spirituality, points beyond the impossible dualism in which Julian finds himself trapped. Now, though, it is too late. Julian's brutality has gone too far. His rise to power has led to the religious and existential paranoia that brings about his downfall.

---

[18] Ibsen borrowed Strauß's study of Julian from the Scandinavian Library in Rome in 1866. See Anker, "Ibsen og den skandinaviske Forening i Roma," 171.

[19] The emphasis on learning, teachers, and teaching will then run through the later works, including *Pillars of the Society, A Doll's House*, and *An Enemy of the People*. I discuss this point in Chapters 4 and 6 in particular.

[20] In *Pillars of Society*, we encounter bourgeois coldness turning into plain evil. An example of this is Berenick's willingness to let his ship go down with the sailors to be able to cash in the insurance. Here, though, the façade remains intact, thus mirroring the horizon of late modernity and a new orientation toward wealth and monetary value. In *Emperor and Galilean*, no such façade is present.

Ibsen's first Roman play, *Catiline*, drew on his high school curriculum.[21] Moreover, Ibsen's short stint at the University of Christiania involved a mandatory entrance exam covering classical texts such as Sallust's *The Conspiracy of Catiline* and Cicero's *Catilinarian Orations*.[22] Indeed, the emphasis on the ideal of a classical education was concretely expressed in the newly erected university, which was planned with the aid of Karl Friedrich Schinkel. Ibsen's interest in classical culture may also have been strengthened through his affiliation with the so-called Dutch Circle (The Learned Holland), whose members had been in favor of retaining the final high school exam in Latin.[23] The interest in the Bacchaean-Dionysiac—vine leaves figure centrally in *Brand* and *Emperor and Galilean*, and, in a faded form, in *Hedda Gabler*—was a staple of this circle.[24]

After *Catiline*, Ibsen had been concerned with the differences between the ancient (classical) material and the historical material of the saga literature. In his 1857 essay on the ballad, Ibsen criticized contemporary attempts at reinvigorating Scandinavian historical material through a return to classical form.[25] A similar attitude—anti-classicist and attentive to historical distance—saturates *The Vikings at Helgeland* (see Chapter 1). If Ibsen had established himself as a playwright with a particular gift for historical drama, he was now ready to expand his use of historical-dramatic material and -form.[26] In returning to Roman antiquity, Ibsen motivates his choice of material by reference to the new philosophical-historical orientation of the play. He describes his own time as "void of meaning [en *meningsmørk* tid]."[27] Humankind, he fears, has gone astray.[28] Yet he insists that *Emperor*

---

[21] Faaland, *Henrik Ibsen og antikken*, 43.

[22] For a discussion of this point, see Andrew Runni Anderson, "Ibsen and the Classic World," *The Classical Journal*, vol. 11, no. 4 (1916): 216–225.

[23] The importance of this group for Ibsen's (early) work is discussed in Fredrik Ording, *Henrik Ibsens vennekreds Det lærde Holland. Et kapitel av norsk kulturliv* (Den norske Historiske Forening. Grøndahl & Søns Boktrykkeri. Oslo 1927), especially Chapter 10.

[24] See Faaland, *Henrik Ibsen og antikken*, 14.

[25] In particular, he had criticized Oehlenschläger. For Oehlenschläger, though, history was the very peak of poetry, and poetry, in turn, was seen as dedicated to that which was "peculiar to a particular nation ['Dette eiendommelige Nationale er Poesiens ædleste Blomst']." For a discussion of this point, see Hemmer, *Ibsen*, 191.

[26] There are diverging opinions on the stylistic features of *Emperor and Galilean*. While Faaland takes the play to draw on classical metrics, Moi views it as a work that cultivates an awareness of the ordinary. See Faaland, *Henrik Ibsen og antikken*, 168–169, and Moi, *Henrik Ibsen and the Birth of Modernism*, 191. However, while the play is free in its form, there are still passages that, rhythmically and stylistically, evoke classical meter.

[27] The poem "Ved Tusendårsfesten," July 18,1872 (P 130; HIS XI 607, trans. modified).

[28] Letter to Brandes, September 24, 1871: "hele slegten er på vildspor, det er sagen," HIS XIII 187.

and Galilean conveys the positive worldview that his critics had so long been asking for.[29]

It is possible that Ibsen's pledge to offer a positive worldview has contributed to the Hegelian reading of *Emperor and Galilean*. Within the German and Scandinavian receptions alike, readers have suggested that the dialectical structure of the play gives rise to a synthetic merging of the ideals of the ancients and those of Christianity. In his study of Norwegian Hegelianism, Ole Koppang argues that "[i]n shaping the motif of Julian's world-historical mission, Ibsen, to a large extent, has made use of the constructions of Hegelian dialectics."[30] These constructions, he further proposes, lead to the point at which someone new (i.e., Julian) "will rule the Third Empire, somebody who remains above the opposition between 'emperor' and 'Galilean.' "[31] Similarly, Douglas Abel argues that "[r]eal human and intellectual progress occurs as the two idea-systems of the play clash dynamically to produce an essentially Hegelian synthesis that both embodies and transcends those original systems."[32] However, given Ibsen's ambivalent approach to Hegel in *Peer Gynt*, we need to ask: How plausible is it that Ibsen, some few years later, would adopt a Hegelian outlook through and through?

Drama and Dialectics

In viewing *Emperor and Galilean* as a Hegelian-dialectical play, Ibsen scholars have made a number of assumptions. They have assumed, for example, that the Hegelian resonance in the play can be exhausted by reference to its dialectic nature, that dialectics is a distinctively Hegelian movement of thought (i.e., that any model that is dialectical is by implication also Hegelian), and that the play is structured around such a dialectical sublation of opposites. Each of these assumptions is in need of further probing.

It would be difficult, perhaps even foolhardy, to deny that in some sense or other Hegel's philosophy is dialectical. In addition to *The Phenomenology of Spirit*, initially written as the historical introduction to his philosophical system,

---

[29] Letter to Frederik Hegel, July 12, 1871 (HIS XIII 15).
[30] Koppang, *Hegelianismen i Norge*, 178 (my trans.).
[31] Koppang, *Hegelianismen i Norge*, 182 (my trans.).
[32] Douglas Abel, "Wisdom! Light! Beauty! A Thematic Analysis of Ibsen's *Emperor and Galilean*," *Modern Drama*, vol. 43, no. 1 (2000): 80. Going beyond his merely structural point, Abel further suggests that "[a]t the same time, Ibsen's application of Hegelian philosophical principles to analyze social phenomena is an approach shared with Marx and Engels." Ibid., 81, n. 12.

the notion of dialectics figures centrally in Hegel's logic, his philosophy of nature, his philosophy of right, and his lectures on the history of philosophy. In effect, the concept of dialectics permeates Hegel's entire philosophy, at least in its mature form. The term "dialectics" refers to an ontological principle of reality; it is taken to represent the dynamic structure of philosophical reasoning; and, finally, it is indicative of the very relationship between thought and reality (as reality is conceptually grasped through thinking).[33]

At stake in Hegel's work is a philosophical reconstruction of a historical process through which concepts, categories, values, practices, and worldviews turn out to be inherently self-contradictory, run up against their limitations, and eventually spawn new, more satisfactory alternatives.[34] These, in turn, will be pushed toward their own internal limits and give rise to further conceptual and philosophical developments. History, as Hegel puts it, advances along a path of doubt and despair (PS 49–50; HW III 72). For Hegel, this process develops through the modern period and reaches a point of culmination in his own time. That is, like other historical periods, modernity grows out of earlier cultures and practices. But unlike previous periods, modernity eventually reaches a full conceptual understanding of this process. With the advent of Absolute Idealism, the historical development is thus replaced by the systematic ambitions of philosophical logic.

The vague and non-committal formulations of dialectics that undergird the readings of *Emperor and Galilean* ignore, by and large, the systematic ambitions of Hegel's philosophy.[35] Moreover, any early Christian (or even pre-modern) synthesis would, for Hegel, be merely preliminary and offer no historical stability or philosophical point of culmination.

---

[33] For an overview of Hegel's dialectical method, see Michael N. Forster, "Hegel's Dialectical Method," in *The Cambridge Companion to Hegel*, ed. Frederick C. Beiser (Cambridge: Cambridge University Press, 1993), 130–170.

[34] In this sense, there is an affinity between Hegel's philosophy and drama, widely conceived. *The Phenomenology of Spirit* is sometimes seen as a philosophical contemplation on the kind of educational development (*Bildung*) we find structuring Goethe's *Wilhelm Meister*, which, if not itself a drama, is nonetheless a work in which reflections on drama feature prominently.

[35] Further, the dialectically-oriented readings deviate from Hegel's understanding of drama in his *Lectures on Fine Art*. In his lectures, Hegel analyzes tragedy along dialectical lines. However, he never argues that tragedy, for this reason, is dialectical in the philosophical sense, i.e., that it develops progressively and through gradually more universal articulations of concepts. Further, while we could grant a loosely dialectical dimension to his analysis of the ancient chorus (it mediates the opposing standpoints of the protagonists [LFA 1210; HW XV 540]), Hegel emphasizes that modern tragedy stages a tension within a single individual and therefore lacks the kind of communal-dialectical reference point that the chorus represents in ancient tragedy (LFA 1183; HW XV 507). For him, the tragic consists in a conflict that is beyond a dialectical resolution.

A further challenge emerges if we broaden our scope and take into account that the notion of dialectics has a history that goes far beyond Hegel's philosophy.[36] It is, in other words, not self-evident that a dialectical structure needs to be Hegelian. For example, we find discussions of dialectics, as well as dialectical structures of thought and conversation, throughout the Platonic dialogues.

In the first part of *Emperor and Galilean* alone, Plato is mentioned ten times. Among Julian's teachers, Libanius is presented as a false spokesman of the Socratic-Platonic tradition (OI IV 237; HIS VI 332). The Socratic-Platonic tradition, we learn, is one in which the philosopher lives as he teaches and, as such, lives and teaches in beauty (OI IV 237; HIS VI 332). Beauty is not opposed to truth; rather it is the emanation of truth itself (Plato has thrown "the light of interpretation" over everything, as Libanius puts it [HIS VI 351, my trans.; the translation at OI IV 274 misses this point]). This, indeed, is what distinguishes a Socratic-Platonic position from a later Christian worldview. Thus, the celebration of beauty, which is also a celebration of life, emerges as a good in itself—as life celebrating life. In *Emperor and Galilean*, Julian makes references to the symposium, i.e., the kind of setting that typically occurs in Greek and Roman antiquity (OI IV 241; HIS VI 341). In this context, dialectics refers to the way in which each asserted view, through the permutations of an open-ended dialogue, is criticized from within its own horizon.[37] This differs from the larger, historical model—with its alleged "thesis-antithesis-synthesis"-structure—that bolsters the Hegelian readings of Ibsen.

By identifying the general dialectical aspects of *Emperor and Galilean* with Hegelian dialectics in particular, we risk overlooking how *Emperor and Galilean* gestures toward a capacious, poetically mediated idea of dialectics that should not be reduced to one figure or position.[38] This leads us to a

[36] For a systematic and historical overview of the term "dialectics," see Claudia Wirsing, "Dialectics," in *The Oxford Handbook of German Philosophy in the Nineteenth Century*, ed. Michael N. Forster and Kristin Gjesdal (Oxford: Oxford University Press, 2015), 651–673.

[37] For a well-known reading of Plato's dialogical dialectics, see Hans-Georg Gadamer, *Plato's Dialectical Ethics: Phenomenological Interpretations Relating to the Philebus*, trans. by Robert M. Wallace (New Haven: Yale University Press, 1991); *Gesammelte Werke* (Tübingen: J. C. B Mohr [Paul Siebeck]), 1985), vol. V, 3–164. For a discussion of the dialogical element of Ibsen's drama, with a special emphasis on *Hedda Gabler*, see Kristin Boyce, "Philosophy, Theater, and Love: Ibsen's *Hedda Gabler* and Plato's *Symposium*," in *Ibsen's Hedda Gabler: Philosophical Perspectives*, ed. Kristin Gjesdal (Oxford: Oxford University Press, 2018), 132–152.

[38] This should be kept in mind as we approach, in the second half of this study, the Nietzschean reverberations in Ibsen's drama: In *Emperor and Galilean*, Ibsen presents a different and far more affirmative image of Socrates and Plato than what we later find in Nietzsche's *The Birth of Tragedy*. A more affirmative interpretation of Socrates can at times be found in Nietzsche's later work (e.g., *Ecce Homo*, §2). I return to this point in Chapter 6.

final question, namely to what extent Ibsen's play really unfolds as a (quasi-Hegelian) harmonious sublation of opposites into a higher unity.

Julian approaches the development of history in terms of its becoming. The very term "becoming [vorden]" captures the transition from that which is to that which will be. This is what Julian calls "the kernel of life [livets kerne]" (OI IV 250; HIS VI 358; Meyer, 170, gives us "the meaning of life," which is not an apt translation). The "kernel of life" is revealed to Julian in a dream: "But up above in the endless firmament, which before had seen mere emptiness . . . *there* was life; there the invisible took on shape and the stillness became sound. Then I perceived the great redemptive revelation [Da fatted jeg den store forløsende erkendelse]" (OI IV 251; HIS VI 360). This wisdom, further, is the following: "That, which is, is not, and that which is not, is" (OI IV 252; HIS VI 360). Bordering on the paradoxical, Julian's nightly vision marks the beginning of a new kind of insight. In seeking to realize his vision—in seeking "a new family [slægt] in beauty and harmony" (OI IV 254; HIS VI 365, trans. modified)—Julian finds his mission. As he now sees it, "the way and the goal are *one*" (OI IV 255; HIS VI 365). With this revelation in mind, Julian sets out to bridge the perceived opposites of knowledge and faith, ancient culture and Christianity, or, as he puts it, "the road to the school and the road to the church" (OI IV 255; HIS VI 366, trans. modified).[39]

Ibsen, though, offers no redemptive ending to Julian's suffering. *Emperor and Galilean* finishes with bloodshed, pain, the Emperor's madness, and only a vague and feeble gesture toward a possible realization of a Third Empire. As the play is about to close, Basil, a devoted Christian, comments that Julian's violence might have served to purge and thus strengthen the Christian community:

> BASIL. Christ, Christ, where were thy people, that they did not see thy manifest purpose? The Emperor Julian was a rod of correction . . . not for our death, but for our resurrection. (OI IV 459; HIS VI 744)

The character of Macrina then responds that if Julian *had* to act as he did, she hopes he will be judged accordingly:

---

[39] In using the (Greek-based) term "school [skolen]," Ibsen anticipates the orientation toward education in his later plays.

MACRINA. Oh Brother, let us not seek to the bottom of this abyss. [*She bends over the body, and covers the face.*] Erring human souls . . . if you were *forced* to err, allowance will indeed be made on that great day when the Mighty One shall come in a cloud to judge the living dead and the dead who live! (OI IV 459; HIS VI 744)

Rather than seeing this end as invoking a higher synthesis,[40] I take the silence that follows Macrina's closing line to leave the reader with the same questions that Julian has asked himself throughout the play: Is there a meaning to history? And, if so, how would this meaning manifest itself? The tragic end of the philosopher-emperor, the devastation of his life and his world, does not grow out of his *asking* such questions, but rests with his insistence, once he is overpowered by a need to put an end to agony and speculation, that he has found a clear and absolute answer to them: namely that *he himself*, as he calls for the return to a long-gone past, incarnates the values of the future.

In this sense, a close identification of Julian's historical-philosophical position with Hegel's dialectics risks undermining the tragic-dramatic complexity of Ibsen's work. However, even if we want to caution against a reductive interpretation of *Emperor and Galilean* in light of Hegelian dialectics, it could still make sense to see it as a Hegelian work. This, however, requires a move from Hegel's dialectical teleology to his philosophy of art, and of drama in particular.

Hegelian Recuperations

Hegel was a philosopher of religion, culture, and history—*and* a philosopher of art. Drama, and especially tragedy, plays an important role in his aesthetics.[41] With Heiberg, Monrad, and others, this part of Hegel's philosophy had featured centrally in Ibsen's circles.[42] Heiberg, further, had led Ibsen

---

[40] Even though the synthesis Julian has in mind—but fails, in the end, to realize—is one between the classical world and Christian religion, there is a tendency in the scholarship to interpret it in a particularly Christian light. See for example Koppang, *Hegelianismen i Norge*, 179. As Koppang puts it, we here encounter the idea that a "fall [undergang] is a necessary aspect of the development and all development involves the realization of divine thoughts" (my trans.).

[41] For a discussion of this point, see Lydia L. Moland, *Hegel's Aesthetics: The Art of Idealism* (Oxford: Oxford University Press, 2019), Chapters 4 and 10.

[42] While Heiberg attended Hegel's lectures on aesthetics, he did not have access to the written version (which was based on student notes and only published later). It is thus likely, as Stewart argues, that Heiberg's version of Hegelian aesthetics was watered down by impulses from, among others, Jean

to Hermann Hettner's (Hegelian) study of modern theater, which Ibsen describes as "a manifesto and a program for reform in the theater."[43] Another name worth mentioning is Gustav Freytag, whose work would later be the subject of Nietzsche's scorn.[44] Closer to home, Brandes published essays on tragedy and comedy, later included in his *Aesthetic Studies*. In a Hegelian spirit, *Aesthetic Studies* summarized a century's worth of philosophy of drama in a German language context. In fact, Brandes, in his essay on tragedy, suggests that the spirit of tragedy is world-historical ("Den Aand, der vifter gjennem det tragiske Drama, er Verdenshistoriens Aand"). Stronger still, he proposes that it is "drama that makes up the basis for philosophy of history."[45]

I return to Brandes—whom Ibsen first met in Dresden in 1871—in Chapter 4. What matters here is how, for Hegel, modern art is associated with the romantic era, which, in turn, is supposed to have Christian beginnings. The breakthrough of Christianity is, in other words, key to Hegel's under- standing of modern (romantic) art. As pagan religion lost influence, it became, in Hegel's view, increasingly oriented toward power, glory, and ma- terial concerns. Indeed, in his narrative, even the Roman gods would even- tually be understood in a purely utilitarian fashion. In this environment, the societal and cultural conditions for great art are no longer present.[46] As Hegel concludes, "we find no beautiful, free, and great art in Rome" (LFA 514; HW XIV 124). The classical harmony between sensuousness and spiritual form is now a thing of the past.

Paul. See Jon Stewart, *A History of Hegelianism in Golden Age Denmark, Tome I, The Heiberg Period, 1824–1836* (Copenhagen: C. A. Reitzel, 2007), 179.

[43] Halvdan Koht even claims that during his first stay in Dresden, nothing preoccupied Ibsen more than Hettner's study. See Koht, *Henrik Ibsen*, 84–85; *The Life of Henrik Ibsen*, 80–81. For Hettner's reinterpretation of historical drama, see Hermann Hettner, *Das moderne Drama. Aesthetische Untersuchungen* (Braunschweig: F. Vieweg, 1852), 1–60.

[44] Freytag was himself a novelist and playwright. His *Graf Waldemar* was translated by Ibsen's wife, Suzannah, and staged in Christiania in 1861. See Astrid Sæther, *Suzannah. Fru Ibsen* (Oslo: Gyldendal, 2008), 83 and 368 (footnotes 34 and 35). For Nietzsche's resentment of Freytag and other authors producing a "historical malady," see Christian J. Emden, *Friedrich Nietzsche and the Politics of History* (Cambridge: Cambridge University Press, 2008), 145. For Freytag's work on drama, see Gustav Freytag, *Die Technik des Dramas* (Leipzig: Hirzel, 1886).

[45] Georg Brandes, *Æsthetiske Studier*, 2nd edition (Kjøbenhavn: Gyldendal, 1888 [first edi- tion: 1868]), 74, my trans.

[46] With Hegel: "The spirit of the Roman world is domina[ted] by abstraction [i.e., by dead law], the demolition of beauty and joyous customs, the suppression of the family *qua immediate* natural ethical life, in general the sacrifice of individuality which now surrenders itself to the state and finds its cold-blooded dignity and intellectual satisfaction in obedience to the abstract law" (LFA 514; HW XIV 124).

However, out of the ruins of the ancient culture of sensuous perfection, a new religion emerges: that of Christianity. Christianity, Hegel points out, represents a retreat to the inner. Now "spirit is pushed back into itself out of its reconciliation in the corporeal into a reconciliation of itself within itself. . . . The spirit, which has as its principle its accord with itself, the unity of its essence with its reality, can find its correspondent existence only in its own native spiritual world of feeling, the heart, and the inner life in general" (LFA 518; HW XIV 128). In early Christianity, the gods no longer play a utilitarian role, and the world of human affairs, laid bare through a battle for power and satisfaction, emerges as corrupt and void of meaning. Failing in its quest to find satisfaction in society and shared practice, spirit turns inward—"absolute inwardness" is Hegel's term (LFA 519; HW XIV 129). Tradition is no longer a guarantor of meaning for the individual. The individual is thrown back at itself and one's faith becomes a personal matter rather than a function of membership in a community. Under such circumstances, the gods of the classical age can no longer survive; the very idea of a panoply of (external) gods becomes implausible (LFA 519; HW XIV 130). What is more, we see, in this era, the speculative preconditions for modern subjectivity as it is marked by reflectiveness—though, in Hegel's view, this reflectiveness still has to be fully developed and reach later, more mediated forms.

A new religion—and a new worldview—requires new art.[47] For Hegel (and again he follows the conventions of the time), this new artistic paradigm is that of romanticism, which stretches all the way from the early Middle Ages to his own time period. Hence, modern art is traced back to its roots in Christianity. While fine art had always been the expression of freedom, subjectivity now turns into its own object of investigation. Rather than representing the gods, art mediates religious longings, feelings, and passions.

In Hegel's system, each art-historical period finds its most adequate articulation in a particular artistic medium. While the preceding periods find the high point of their expressions in architecture (symbolic art) and sculpture (classical art), romantic art is most evidently manifest in painting, music, and, ultimately, poetry. Poetry, for Hegel, expresses inward longing (LFA

[47] In Hegel's words: "The different moments which constitute the totality of this world view as the totality of truth itself . . . find their appearance in man in such a way that content and form are not afforded either by the natural as such, as sun, sky, stars, etc., or by the beautiful group of the Greek gods, or by heroes and external deeds wrought on the ground of family obligations and political life; on the contrary, it is the actual individual person in his inner life who acquires infinite worth, since in him alone do the eternal moments of absolute truth, which is actual only as spirit, unfold into existence and collect together again" (LFA 520; HW XIV 131).

961; HW 225). It synthesizes the externality of painting and the inwardness of music, the precursors to romantic poetry. In this way, poetry is in a certain sense superior to the other arts.[48]

If all art, for Hegel, manifests spirit in a sensuous form, poetry holds a maximum of spiritual content. It is, as Hegel puts it, "the most universal and widespread teacher of the human race" (LFA 972; HW XV 239–240). There is little holding Hegel back in his description of poetry. He emerges as a philosopher who, along the lines of Herder and the romantics, venerates poetry and sees it as the artform of his time. While eager to criticize romantic philosophy, Hegel still appreciates romantic poetry, which he situates within this larger, historical-speculative context.[49]

Following the conventions of the time, Hegel distinguishes between epic, lyric, and dramatic poetry. Within this division, dramatic poetry is assigned a special place. If all poetry testifies to the expression of human freedom, dramatic poetry gets to the center of this freedom as it manifests itself through action. In Hegel's view, dramatic poetry is action realized in words (i.e., in a spiritual medium). Understood as the presentation of human action, drama shows us the entire scope of humanity embodied in concrete characters and actors. Drama retains a focus, prevalent in epic narrative, on action. Yet, it also remains close to lyrical poetry. Historically, and in terms of its systematic features, dramatic poetry synthesizes the other poetic forms—epic and lyrical poetry—and thus completes the development of poetry (LFA 1158; HW XV 474; for a similar point in Ibsen's work, see HIS XVI 144).

Drama takes the form of comedy and tragedy, both of which are defined through a depiction of human conflict. Each of these poetic sub-genres develop throughout the ages. From *The Phenomenology of Spirit* onward, Hegel takes a special interest in tragedy, in particular Sophocles's *Antigone*, which, in his work, reflects the opposition between, on the one hand, an orientation toward family and religion (Antigone), and, on the other, that of publicly

---

[48] As Hegel puts it: "The subject-matter really corresponding to poetry is the infinite wealth of the spirit. For language, this most malleable material, the direct property of the spirit, of all media of expression the one most capable of seizing the interests and movements of the spirit in their inner vivacity, must be used, like stone, colour, and sound in the other arts, principally to express what it proves most fitted to express. Accordingly, the chief task of poetry is to bring before our minds the powers governing spiritual life, and, in short, all that surges to and fro in human passion and feeling or passes quietly through our meditations—the all-encompassing realm of human ideas, deeds, actions, and fates, the bustle of life in this world, and the divine rule of the universe" (LFA 972; HW XV 349).

[49] For a discussion of this point, see Moland, *Hegel's Aesthetics*, Chapter 4.

recognized law (Creon).[50] Ancient tragedy of this kind represents a collision of ethical horizons (LFA 1217; HW XV 549). As such, it comes to reflect the dissolution of a coherent worldview. In this sense, Greek tragedy dies from within. As the classical culture evolves, the panoply of gods expands, the values they represent are in conflict, and we witness a turn to the inner as a source of religious satisfaction. Christianity emblematically expresses this. As a religion of subjective faith, it harbors within itself the conflict between the divine and the human, infinite and finite. This is the material out of which modern drama grows.[51]

Like many of his contemporaries, Hegel finds that modern drama—with its historical-philosophical preconditions—obtains its most pregnant expression in Shakespeare. This point of view, anticipated by the *Sturm und Drang* movement (see Chapter 1), is reiterated by Hettner and Brandes.[52]

There is no need, at this point, for a detailed discussion of Hegel's reading of Elizabethan drama.[53] Yet it must be mentioned that, in his interpretation of *Hamlet*, Hegel focuses on how the play's protagonist is in conflict with himself. As such, Hegel, while recognizing the historical roots of the play, finds in Shakespeare's Hamlet a profoundly modern character. In *Hamlet*, we see how an agent comes to realize that subjectivity itself is the source of all values—and the utter disappointment, melancholy, and sorrow that follow from this realization. For if values depend on subjective approval, they can also appear as arbitrary and haphazard.[54] Moreover, if values prove contingent on subjective action and endorsement, then the world itself may appear disenchanted—without inherent value and pre-constituted sites of self-realization. If the subject now emerges as all-powerful, then the world he or she reigns over is potentially drained of the qualities that made

---

[50] Hegel judges *Antigone* to be the most important work of tragic art: "Of all the masterpieces of the classical and the modern world . . . the *Antigone* seems to me to be the most magnificent and satisfying work of art of this kind" (LFA 1218; HW XV 550).

[51] In Hegel's words, "Modern tragedy adopts into its own sphere from the start the principle of subjectivity. Therefore it takes for its proper subject matter and contents the subjective inner life of the character who is not, as in classical tragedy, a purely individual embodiment of ethical powers, and, keeping to this same type, it makes actions come into collision with one another as the chance of external circumstances dictates, and makes similar accidents decide, or seem to decide, the outcome" (LFA 1223; HW XV 555).

[52] See Hettner, *Das moderne Drama*, 18, and Georg Brandes, *William Shakespeare* (Kjøbenhavn: Gyldendal, 1895–1896); *William Shakespeare: A Critical Study*, trans. William Archer et al. (London: William Heinemann, 1898).

[53] For Hegel's reading of Shakespeare, see my "Reading Shakespeare, Reading Modernity," *Angelaki: Journal of the Theoretical Humanities*, vol. 9, no. 3 (2005): 17–31.

[54] As Hamlet puts it, time is out of joint (1.5.186) and "this goodly frame the earth seems . . . a sterile promontory . . . a foul and pestilent congregation of vapors" (2.2.264–268).

it a worthwhile investment in the first place. In spite of its newly acquired powers, modern subjectivity emerges as isolated, alienated, and powerless.

With this analysis in mind, we return to Ibsen. For the experience of hypostatized selfhood and lost values, of a gap between mind and world, is also a central topic in *Emperor and Galilean*. In my view, it is this—rather than the reference to a grand, dialectical-teleological synthesis—that makes up the most plausible philosophical-dramatic backdrop of *Emperor and Galilean*.

Faith and Certainty

In his stage instructions, Ibsen offers a detailed description of Julian's time and milieu. As the play begins, the landscape is open, the audience glimpses the Strait of Bosporus, and we are presented with a mass gathering outside of the illuminated church in Constantinople. Something is not quite right. Monuments are overturned. Turmoil lurks even as we hear psalm music resound from the church (OI IV 201; HIS VI 263). At the church entrance, there are beggars. Everyone is waiting for Emperor Constantius, Julian's cousin, to emerge. Colloquial exchanges among those awaiting his entrance reveal that the Emperor has recently let it be known that he, a Christian, disapproves of Christian interaction with the pagans. The Christian faith is in need of purification—the protection of "the true members of the church [kirkens rene lemmer]" (OI IV 202; HIS VI 266), as the barber, Eunapius, puts it. Bewilderment and skepticism prevail. The Emperor is no exception. In Ibsen's directions, the insecurity of the Emperor is palpable: "his eyes are gloomy and suspicious; his gait and his whole being betray uneasiness and infirmity [forråder uro og svækkelse]" (OI IV 203; HIS VI 268).

With Emperor Constantius is his young cousin Julian. Julian is evidently tense: "*He has black hair, an incipient beard, and sparkling, darting brown eyes; his court dress does not become him; he is strikingly awkward and impetuous in his manner*" (OU IV 203; HIS VI 268). Ibsen details Julian's physique, both as far as he is described in the stage instructions and as far as the other characters' conversations go. The Emperor is short, thin, and dressed in ragged garb. His soul is split, we learn. He is thinking about religion— religion, it seems, is everywhere and on everyone's mind—but without the commitment of the unwavering believer. Julian longs for certainty, and yet he knows that such certainty cannot be found, at least not in the Emperor's Constantinople:

JULIAN. I shall not brood, if only you will let me [leave]. . . . Here the anguish of my soul grows worse every day. Evil thoughts crowd in on me. For
nine days I have worn a hair shirt, and it has not protected me; for nine
nights I have whipped myself with scourges, but that does not drive my
thoughts away. (OI IV 205; HIS VI 271)

What plagues Julian is not simply a longing for a new religion, but, even more
markedly, a quest for something that can set his mind to rest. He is beset by a
gnawing suspicion that whatever can ease his agony, it is constitutively out of
reach—at least it appears to be out of reach within Christianity, a religion that
places faith at its center and locates the relationship to God in the individual
heart and mind.[55] As Julian puts it: "At times, to my horror, I feel sickened by
the nourishment of the Faith and the Word [jeg ækles ved troen og ordets
føde]" (OI IV 212; HIS VI 284).

Julian's time is one of religious backlash. In the Christian community, religious agony is vented by lashing out against the pagans. Bouts of revenge
are triggered by the slightest of suspicions (OI IV 243–244; HIS VI 345). If
he were to admit his doubt, Julian would be vulnerable to such revenge. It
is no wonder that he is overcome by fear, or as Ibsen puts it, in an almost
Hamletian language, by disgust (ækel). Seeking to overcome his disgust,
Julian embarks on a journey to find himself as a believer. He is out to fight
for Christianity and yet his path turns out to be different from what he had
initially envisioned. The old pagan religion into which he was initially born
represents a permanent temptation, the teachers of wisdom an omnipresent
lure. Theirs is an emphasis on this world. They do not view truth as "the
enemy of beauty" (OI IV 241; HIS VI 341, trans. modified), but see wisdom
and beauty as one.

Julian has a mind of learning. He is a philosopher of sorts, and his life is
one of bookish wisdom. Yet, with his restlessness, Julian finds that books
cannot yield what he is asking. Not learning, but life is what it would take to
quell Julian's doubts and existential quandaries:

JULIAN. The same counsel of despair. Books, . . . always books! When
I went to Libanius the answer was: books, books! When I came to you, . . .

---

[55] Hegel makes an exception for the early Christian religion. See Hegel, The Spirit of Christianity and
Its Fate, in Early Theological Writings, trans. T. M. Knox (Philadelphia: the University of Pennsylvania
Press, 1975), 182–302; Hegels theologische Jugendschriften, ed. Herman Nohl (Tübingen: J. C. B.
Mohr, 1907), 241–342.

books, books, books! Stones for bread! Books are no good to me; . . . it is life
I am hungry for, communion with the spirit, face to face. (OI IV 244; HIS
VI 346)

Christianity, the new religion, cannot offer life and vitality.[56] Julian lives in
a period of transition and uncertainty: "The old beauty is no longer beautiful, and the new truth is no longer true" (OI IV 245; HIS VI 447). Only a
miracle—a revelation—can get him beyond this predicament: "Yes, a revelation! Oh, Basil, if only your prayers could bring me *that*!" (OI IV 245; HIS
VI 347).[57] Is this madness (as his teacher Libanius suggests [OI IV 247; HIS
VI 351]) or is it the highest wisdom (as Julian is prone to thinking)? It is in
between these two poles—those of doubt and certainty—that Julian's faith is
played out.

At the end of Part One, Julian is crowned. Geographically, his rule is vast.
Existentially, however, he is poor. The past cannot be retrieved, and the world
is experienced as nothing but a heap of rubbish:

JULIAN. Isn't the whole world a heap of rubbish?
MAXIMUS. But you have proved that what has fallen can be rebuilt.
JULIAN. Don't be sarcastic! In Athens I saw a cobbler who had set up a little
    workshop in the temple of Theseus. In Rome I hear that a corner of the
    Basilica Julia has been converted into an ox-stall. You might call *that*
    rebuilding too! (OI IV 399; HIS 632)

It is no wonder that neither worldly goods nor wisdom can offer deeper satisfaction. Julian has lost his Christian faith, is seeking a return to his pagan
past, and yet this past evades him.

When Julian is presented with the idea of a Third Empire, a synthesis of
paganism and Christian faith, the overtly reflective emperor struggles to believe in this as well. The notion of a Third Empire is, as it were, too closely tied
to his own subjective fate; there is no way of knowing whether it has objective
reality. Thus, when Julian, in Part Two, seeks to realize the idea of a Third
Empire, his despair only increases. His credo, at first a message of religious
tolerance, turns into a terror of the most intolerable kind.

---

[56] He who has been under Christ can never be free, Julian remarks, anticipating Nietzsche's ethos
from the later *Genealogy of Morals* (to which I return in Chapter 8).

[57] This is the kind of skepticism Hegel finds in the early modern era—a skepticism that is somewhat
similar, yet caught in a language different from the Cavellian skepticism Moi traces in Ibsen's work.

Julian dies without hope. His kingdom is a wasteland, his rule a failure, his reputation in tatters. The Emperor who once was everyone's hope turned out to be a disappointment—not only to his subjects, but also to himself. Julian's final words—representing a twisted version of Christ's most desperate moment (and a proto-version of Oswald's longings in *Ghosts* some eight years later)—resounds as a plea: "Oh, sun, sun, why did you deceive me" (OI IV 458; HIS VI 741, trans. modified [the Oxford translation renders this in a more old-fashioned Biblical language that breaks with Julian's tone of voice]). A new emperor is called for and Julian is "forgotten before [his] hand is cold" (OI IV 458; HIS VI 742).

Emperor and Galilean is neither a drama of forward-looking dialectics,[58] nor of ideas, at least not in the traditional meaning of the term.[59] Rather, it is a drama of doubt and agony. Julian's enemies are everywhere, including within him. He fails to come to terms with his faith and the world. There is no progress here, no history to speak of. All we have is a long, nihilistic standstill. It is as if the sheer length of Ibsen's play, the endurance it would take to sit through the ten acts (surpassing even *Brand* and *Peer Gynt*), is but a way to evoke in the audience a sense of ennui. In a world where past and future have lost their meaning, temporality is experienced as vacuous. Julian's fight is a fight against the void in him, and this void in him is also mirrored in his outlook on the world. It is in this sense—not as a champion of historical-progressive synthesis, but as an early formation of the perils of modern selfhood—that Julian emerges as a proto-modern dramatic character in Hegel's sense of the word.

Along with his philosophy of art, Hegel's philosophy of religion had a central place in Norway.[60] For Hegel, Christianity, precisely *in* being a religion of subjectivity, prepares for modern philosophy.[61] It is a religion that links belief with individual conscience and passion, allowing spirit to turn toward itself.[62] In religion, this reflective turn culminates in Protestantism,

---

[58] As argued in Koppang, *Hegelianismen i Norge*, 182–185.

[59] This applies whether the ideas in question are part of the proto-religious reading we find in Faaland's *Ibsen og antikken* (see for example p. 173) or the non-religious reading suggested by Meyer (see Meyer, *Henrik Ibsen* II 186).

[60] Johan Sebastian Welhaven, who had been appointed as professor of philosophy in the 1840s, had been teaching Hegel's philosophy of religion early on. Koppang, *Hegelianismen i Norge*, 41.

[61] Here we should note the difference between the young Hegel's praise of the early, Christian communities and his later focus on the figure of Christ.

[62] In Hegel's words: "In this new period the universal principle by means of which everything in the world is regulated, is the thought that proceeds from itself; it is a certain inwardness, which is above all evidenced in respect to Christianity, and which is the Protestant principle in accordance with which thought has come to the consciousness of the world at large as that to which every man has a claim." LHP, III 217; HW XX 120.

but it also prepares for spirit's search for itself in a medium beyond art and religion, i.e., in conceptual thought. As philosophy, this reaches its most pregnant expression in the Cartesian *cogito* and the I's turn toward its own thinking.[63] And just like the world, in the view of the struggling Christian, is sometimes presented as a realm void of meaning—of emptiness, dust, and finitude, nothing like the eternal joy of God—so is the Cartesian philosopher, in Hegel's view, beset by skepticism.[64] In Hegel's presentation, the uneasy mindset of a protestant Hamlet is but the other face of the Cartesian turn toward the thinking I.[65] For Hegel, only absolute idealism, his own system, will provide the ultimate antidote to this skepticism.

In *Emperor and Galilean*, Ibsen introduces no idealist synthesis that can mend the gap between the subject and its world. The work reflects the moment of budding Christianity as it, in hindsight, lays the groundwork of a modern mindset. For Ibsen (as for Hegel), this is a point of no return. It is, on Ibsen's scheme, as if the very subjectivity of Christianity, even after Julian loses his faith, makes it impossible for him to restore the previous order. The impossibility of retrieving the past—historically, existentially, *and* aesthetically—is, as we saw in Chapter 1, something that preoccupies Ibsen throughout his early period. On this basis, *Emperor and Galilean* sheds light on the genuinely modern mindset that permeates the romantic-historical plays. For as Ibsen makes it clear—and here he follows Hegel's speculative thought—romanticism is born out of the Christian era (HIS XVI 146).

As the final act propels Julian toward increasing madness, Ibsen's exploration of the modern mindset culminates in the image of Julian as a self-postulated God. In Ibsen's view, as in Hegel's, what matters in this regard is the fact that belief is now a question of personal conviction. The emphasis on how commitments get a grip on us—on how they start mattering as subjective faith, and how, if or when they stop mattering, their downfall is experienced as a threat to the self itself—is one that we found in Ibsen's early plays (*Catiline, The Vikings at Helgeland, Peer Gynt*, possibly also *Brand*[66]) *and* that

[63] With the Cartesian cogito's reflection on its own activity of thinking, modern philosophy is finally on its "own proper soil," as Hegel puts it in his *Lectures on the History of Philosophy* III 217; HW XX 120.

[64] See for example Hegel, LHP III 551–552; HW XX 460–461.

[65] As Hegel describes Hamlet: "his noble soul is full of disgust with the world and life, what with decision, proof, arrangements for carrying out his resolve, and being bandied from pillar to post, he eventually perishes owing to his own hesitation and complication of external circumstances" (LFA 1226; HW XV 559).

[66] Helge Rønning remarks on the parallel between the ending of *Brand* and that of *Emperor and Galilean*. His approach, though, differs somewhat from mine in that he sees both works as centering,

resounds in later plays such as *The Wild Duck, Little Eyolf, Ghosts, The Master Builder*, and *When We Dead Awaken*. While many of Ibsen's protagonists (Nora and Hedda are cases in point) are thirsting for beauty, *their* beauty, as we will see in the following chapters, is not one of aestheticism. It is associated with the hope, however frail, that their world and their ideals will once again cohere.

In *Emperor and Galilean*, Ibsen explores the difficult historical-existential moment of a consciousness that suffers the costs of its own progress. This, further, is what ties the play's two parts together. Unlike the critics who see the work as fragmented, I view the existential Part One and the historical-panoramic Part Two as deeply intertwined. If Part One focuses on an individual who struggles to commit to, and realize, his values, Part Two explores the impossible quest to find certainty by externalizing, initially through religious tolerance and then through surging terror, a set of values to which inner subjectivity can no longer commit.[67] Julian's return to classical values represents a futile historical mission; it is twisted and doomed from the very start. Psychologically, it also represents an impossible quest: to the grown-up emperor, the outlook of wholesome infancy is forever lost. As a dictator of the self—his quest for omnipotence betraying his impotence—Julian tries to retrieve the past by rebelling against time.

Theater of Historicity

In *Emperor and Galilean*, Ibsen stages a moment at which history and individual existence merge. History takes on an existential meaning, and existence is felt as profoundly historical. It is from this point of view that Julian, upon his return to the old faith, experiences a lamentable apathy (*sørgelig ligegyldighed*, OI IV 325; HIS 496). Old ideals can no longer be brought to life; their historical moment is over.[68] Julian's belief that his studies can bring him back to the "teachings and customs" of the past is illusory (OI IV 326, trans. modified; HIS VI 497). As the tax collector, Ursulus, utters

first and foremost, on the notions of freedom and necessity, including the question of freedom in history. See Rønning, *Den umulige friheten*, 142.

[67] For Julian's early commitment to tolerance, see for example OI IV 325; HIS VI 496.
[68] Hegel, too, had made this point, especially in his discussion of Goethe's *Hermann und Dorothea*. I thank Lydia Moland for this point.

in a moment of truthfulness: "I cannot bear to see your fair and rising glory stained by wearing borrowed plumes" (OI IV 333; HIS VI 510).[69] That which is over historically can no longer be brought back—at least not as *mattering* in the way it once did. This, it seems, is the "philosophy of the time," which is very different from what Ibsen had rejected as a "moral of the story."

When Julian returns to Dionysus, seeking the liberated jubilation (*den frigjorte jubel*) that marks life and beauty (OI IV 337; HIS VI 517), his gesture resounds with emptiness. His parade ends up as sheer spectacle, marked, in Ibsen's text, by the dumb amazement of the onlookers (OI IV 341; HIS VI 524).[70] Later, Julian compares the celebration of Dionysus with a theater (OI IV 375; HIS VI 588), though hardly of the kind to which Ibsen would aspire—neither in his historical drama (which, as we saw in Chapter 1, problematizes the very idea of a return to the past), nor in the contemporary plays to follow. Julian's staging of a return to the past, his retrieval of that which has sunk,[71] is a contorted farce. Pointing to an overturned statue of Apollo, Julian observes: "Look at his face without a nose. Look at this shattered elbow . . . these splintered loins. Does the sum of all this ugliness add up to the divine perfection of former beauty?" (OI IV 399; HIS VI 632). And in this world of ugliness and hollow ideals, Julian's despair—originally fueled by his quest for a certainty about values and meaning—reaches new heights. He is, as Ibsen has Macrina put it, a lost soul.[72]

Whereas Voltaire had seen Julian as a champion of secularism, and Strauß had seen his return to paganism as the act of an impostor, in Ibsen's drama there is a crystallization of a historical moment, that of early Christianity, in which, along the lines of Hegelian thinking, personal doubt and historical loss cohere. This merging of individual and historical fate is the moment in which a proto-modern subjectivity breaks through. If Hjørdis of *The Vikings at Helgeland* presents us with the pain of experiencing a vanishing old world,

---

[69] Julian realizes this while speaking of his studies: "It has cost me many a night's sleep to find out from ancient books what used to be the common way [været brugeligt]" (OI IV 325; HIS VI 497, trans. modified).

[70] Hence, the onlookers (watching the many parades and celebrations in this play) represent but a version of the modern chorus as it, in the work of A. W. Schlegel's Kant-infused rhetoric, had taken on the role of the disinterested spectator. For an elaboration of this point, see my "The Theater of Thought: A.W. Schlegel on Shakespeare, Modern Drama, and Romantic Criticism," in *The Philosophy of Theatre, Drama and Acting*, ed. Tom Stern (London: Rowman and Littlefield, 2017), 43–65. Hegel, as pointed out, questions the use of chorus in modern tragedy and asks to what extent modern audiences can even appreciate the ancient chorus (LFA 1183; HW XV 507).

[71] He aspires, in the Norwegian original, to *genoprejse det sunkne*, OI IV 399; HIS VI 632.

[72] Ibsen uses an active inclination in the Norwegian original: *en vildfarende menneskesjæl*, HIS VI 744; a possible translation could be: "a human soul going astray."

and if Peer Gynt is the emperor of an inherently fragile modern self, then Julian brings to life the story of how such a self came to be in the first place. With *Emperor and Galilean*, the experiences of Peer Gynt, the Emperor of Self, is given a historical context.

In this way, *Emperor and Galilean* is a key work in Ibsen's dramatic oeuvre—and, we could add, in the understanding of his modernity. It shows how Ibsen's modernity grows out of, and remains linked up with, the way history and historicity are reflected in his work. The kinds of gains and losses that, in Hegel's philosophy, prepare for the modern world, are presented in Ibsen's drama through the agony of the young Emperor.

While Hegel speaks of the emerging, new religion in general philosophical terms, Ibsen reminds us that *as* lived and individualized, the mindset disclosed in early Christianity cannot be discussed in general terms without also being deprived of that which is distinctive of it. As Kierkegaard would have pointed out, philosophy, seeking to initiate a turn to reflective subjectivity, will run up against its own boundaries. Drama, by contrast, can stage this lived experience. As such, Ibsen's *Emperor and Galilean* offers no philosophical conclusions or didactic closing lines. It is as if Ibsen, with the tragic ending of *Emperor and Galilean*, sets the stage for a turn, in his contemporary drama, to a full concentration on modern life and its relation to history. This, I want to argue, is definitely the case with *A Doll's House*, a work that explores the call to take responsibility for oneself and, if needed, break with tradition when it no longer appears conducive to the future.

4

Modern Values (*A Doll's House*)

Six years set *A Doll's House* apart from *Emperor and Galilean*. In between these works, Ibsen published *Pillars of Society*, one of his few straightforwardly political plays. At this point, we have reached Ibsen's so-called contemporary drama, though, as I have argued, the historical works are also, in a certain sense, profoundly "contemporary." *A Doll's House* is Ibsen's most frequently staged play and one of the most frequently staged dramatic works of all time. With this play, Ibsen turns to the bourgeois interior.[1] Gone are the world-historical ideas and extravagant plots of the earlier plays. Also gone are the monuments, parades, and processions. The bourgeoisie emerges as the class of trade and finance.[2] We encounter a panoply of individual characters who seek to find fulfillment in the private sphere—or, more often, responding to the futility of this exercise. With brutal honesty, Ibsen continues to dramatize the nineteenth-century mindset, now by way of scrutinizing the conditions, contradictions, and painful self-discovery of the bourgeoisie.

In *A Doll's House*, Ibsen takes the now familiar thirst for meaning—embodied in characters such as Hjørdis and Julian—from the domain of shared history into the domestic quarters of the nuclear family. He offers a portrait of Nora and Torvald Helmer as they desperately seek (and spectacularly fail) to develop a relationship of genuine love and understanding. Nora and Torvald speak different languages and pursue different goods. In addition to his concern for money, Torvald is obsessed with a traditional image of the family. The home, for him, contains a kind of beauty that is free from the

---

[1] For a study of houses and homes in Ibsen's work, see Mark B. Sandberg, *Ibsen's Houses: Architectural Metaphor and the Modern Uncanny* (Cambridge: Cambridge University Press, 2015).

[2] In this sense, it is significant that *A Doll's House* follows *Pillars of Society*, a play that, centering on shady, financial speculations, serves as a perfect example of what Franco Moretti has described as Ibsen's willingness to expose the gray area of bourgeois life. As Moretti puts it: "This is what the gray area is like: reticence, disloyalty, slander, negligence, half truths . . . As far as I can tell, there is no general term for these actions [. . .] But with the gray area, we have the thing, without the word. And we really *do* have the thing; one of the ways in which capital develops is by invading ever new spheres of life—or even *creating* them, as in the parallel universe of finance—in which laws are inevitably incomplete, and behavior can easily become equivocal: not illegal, but not quite right either." Franco Moretti, *The Bourgeois: Between History and Literature* (London: Verso, 2013), 172.

The Drama of History. Kristin Gjesdal, Oxford University Press (2021). © Oxford University Press.
DOI: 10.1093/oso/9780190070762.001.0001.

dynamics of history.[3] He seeks to secure a beautiful existence for himself and his family. Initially, Nora is happy to play along. She too seeks a beautiful life. Throughout the play, though, she demonstrates a growing desire to break out of this picture and create a space in which she, as a woman, can find meaning. While Torvald remains stuck in a petrified image of gender roles and family life, Nora is impelled to leave her family in order to figure out whether the prevailing social norms permit her to live with values that she can recognize as meaningful. While acknowledging the costs of her endeavor, she sets out to pursue what she, not without a utopian tint, views as "the wonderful" (*det vidunderlige*, typically translated as "a miracle"). Unlike Torvald's commitment to a static beautiful existence, Nora seeks the kind of self-education and change that will disclose new historical spaces.[4] In his 2002 Schaubühne production of *A Doll's House* (*Nora*, as the play is called in German), Thomas Ostermeier makes an explicit point out of this in that he gives Nora, played by Anne Tismer, a pistol and, in the end, has her kill her husband, thus in effect seeking to eradicate the set of repressive, traditional expectations (in this version, the doll is associated with a Barbie) that he had come to represent (see color plate 5).

In the period around *A Doll's House* Ibsen develops a series of female characters who question a traditional identification of women with the (modern) home *and* expand the professional opportunities of female actors and audiences.[5] With Nora leaving her husband and her children in order to make sense of her life, *A Doll's House* has been read as a feminist manifesto.[6]

---

[3] With its focus on the contrast between financial, aesthetic, and human values it should not be a surprise that the play caught the interest of Karl Marx's youngest daughter, Eleanor, who organized an early reading of *A Doll's House* in London, with herself as Nora and George Bernard Shaw as Krogstad, the infamous moneylender. See Bernard F. Dukore, "Karl Marx's Youngest Daughter and *A Doll's House*," *Theatre Journal*, vol. 42, no. 3 (1990): 308–321.

[4] Ibsen is here in line with the position of Camilla Collett and other feminists, who, in this period, insisted that the path to equality must involve education. See Kristin Ørjasæter, "Mother, Wife, and Role Model: A Contextual Perspective on Feminism in *A Doll's House*," *Ibsen Studies*, vol. 5, no. 1 (2005): 19–47. It is also worth noting that, in *An Enemy of the People*, Ibsen presents Stockmann's daughter as a brave and clear-minded teacher, whose calling Stockmann eventually seeks to follow. I return to this point in Chapter 6.

[5] The actress Elizabeth Robins puts it as follows: "without the help of the stage the world would not have had an Ibsen to celebrate; and without Ibsen the world would not have had the stage as it became after his plays were acted." Elizabeth Robins, *Ibsen and the Actress* (London: Woolf, 1928), 7–8. See also Penny Farfan, *Women, Modernism, and Performance* (Cambridge: Cambridge University Press, 2004), 11–34.

[6] The feminist reading, however, was undermined by the so-called German ending, in which Torvald drags Nora to see her sleeping children and has her decide to stay. Ibsen wrote this alternative ending in response to the scenario of German directors producing their own ending (in order recruit actors for the controversial role as Nora). Later modifications of the play have been conducted in a different spirit. Responding to a culture in which children would be left with their father upon divorce, Dariush Merhrjui's film adaptation, *Sarah* (1992), has Nora leave with her daughter. For a

In concentrating on a female protagonist, Ibsen follows a larger trend in European realism *and* in Norwegian literature.[7]

With its emphasis on Nora's emancipation, *A Doll's House* has been viewed as an anti-Hegelian contribution. As Toril Moi argues, "*A Doll's House* can be read as a rebuff of Hegel's conservative understanding of women's role in marriage and the family."[8] Elaborating, she explains that she does not "mean that Ibsen set out to illustrate Hegel. (No claim would have annoyed him more.)" The point is, rather, "that Hegel happens to be the great theorist of the traditional, patriarchal, and sexist family structure that *A Doll's House* sets out to investigate."[9] Moi's argument can hardly be denied: Hegel's account of marriage is reactionary while Ibsen's finished version of *A Doll's House* is not.[10] Yet, Hegel's philosophy goes beyond his reactionary views on gender.

discussion of this point, see Frode Helland, *Ibsen in Practice: Relational Readings of Performance, Cultural Encounters and Power* (London: Bloomsbury Methuen, 2015), 100–102. In his Schaubühne production, Thomas Ostermeier has Nora kill Torvald, reasoning that a mother leaving her children is no longer unheard of: while it was "very shocking at the end of the Nineteenth Century that a woman should leave her husband and her children[,] we can't nowadays have the same moment of shock when two thirds of families split up." Quoted from Greene, *Home on the Stage*, 34–35.

[7] This includes a handful of very strong but still underappreciated women writers. In particular, I have in mind Camilla Collett, the author of the first realist novel in Norway, who had stayed with the Ibsens in Dresden, and the slightly younger Amalie Skram, who would offer thoughtful responses to his work. While Ibsen, in letters to male friends, describes his sparring with Collett during her stay, he writes her from Munich, in 1879, with a copy of a newly published play, presumably *A Doll's House*. See letter to Camilla Collett, November 20, 1879, HIS XIII 525. Ibsen also served as a mediator between Collett and his publisher, Hegel, in Copenhagen. For a discussion of the significance of Collett's influence (and the nature of her feminism), see Ørjasæter, "Mother, Wife, and Role Model."

[8] Moi, *Henrik Ibsen and the Birth of Modernism*, 12. As previously mentioned, Moi brings Ibsen closer to Nietzsche. However, even in Ibsen's own time, Nietzsche was seen as an anti-feminist. Brandes would emphasize that his views on this issue deviate from Nietzsche's. Later, Hedwig Dohm would sum up her criticisms in her 1902 *Die Antifeministen. Ein Buch der Verteidigung* (Berlin: Ferd. Dümmler, 1902). Vigdis Ystad notes that Ibsen may have been familiar with Dohm's earlier work (HIS VII/B 415–416). I return to this point in Chapter 5.

[9] Moi, *Henrik Ibsen and the Birth of Modernism*, 226.

[10] For a volume that includes more constructive readings of Hegel's potential for feminist thought, see *Hegel's Philosophy and Feminist Thought: Beyond Antigone?*, ed. Kimberly Hutchings and Tuija Pulkkinen. (New York: Palgrave Macmillan, 2010). Further, Amalie Skram's review of *A Doll's House* offers observations that could have been taken straight out of the master–bondsman dialectics in *The Phenomenology of Spirit*: "This animated reproduction of life stands among us as a sign and a warning and a judgement. When the woman wakes and gains full consciousness of her human dignity, when she rightly has her eyes opened to all the wrongs which have been done to her throughout history, then she will arm herself against the one she was given to assist her, and she will break asunder all bonds, cross all the walls which society and the institutional authorities have built up around her. Her resistance will perhaps lead her far beyond the borders of all reason, and that is when it will be strongest, when something is being done to reconcile, equalize and restore. History and the individual have at all times shown that the sufferer is always the one who tries to compromise, because confessions offer the insight of the sprouting liberation into how big the wrongs have been." See Amalie Skram, review of *A Doll's House*, *Dagbladet* January 19, 1880, trans. Mai-Brit Akerholt. See http://ibsen.nb.no/id/11186656.0 (Accessed June 7, 2019).

One way in which this happens is through his critique of aesthetic conscious-ness; another is his dialectics of recognition—a notion that has also been of fundamental importance to later thinkers such as Simone de Beauvoir.[11] Further, from our readings of *Peer Gynt* and *Emperor and Galilean*, we know that Ibsen's work, rather than being for or against Hegel's system, maneuvers Hegelian ideas with artistic freedom and inventiveness. Thus, even though *A Doll's House* clearly breaks with a Hegelian understanding of marriage, it can still be a work that resonates with Hegelian insights.

In the spirit of the previous chapters' discussion of selfhood, historicity, and existential meaning, my interpretation of *A Doll's House* seeks to show how Nora's worldview is shaped in interaction with a traditional under-standing of marriage and the good life.[12] As I see it, the increasingly claus-trophobic interaction between Nora and Torvald—but also Nora's reflections on her life and marriage—explores, in drama form, the pressures of modern life that Hegel so aptly analyzes. Nora's revolt is not only opposing the confines of the bourgeois marriage, but is also a heroic attempt to shatter a confining, ahistorical image of the beautiful life. In this way, Nora discloses a path to self-discovery and edification, enabling an authentic appropria-tion of the past and thereby also a genuinely future-oriented existence. The play's questioning of the idea of a petrified, ahistorical existence—its fol-lowing, at this point, in the footsteps of Hegel—significantly contributes to the dramatic novelty and the philosophical valor of Ibsen's mature work. Yet it clearly points beyond Hegel's understanding of the end of art in reflective romantic art and poetry and performs a realist turn that Hegel would not have been able to envision.

[11] See Nancy Bauer, *Simone de Beauvoir, Philosophy, and Feminism* (New York: Columbia University Press, 2001).

[12] This, though, is not to undermine the political power of Ibsen's play. Hence, I do not agree with Meyer, who simply refuses to see the play as being about women's rights. Seeking to defend the play against Shawn's objections in *Quintessence of Ibsenism*, Meyer suggests that "*A Doll's House* is no more about women's rights than Shakespeare's *Richard II* is about the divine right of kings, or *Ghosts* about syphilis, or *An Enemy of the People* about public hygiene." Meyer, *Ibsen*, 478. In my view, *A Doll's House* integrates, in its very core, the question of women's right to lead fully human lives. For a powerful criticism of Meyer's reading (and other, similar readings), see Joan Templeton, "The Doll House Backlash: Criticism, Feminism, and Ibsen," *PMLA*, vol. 104, no. 1 (1989): 28–40.

The Dissatisfactions of Modern Life

Ibsen started working on *A Doll's House* in Rome and finished the play about half a year later in Amalfi (HIS VII/B 219). In his notes, he describes the new work as a "contemporary tragedy" or a "tragedy about our time" (*nutidstragedie*, HIS VII/B 210). No other drama, he writes, has given him more satisfaction in working through the details.[13] From its premiere in Copenhagen in December 1879, the play was widely discussed—and widely successful. In fact, the original production was part of the repertory in Copenhagen for no less than twenty-eight years.[14]

Maintaining the unity of place and time—though allowing for the characteristically Ibsenesque technique of retrospective self-discovery—*A Doll's House* presents us with a tightly-knit group of characters. Ibsen's previous play, *Pillars of Society*, features nineteen named characters. In *A Doll's House*, the action concentrates around five. In addition to Nora and Torvald Helmer, there is Nora's childhood friend Kristine Linde, the house-friend Doctor Rank, and Krogstad, a fallen money lender and former acquaintance of Torvald.

Even though *A Doll's House* is well-known, a quick plot summary is in place. As the play begins, it is Christmas in the house of the Helmers. Nora, Torvald, and their children are getting ready for the holidays. There is a lot to celebrate, including Torvalds promotion in the *Aktiebank*. One after the other and in each case quite unexpectedly, two guests from the past arrive: Kristine Linde and Krogstad. Kristine Linde has lost her husband and has come to look for work. Krogstad's business is less honorable. Long ago, he had lent Nora money behind her husband's back. Her father was dying, her husband was sick, and, following the doctor's advice that Torvald should convalesce in Italy, Nora had forged her father's signature on the IOU and received the money needed for the trip abroad. Fatally, though, she signed the paperwork a day after her father died. Krogstad had himself been accused of fraud. Now he wants his name rehabilitated—even if this involves blackmailing Nora Helmer. If Nora does not help him get a position in the bank, Krogstad will tell Torvald about the forged signature. And, if that is not enough, he will let the entire world know. Nora, however, does not budge. She imagines that Torvald will stand up to Krogstad's accusations and even take the blame in order to rescue her. In a potlatch of love, she then plans to

---

[13] Letter to Hegel, September 15, 1879 (HIS XIII 505).

[14] Marker and Marker, *Ibsen's Lively Art*, 54. For the reception of *A Doll's House*, see also Fulsås and Rem, *Ibsen, Scandinavia and the Making of a World Drama*, esp. 93–95.

take her life in order to save her husband from scandal and demotion. As she later renders her plans to Torvald:

> All the time Krogstad's letter lay there, it never so much as crossed my mind that you would ever submit to that man's condition. I was absolutely convinced that you would say to him: Tell the whole wide world if you like. And when that was done ... [...] When that was done, I was absolutely convinced you would come forward and take everything on yourself and say: I am the guilty one. (OI V 284; HIS VII 374)

What happens, we know, is very different from what Nora, in her romantic reveries, envisions. Torvald scolds her for having broken the law, blames everything on her father's lack of moral spine,[15] and demands that she stay away from the children while maintaining the façade of a well-functioning family. Nora, on her side, emphasizes the spirit in which she had signed the paperwork. Her forgery was motivated by love for her husband and concern for her dying father's peace of mind. If it was illegal, it was still conducted with a pure heart. As she asks:

> Isn't a daughter entitled to try and save her father from worry and anxiety on his deathbed? Isn't a wife entitled to save her husband's life? I might not know very much about the law, but I feel sure of one thing: it must say somewhere that things like this are allowed. (OI V 229; HIS VII 267).[16]

Nora, in other words, is hoping for sympathy. When Torvald responds to the forgery with vanity and concern for his reputation, Nora realizes that she has spent years with a man she does not know. Following this revelation, Nora sets off on a path of self-discovery. She realizes that, in transitioning from the role of her father's daughter to that of her husband's wife, she has lived in the image of others. It is with this realization, tragic but also empowering, that Nora decides to leave her husband and her children.

---

[15] As in many of Ibsen's plays (including *Ghosts* and *Hedda Gabler*), the topic of the dead father looms large. Torvald blames Nora's forgery on her dead father (OI V 276; HIS VII 358–59). Dr. Rank, the house friend, suffers from a disease inflicted on him by his father's lavish meals (OI V 246; HIS VII 298, see also OIV 276; HIS VII 358–539).

[16] Yet Nora, too, has a cynical side. She confides in Kristine Linde that, regardless of Krogstad's appearance, she might tell Torvald what she did for him if she needs a card to play out (OI V 215; HIS VII 239).

Upon leaving, Nora defends her newly acquired insight by conveying that if anything were to bring her and Torvald back together, it would have to be a different kind of relationship and a different kind of selfhood:

HELMER. Can't I help you if ever you need it?
NORA. I said "no." I don't accept things from strangers.
HELMER. Nora, can I never be anything more to you than a stranger?
NORA [takes her bag]. Ah, Torvald, only by a miracle of miracles. . . .
HELMER. Name it, this miracle of miracles!
NORA. Both you and I would have to change to the point where. . . . Oh, Torvald, I don't believe in miracles any more.
HELMER. But I will believe. Name it! Change to the point where . . . ?
NORA. Where we could make a real marriage of our lives together. Goodbye!
     [She goes out through the hall door] (OI V 286; HIS VII 378–379)

Upon Nora's departure, Torvald sinks down on his chair, covers his face in his hands, and then, calling her name to no avail, exclaims with a sudden hope: "The miracle of miracles . . . ?" (OI V 286; HIS VII 378–379).[17] Thus the play ends, following the ellipsis, with a silence that is only broken by the loud sound of the gate being slammed ([in Norwegian: a drønn] OI V 286; HIS VII 379).[18]

Love versus law—this opposition, known from classical tragedy, still has reality for Nora, but not for Krogstad and Torvald.[19] The play, further, has a structural transparency evoking classical forms. Contemporary audiences thus discussed whether or not a Norwegian housewife, abandoning her family with the slam of a door, could be a tragic hero.[20] Did Ibsen, when he left his initial idea of a "Contemporary Tragedy" for the neutral "A Play in Three Acts" (and then published Ghosts: A Domestic Drama in Three Acts two

---

[17] Ibsen uses the term "det vidunderlige" also in Emperor and Galilean (HIS VI 364).
[18] In the version Ibsen added for the German audiences, which he later characterizes as barbaric, he ends the play by having Nora return and Torvald joyfully and softly (Ibsen's instructions) mumbling his wife's name: Nora! (OI V 288).
[19] Or, in Torvald's rendering, what Nora lacks is not only (as Krogstad already has pointed out to her) an understanding of the law, but also of the society (samfund) she lives in—a dimension of modern life that, in all its lack of morality, has already been exposed in Pillars of the Society. The reference is to OI V 238; HIS VII 372.
[20] Needless to say, this does not mean that the play should be read as a tragedy only. The subplot of the reunion of Mrs. Linde and Krogstad, and Krogstad's swift transformation from cynical money-lender to tender lover, gives the play a lighter undertone. Further, the suspense related to Krogstad's comings and goings—Will Torvald learn about Nora's forgery? When will he know?—situates the play with the popular drama of intrigue.

years later), also leave behind his commitment to tragedy? Or did he, rather, shape the genre so as to adapt it to his own time period?

Ibsen's work, we have seen, is preceded by a century of philosophy of drama that revolved around such issues as history, historicity, and the contemporary relevance of traditional forms, tragedy included. Hegel, on his part, had paid ample attention to tragedy and described *Antigone* as the most perfect work of art ever made. Albeit less committed to classical ideals, there were also the works of Friedrich Theodor Vischer and Georg Gottfried Gervinus. Closer to home, there were Heiberg's writings on drama and Brandes's discussion of tragedy in *Aesthetic Studies*.

In the context of *A Doll's House*, Brandes's approach is particularly relevant. While Ibsen and Brandes, toward the end of the 1870s, appear to have temporarily drifted apart (there are no preserved letters between the two in the years between 1877 and 1881), Ibsen had been reading and communicating with Brandes in the earlier period.[21] Brandes, at the time, wrestled with his Hegelian commitments. In an effort to move with, but also get beyond Hegel, he sees tragedy as synthesizing (or, in Hegel's lingo: sublating) the metaphysical and the ethical. Brandes discusses the problem of modern love in particular. He points out that Hegel dismisses modern (individual) love as a topic for genuine tragedy.[22] For Hegel, modern love is not about family ties, but subjective feelings. As such, it risks being contingent. Art, by contrast, addresses the essential.[23] Against this view, Brandes objects that even though modern love may be contingent on feeling, and thus not meet the call for objective necessity, tragedies of love allow the modern audiences to identify with the characters. Thus, he notes, tragedies of love can initiate a response as broad and universal as the judgment on pure beauty within the Kantian system.[24] Love, in other words, can serve as an artistic placeholder for the subjective-universal: it unites an (ideal) community of audiences and

[21] The letters of 1872 are of particular interest. See for example letter of April 4, 1872 (HIS XIII 57–60), April 30, 1873 (Ibsen anticipates Brandes's new work on the romantic school), and October 16, 1873 (Ibsen makes it clear that he has read the book, HIS XIII 153–154). There is no sign of animosity when Ibsen, in 1882, writes Brandes to thank him for his review of *Ghosts*. On the contrary, he writes that he "unconditionally" trusts him (with respect to his new lecture and essay) "in this as in everything else" (January 3, 1882; HIS XIV 109).

[22] Hegel, however, is positive to Shakespeare's *Romeo and Juliet*. But in this case, the crux of the tragedy is the long-standing feud between the Capulets and the Montagues. I thank Lydia Moland for this point. See also her discussion of Hegel's view of tragedy in *Hegel's Aesthetics*.

[23] As Brandes quotes Hegel, there is nothing substantial in the fact that a hero simply fell for a particular young lady. Brandes, *Æstetiske Studier*, 69.

[24] Brandes, "Begrebet: den tragiske Skæbne (1863)," *Æstetiske Studier*, 69.

judges of taste.[25] In Brandes's reading, love invites the same kind of broadened mindset that we, in Kant's *Critique*, may·reach through disinterested (that is, pure) aesthetic judgment. Provocative as it is, this philosophical move tells us a great deal about the intellectual landscape in which Ibsen situates himself in the period leading up to the publication of *A Doll's House*.

Brandes would later review *A Doll's House*. By and large, his review is positive. Recognizing the influence of Bjørnson and Camilla Collett, he notes that although Ibsen was not originally a feminist, the drama has feminist implications.[26] Further, he notes how Ibsen, in his exploration of modern art and life, turns precisely to the topic of love and marriage.

The Helmers are of course not high-born, tragic heroes in the classical sense. Nor are they clearly chiseled characters, each of whom embodies a set of values (which Hegel takes to be a key element of ancient tragedy). Rather, we face two individuals who struggle to know who they are and how best to live—individually and together. When the curtains part, we encounter a happy, youthful family; when they fall, the home has the feel of an involuntary confinement. And yet we must imagine that this disintegrating home—Ibsen offers detailed accounts of furniture, doors, and back rooms; he clearly wants a particular kind of atmosphere—is disturbingly similar to the domestic quarters to which his audiences will return after a night in the theater.[27] From this point of view, it makes sense for Ibsen to avoid narrow genre specifications and, in spite of the parallels between Greek tragedy and *A Doll's House*, make the shift from "A Contemporary Tragedy" to simply "Drama in Three Acts." This shift confirms the move, initially made by Herder and A. W. Schlegel (and later taken up by Hegel), to see modern drama as a synthetic form.[28]

With this genre specification, Ibsen corroborates his will to take part in a new, dramatic era. What is new is not simply that Ibsen spells out the problems of modern marriage and the role of the modern woman, whose paradoxical condition is that she is brought up to freedom and yet it is denied

[25] Prior to Hegel's aesthetics lectures, A. W. Schlegel, in his lectures on dramatic art, connects the disinterested (subjective universality) to the work of art, more precisely to tragedy and the chorus. Brandes routinely refers to Schlegel's work.

[26] Brandes, who had translated Mill's *The Subjection of Women* into Danish, recalls how Ibsen would ridicule the co-authorship of John Stuart Mill and Harriet Taylor Mill's feminist treatise *The Subjection of Women*. Brandes, *Henrik Ibsen* ("Andet Indtryk," 1882), 90–91.

[27] For instance, the Helmers' living room is described as "tastefully but not expensively furnished" (OI V 201; HIS VII 213).

[28] For a discussion of this point, see my "The Theatre of Thought: A.W. Schlegel on Shakespeare, Modern Drama, and Romantic Criticism."

to her, but also that the drama is in direct continuation with the lives of his modern audiences. (The dramatic potential of this continuity is even more effectively utilized in *Ghosts*, which will be discussed in Chapter 5). Thus, *A Doll's House* sets into play a sense of identification (the stage is no longer limited to the theater but extends into the very heart of the domestic sphere) and a process of reflection (it promotes scrutiny of one's own choices or lack of such).[29] This dimension of the work is reflected in character development, dialogue, stage description, *and* Ibsen's willingness to put the modern family on the stage for display and dissection.[30] *A Doll's House* (or, rather, a Doll's *Home*, as the literal translation would be[31]) is well-named: Within the relatively safe framework of theater and dramatic literature, the middle class is invited to observe their historical situation and the lives they are living.

This, surely, is a kind of drama that, on the face of it, has left behind the framework of Hegel's philosophy of tragedy and questioned the notion that art, after the reflective turn of romanticism, cannot make historical progress. Yet it is not, for that reason, a drama that has cut all ties to Hegelian thought. To get a better sense of the Hegelian resonances in the play, we need to ask what kind of life the Helmers lead—and what kind of lives, further, they share with their audiences. How, in short, does Ibsen present the conditions of modern life? And how, further, would these conditions be viewed in and around Ibsen's quarters? Few philosophers have explored the gains and costs of modern life with more consistency than Hegel.

---

[29] In this sense, Ibsen's drama mirrors the return, in the work of Kierkegaard and the existentialist philosophers, to an ideal of a philosophy that addresses an individual reader as a first-person singular (rather than as somebody who is committed, in a disinterested way, to a universal truth). This form is explored in Jean-Paul Sartre's and Simone de Beauvoir's philosophical, literary, and autobiographical works and can shed light on the connection between philosophy and drama in twentieth-century existentialism.

[30] Hence, it is no coincidence that when Ibsen turns to modern marriage, his play also features a limited group of characters *and* a stage that, basically, is the interior of a living room. For an analysis of this aspect of the play, see Greene, *Home on the Stage*, 16–20. Marker and Marker include some helpful drawings from the 1879 production in Copenhagen and the Norwegian premiere the following year. In both cases, the stage presents a lavishly decorated urban apartment, emphasizing the impression of this being the home of a solid middle-class family. See Marker and Marker, *Ibsen's Lively Art*, 54–55.

[31] For a discussion of this point, see Sandberg, *Ibsen's Houses*, 68–85.

Hegelian Interlude

In the previous chapter, we saw how Hegel—and, in dramatic form, Ibsen—interprets the transition from ancient Rome to Christianity as a move toward subjectivity and inwardness. The purity of the soul is achieved by abandoning that which is external, turning from outer symbols and practices (e.g., buildings, sculptures, parades) to the individual self as a nucleus of faith. According to Hegel, the transition to this new worldview is one in which, as he puts it, "[t]he simple solid totality of the Ideal is dissolved and it falls apart into the double totality of a subjective being in itself and the external appearance" (LFA 518; HW XIV 128, trans. modified). To the extent that modern life grows out of and is historically conditioned by such experiences, it is marked by alienation.[32]

As a philosopher of modernity, Hegel's position is designed to overcome this predicament.[33] If the overcoming of past ideals is not without a sense of loss and tragedy (PS 49; HW III 72), spirit still feeds off historical development and is educated in and through historical change (PS 50-51; HW III 72–74). This is also true of the transition to modernity. In responding to modern alienation, subjectivity turns toward itself. Here it discovers a dimension of freedom in "its own native spiritual world of feeling, the heart, and inner life in general" (LFA 518; HW XIV 128). At stake is an elevation of spirit to itself; spirit wins, as Hegel puts it, "its objectivity, which hitherto it had to seek in the external and sensuous character of existence" (LFA 518; HW XIV 128). With this reflective turn, however, art can no longer hold the position it once had. The highest spiritual content is too abstract; it is no longer in need of sensuous expression. Art is no longer the medium through which spirit makes progress in history.

When addressing modernity, Hegel speaks of "a new epoch" (LHP III 551; HW XX 460) characterized by individuals that seek to gain an adequate conception of the world and its structure, which now emerges as dependent of the subject. Thus conceived, modernity is the era of self-reflection. In Hegel's

---

[32] In Ibsen's early character gallery, no one suffers from a more severe case of alienation than Julian. Born into an old, holistic worldview, Julian cannot find peace in the schism that, with Christianity, has opened up between inner and outer, faith and life, truth and beauty. Yet, a return to the old values does not work. This, precisely, is his tragedy—and, we could add, the tragedy of Furia (of *Catiline*) and Hjørdis (of *The Vikings at Helgeland*). In this way, Ibsen's early characters strike us as peculiarly modern.

[33] Robert Pippin lays out his reading of Hegel as a late modern philosopher in *Idealism as Modernism: Hegelian Variations* (Cambridge: Cambridge University Press, 1997), esp. the introduction and Chapters 4, 5, and 6.

narrative, such self-reflection begins with the Cartesian *ego cogito* and later leads to the subjective idealisms of Kant and Fichte. In their programs, reason not only claims to know the world, but also aspires to knowledge of the very nature of knowledge itself (PS 17; HW III 33). Self-reflection intrinsically relates to self-determination and freedom. As such, Hegel celebrates modernity.[34]

Yet, in Hegel's dialectical scheme, every step forward indicates that something is left behind. Philosophical modernity is no exception. With Descartes, philosophy tears itself loose from the unexamined authority of the tradition (LHP III 224; HW XX 126–127). Reason emerges as self-grounding. It tries to free itself of its history and does not accept anything as authoritative without having established it as true or valid. Subjectivity strives single-handedly to lay the grounds for its goals, pursuits, and epistemic, ethical, and aesthetic standpoints. In short, it celebrates itself as the genius of its existence, as an artist whose life is his or her ultimate work of art.

This is the birth not only of modern autonomy, which forms the basis of rational behavior in science and morality, but also of an aesthetic consciousness that emerges as its pathological flipside. At stake is a mentality or attitude in which the single individual understands its relation to its surroundings in terms of a thoroughly aesthetic, or even aestheticizing, model. Self-expression and aesthetic experience are cultivated in excess. Ultimately, the entire world emerges as a reservoir for the subject's projections. For the aesthetic consciousness, subjective pleasure is the prime motivating factor.[35] And because the individual I is taken to be responsible for its existence, the I's satisfaction with the world is at the same time reflective of the I's satisfaction with itself. If the ego is threatened, aesthetic consciousness immediately drums up an illusion that makes it possible to retain the image of its sovereignty.

As we saw in Chapter 2, Hegel associates this kind of aestheticism with the philosophy of the Jena romantics. In his history of philosophy, Hegel claims that in romantic philosophy, subjectivity, in turning to itself, eventually also "dies away within itself" (LHP III 510; HW XX 418). Hegel's critique

---

[34] Hegel claims that in the modern philosophical period, our testing of knowledge is "not only a testing of what we know, but also a testing of the criterion of what knowing is" (PS 55; HW III 78). See also Pinkard, *Hegel's Phenomenology*, 191–193.

[35] Hegel's analysis at this point makes it clear how Kierkegaard, even with his anti-Hegelian sentiments, could also borrow from Hegel. For a discussion that pays attention to the complex bonds between Kierkegaard and Hegel(ianism), see Jon Stewart, *Kierkegaard's Relations to Hegel Reconsidered* (Cambridge: Cambridge University Press, 2003), 132–182.

of the Jena romantics is exaggerated and polemical.[36] He does not take into account how, for example, Novalis's philosophy of history and education anticipate his (Hegel's) own position in *The Phenomenology of Spirit* or how Schlegel's appeal to irony lays out a structure of thought that anticipates his own dialectics.[37]

Brandes offers a more nuanced account of romanticism than Hegel does. Among the romantic voices in nineteenth-century Europe, Brandes is particularly fascinated by Germaine de Staël and what he calls her "literature of displacement." Indeed, the bulk of his *Emigrant Literature*, the first volume of *Main Currents*, is dedicated to her "noble and significant writing." However, though Brandes is influenced by the romantic movement, he follows Hegel's criticism in the end. Romanticism, he claims, is dreamy. If classicism had sought to reawaken the ideals of ancient Greek culture, romanticism pursues another kind of a historical and aestheticized life—what Brandes characterizes, in a gesture of flagrant Orientalism, as "a modern India."[38]

The criticism we find in Hegel and Brandes has come to shape our approach to romanticism—*and* the way it was viewed in Ibsen's time.[39] In this context, three aspects of the Hegel-Brandes approach are especially noteworthy. First, aesthetic consciousness is mainly perceived as a modern phenomenon and, as such, is related to the search, on behalf of the individual subject, for complete self-determination and independence. Second, aesthetic consciousness represents a variety of philosophical solipsism; it sees intersubjectivity as derived.[40] Third, aesthetic consciousness is totalizing and cannot be changed or revised in light of external criticism or objections, but

---

[36] For an outline of Hegel's critique of philosophical romanticism, see Otto Pöggeler, *Hegels Kritik der Romantik* (Bonn: Friedrich Wilhelms Universität, 1956 [Dissertation]).

[37] For a discussion of this point, see Fred Rush, *Irony and Idealism: Rereading Schlegel, Hegel, and Kierkegaard* (Oxford: Oxford University Press, 2016), 101–198.

[38] Brandes, *Emigrantlitteraturen*, 253–255.

[39] Neither Hegel, nor Brandes realizes how romanticism was closely affiliated with, and to some extent grew out of, a historical turn in German philosophy (through Herder and others). The work of the Humboldts and the Schlegel brothers did indeed engage in a genuine, intercultural hermeneutics and the India at stake in their work is far from "dreamy." Finally, Brandes's much-admired Staël was herself a romantic philosopher of great merit not only due to her discussions of philosophers such as Rousseau, Kant, and Schelling, and the years she spent in the company of A.W. Schlegel, but also in light of her own analyses of the imagination, literature, freedom, gender, and a wide range of other topics. The point is not that Hegel and Brandes are wrong in criticizing naïvely aestheticizing attitudes—these are indeed problematic strategies for coping with the challenges of modern life!—but that these are not commitments of central importance to romanticism.

[40] In Hegel's view, this is why romanticism needs to be overcome by a philosophical model that, although committed to the notion of self-determining subjectivity, takes into account the sociality of reason and sees subjectivity as constituted through its intersubjective bonds and relations. This aspect of Hegel's philosophy was discussed, with reference to *Peer Gynt*, in Chapter 3.

only by way of an inner crisis.[41] With this framework in mind, we can now return to *A Doll's House* and seek to identify the kind of aesthetic attitudes that saturates the Helmer marriage.

In his analysis of the play, Brandes pays particular attention to Torvald. Specifically, he notes the generosity with which Ibsen treats this character: Torvald is honest, educated, and kind.[42] It is this generosity, Brandes argues, that makes *A Doll's House* a success.[43] While furnishing Nora with a husband who is in no way monstrous or unfaithful (like the deceased Mr. Alving in *Ghosts*, for example), Ibsen nevertheless finds the conditions of love and happiness to be non-existent. Hence, what Brandes had earlier pitched as a positive feature of modern tragedy, namely love and the possibility of reconciliation, he now finds Ibsen dissecting and analyzing down to its most brutal core.

Brandes's reading is dramatically and philosophically perceptive. Only to the extent that Torvald is a reasonably good husband and Torvald and Nora's marriage is, by the look of it, a fairly healthy and happy one, can Nora's plight stand forth as the plight of the modern woman and perhaps even the modern individual: the plight of realizing, in the midst of the familiar, that one has to stand up for one's worldview and that values and existential identity are not given but have to come from within. Further, only to the extent that, at some level or other, the Helmer marriage appears to be in order, only to the extent that it appears to be a marriage of a familiar kind, can *A Doll's House* succeed as a drama of a new bourgeois era.

It could be argued that Brandes overstates Torvald's positive character traits.[44] Yet, he is right in seeing the Torvald character as key to the dramatic development of the play. It is against Torvald's static understanding of their marriage that Nora seeks to position herself. Further, what makes Torvald

---

[41] These aspects of Hegel's critique of aesthetic consciousness will prove to be of crucial importance not only for Brandes, but also for twentieth-century philosophers and their attempts to get beyond romanticism of all forms (we find this in philosophers from Lukács and Adorno to Heidegger and Gadamer).

[42] Brandes, *Henrik Ibsen* ("Andet Indtryk," 1882), 92. Interestingly, Brandes's brother Edvard holds a less favorable view of Torvald as arrogant and indifferent but still maintaining an impeccable façade. As he puts it, "His [Torvald's] brain is stuffed with conventional fragments of thoughts, hers is empty." Edvard Brandes, review of Ibsen's *A Doll's House* in *Ude og Hjemme*, København January 4, 1880 (no. 118, Tredie Aargang, 148–153). http://ibsen.nb.no/id/11193496.0 (Accessed June 1, 2019), my trans.

[43] Ibsen had initially sketched Torvald as somewhat good but later gave him more negative character traits. See Koht, *Ibsen*, vol. II, 105.

[44] As it is, this would be in line with Brandes's Hegelian orientation in this period. For Hegel, tragedies work best when we do not face a scenario of good versus bad, but of good characters being pitched against each other (since their values are incompatible). I thank Lydia Moland for this point.

such a key character is precisely the way in which he, unlike Nora, fails to question the aestheticizing attitudes that initially permeate their marriage. He is not willing to relinquish his desire to create a domestic space of beauty protected from the actual world. It is this aesthetic consciousness—and the ahistorical existence it embodies—that Nora needs to break with in order to find her true self.[45] In dramatically analyzing the temptations and perils of an aesthetic existence, Ibsen links his exploration of selfhood and recognition (as we find it in *Peer Gynt*) with his exploration of the desire for beauty (as we find it in *Emperor and Galilean*).[46]

Petrified Aestheticism

From the first stage directions onward, Ibsen brings to attention the economic backbone of the Helmer household.[47] We are introduced to "*A pleasant room, tastefully but not expensively furnished*" (OI V 201; HIS VII 213).[48] As it gives rise to the couple's first exchange on the stage, Nora's weakness for macaroons is subject to discussion not only because Torvald cares about his wife's appearance, but also because she "has been out squandering money again" (OI V 202; HIS VII 214). The subsequent exchange between Nora and Torvald circles around the financial arrangements for the upcoming holidays, all the while with the insinuation that Nora is incapable of

---

[45] Torvald's dream of an existence beyond (human) history and historicity is also reflected in his addressing Nora as a squirrel, a dove, a bird, etc.

[46] Needless to say, to point out the fact that Ibsen over time pursues a constellation of topics or issues is not the same as to write his work into a teleological model of development.

[47] The topic of dirty, monetary transactions was present in *Pillars of Society* and reemerges in *The Wild Duck*, *John Gabriel Borkman*, and other plays. It is important to keep in mind that money figured prominently in Eugène Scribe's stage plays and, in turn, in Heiberg's. For a discussion of this dimension of Scribe's work, as it is seen to have contributed to his reinvention of the vaudeville genre, see Neil Cole Arvin, *Eugène Scribe and the French Theater, 1815–1860* (Boston: Harvard University Press, 1924), 225. For Heiberg, though, the vaudeville was explicitly connected to his Hegelianism and the Hegelian view that comedy is the most advanced of all the arts (and the point at which great art reaches its end). As he puts it, "I would never have come to write my vaudevilles and in general would never have become a poet for the theater if I had not learned, by means of the Hegelian philosophy, to see the relation of the finite to the infinite and had won thereby a respect for finite things which I previously did not have, but which it is impossible for the dramatic poet to do without." Heiberg's *On the Significance of Philosophy for the Present Age and Other Texts*, ed. and trans. Jon Stewart (Copenhagen: C. A. Reitzel, 2006), 66.

[48] This differs significantly from the opening scene in *The Wild Duck*, where we are presented with Haakon Werle's house: "*The study, expensively and comfortably appointed, with bookcases and upholstered furniture; in the middle of the room a desk with papers and documents; the room is softly lit by green-shaded lamps. Folding doors at the back of the room are standing open, and the curtains are drawn back. The sitting-room, spacious and elegant, can be seen within, brilliantly lit by lamps and candelabra*" (OI VI 131; HIS VIII 11).

handling money, and thus does not understand the material scaffolding of upper-middle-class existence.[49]

Nora, however, understands a thing or two about financial planning. After she took up the loan with Krogstad, she paid down her debt by working behind her husband's back. Her opening exchanges with Torvald and Kristine Linde initially seem to portray a woman who is unaware of, and even insensitive to, other people's financial responsibilities and hardships. However, at least as far as financial responsibilities go, readers and theater audiences will look back at Nora's lines and realize that she cleverly communicates on multiple levels. We find an example of this in her conversation with Torvald about the expenses of housekeeping:

HELMER. You can't deny it, Nora dear. [*Puts his arm around her waist.*] My pretty little pet is very sweet, but it runs away with an awful lot of money. It's incredible how expensive it is for a man to keep such a pet [spillefugl].

NORA. For shame! How can you say such a thing? As a matter of fact I save everything I can.

HELMER [*laughs*]. You are right there. Everything you *can*. But you simply can't.

NORA [*hums and smiles quietly and happily*]. Ah, if you only knew how many expenses the likes of us sky-larks and squirrels have, Torvald! (OI V 204; HIS VII 219).

Nora's body language—her humming and smiling—offers a key to this passage.[50] Her secret work and her show of financial responsibility have opened the door to a real freedom rather than the vacuous freedom that came from her acting the role of the young and charming wife. Hence, it is no wonder that Nora takes pleasure in her work. As she explains to Kristine:

Last winter I was lucky enough to get quite a bit of copying to do. So I shut myself up every night and sat and wrote through to the small hours of the

---

[49] For a study of the problem of money in Ibsen's drama, see Bernard F. Dukore, *Money and Politics in Ibsen, Shaw, and Brecht* (Columbia: University of Missouri Press, 1980). See also Frode Helland, "Henrik Ibsen og det politiske: *Et dukkehjem*," in *Lesing og eksistens. Festskrift til Otto Hageberg på 70-årsdagen*, ed. Per Thomas Andersen (Oslo: Gyldendal 2006), 134–150.

[50] Another key item, as I see it, is the follow-up passage, where Torvald blames Nora's spending on her father, i.e., ascribes it to her genetic disposition. Once the plot of the play is known, however, this exchange could, if anything, be taken to prove that Nora's disposition was precisely not of the kind that Torvald ascribes to her father.

morning. Oh, sometimes I was so tired, so tired. But it was tremendous fun all the same, sitting there working and earning money like that. It was almost like being a man. (OI V 216; HIS VII 240)

If Torvald had known that his recovery was rooted in debt and, equally problematic, that Nora contributes to the financial well-being of the family ("almost like a man," as she puts it), this would have been unwelcome news. It would have, in his eyes, implied that his life was no longer beautiful. In Nora's words:

> But the whole point was that he [Torvald] mustn't know anything. Good heavens, can't you see! He wasn't even supposed to know how desperately ill he was. It was me the doctors came and told his life was in danger, that the only way to save him was to go South for a while. Do you think I didn't try talking him into it first? I began dropping hints about how nice it would be if I could be taken on a little trip abroad, like other young wives. I wept, I pleaded. I told him he ought to show some consideration for my condition, and let me have a bit of my own way. And then I suggested he might take out a loan. But at that he nearly lost his temper, Kristine. He said I was being frivolous, that it was his duty as a husband not to give in to all these whims and fancies of mine—as I do believe he called them. (OI V 214; VII 237–238)

In the house of the Helmers, the financial balance—*and* the distribution of freedom and beauty—is, in other words, more complex than Torvald thinks. While Torvald believes that he is the sole breadwinner and head of the family, the bonds of dependency also run the other way. Nora's alleged "squandering" is in reality her show of financial maturity. Torvald budgets for expensive goods, Nora buys cheap; while Torvald thinks she is preoccupied with domestic beautification projects, she takes care of her secret work. Because Torvald is indebted to Nora and dependent on her (and not just she on him), Nora is, ironically, about to win her freedom—in spite of the fact that this implies that she lives, at least by Torvald's standard, less beautifully than she could expect as the wife of the soon-to-be director of the *Aktiebank*.

In Torvald's view, there is a relationship between financial freedom and a beautiful life. A beautiful life *is*, by definition, a life in financial freedom.

Plate 1 Erik Werenskiold. *Portrait of the Poet Henrik Ibsen*. 1895. Oil on canvas. 121.5 × 71.5 cm. The National Museum of Art, Architecture and Design (Inventory no.: NG.M.04206). Photographer: Børre Høstland. Copyright Nasjonalmuseet for kunst, arkitektur og design.

Plate 2 Edvard Munch. *The Sun*. 1911. Oil on canvas. 455 × 780 cm.
The University of Oslo. Photo © Munchmuseet.

Plate 3 Hans Gude and Adolph Tidemand. *Bridal Procession on the Hardanger Fjord.* 1848. Oil on canvas. 93.5 × 130.1 × 2.9 cm. The National Museum of Art, Architecture and Design (Inventory no: NG.M.00467). Photo: Børre Høstland. Copyright: Nasjonalmuseet for kunst, arkitektur og design.

Plate 4 Werner Rehm as Peer Gynt. From Peter Stein's production of *Peer Gynt* (1971). Schaubühne, Berlin. Photographer: Abisag Tüllmann. Copyright: Theatermuseum München.

Plate 5 Anne Tismer as Nora. From Thomas Ostermeier's production of *Nora* (2003). Photographer: Arno Declair. Copyright: Schaubühne, Berlin.

Plate 6 Edvard Munch. Set Design for Henrik Ibsen's *Ghosts*. 1906. Oil on cardboard. 47.5 × 68 cm. Munchmuseet Photo © Munchmuseet.

Plate 7 Tessman (Lars Eidinger) and Julle (Lore Stefanek). From Thomas Ostermeier's production of *Hedda Gabler* (2006). Photographer: Gianmarco Bresadola. Copyright: Schaubühne, Berlin.

Plate 8 Edvard Munch. *Hedda Gabler*. 1906–07. Watercolor and pencil. 660 × 487 mm Munchmuseet, Oslo Photo © Munchmuseet.

Debt, by contrast, betokens an unfree existence and is, as such, ugly.[51] Within the walls of his home, Torvald is offended by work that is undertaken in a spirit of utility. One example of this is Kristine Linde's knitting, which Torvald bluntly recommends that she leave aside in order to take up more aesthetically pleasing needlework such as embroidery.[52] Whereas knitting "just can't help being ugly," embroidery is "so much prettier" (OI V 268; HIS VII 344).[53] Behind Torvald's judgment is the notion that for a woman, work signals a lack of freedom and therefore also a lack of beauty.[54] In his view, the domestic sphere of the upper-middle-classes is free when women, like Nora, can wholly dedicate themselves to careless beauty.[55]

Nora, by contrast, has a more dialectical understanding of freedom and beauty. She desires a beauty that is obtained by dealing with the realm of necessity; only then can beauty be worth caring about. Unlike Torvald, Nora is thus not averse to treating beauty and necessity as interrelated. Nowhere is this clearer than in the final act's dramatic exposé of Torvald's relationship to Nora. When Nora's fraudulence is uncovered, Torvald demands that they, in order for him to save face, continue as if nothing had happened. At least on the face of it, the beautiful life must continue. Happiness, he emphasizes, is out of the question. "All we can do is save the bits and pieces from the wreck, preserve appearances" (OI V 276; HIS VII 360). Ibsen is here using the term *skinnet*, echoing Hegel's discussion of the aesthetic *Schein*.

[51] This also goes for the finitude of human life. As the couple is confronted with Dr. Rank's progressing illness, Dr. Rank confides in Nora: "There's something I want to ask you. Helmer is a sensitive soul; he loathes anything that's ugly. I don't want him visiting me" (OI V 245; HIS VII 297). And, indeed, a bit later, Torvald describes his friend's imminent death as "this ugly thing [uskønhed]" that has come between him and his wife and from which they need to free themselves (OI V 274; HIS VII 356). We see the same way of thinking in *Hedda Gabler*. Hedda does not want to visit Tesman's dying aunt: "I don't want to look at sickness and death. I must be free of everything that's ugly" (OI VII 239; HIS IX 143).

[52] Similarly, in *The Pillars of Society*, embroidery is used as a class-marker when we first see Adjunct Rørlund socialize with the women of the economic upper classes.

[53] Later, we find a related rejection in Hedda's disgust at her husband's embroidered slippers, again alluding to some level of affinity between these characters, though Hedda is given a capacity for metaphysical longing (and, relatedly, boredom) that Nora does not appear to know.

[54] To a philosophically sensitive reader, the emphasis on a beauty that is remote from all utility evokes the parameters of Kantian aesthetics.

[55] In Rainer Werner Fassbinder's 1974 *Nora Helmer*, this aspect of the play is highlighted as the unhappy Nora, dressed in the most impractical of silk garbs, sleepwalks through a house that itself has the feel of an overly ornamented wedding cake. Nora's life is turned into a stifling, semi-kitschy work of art. Further, the children are taken out and the ever-present maid and ubiquitous mirrors lend a sense of Nora being permanently watched and also, as the dialogues between wife and husband are caught through the filming of mirror reflections (they look at themselves rather than directly at the other), an eerie lack of direct, human interaction.

For a beautiful soul such as Torvald, any real existential challenge is evaded by keeping up one's façade. At this point, Torvald's vision of a beautiful life has surfaced in its true ugliness—as a beauty that is out of touch with the everyday. It is a vision of a petrified beauty, transcending the exigencies of historical existence—a life of mere *skinn*. His desire to be indebted to no one (in more than one sense of the term "indebted") has left him unable to relate to others. His existence is out of touch with the reality of which he is a part. Nora, by contrast, wants to take ownership of her own role—and thus transform necessity into beauty.

For Nora, the real disappointment is not that she is forced to admit her fraud. As she confesses to Kristine, she might have wanted at some point to disclose her secret to Torvald. The real crisis emerges when Torvald, in learning about her fraud, rejects her rationale for acting as she did and refuses to consider the possibility that she, too, acts on reasons (even if these reasons are different from his). In effect, he also rejects the possibility that a relationship can change, that is, that a relationship has its own history. On being asked if she understands what she has done, she responds—looking, according to Ibsen's stage directions, *"fixedly at him, her face hardening"*—that "yes, now I'm really beginning to understand" (OI V 275; HIS VII 358).

Unlike what Kristine Linde had been hoping, this is not a moment that puts an end to deceit and play-acting between husband and wife. Instead of initiating a genuine dialogue, Torvald wants more hypocrisy, more aestheticizing, even if this is going to result in an even more petrified existence.

While insisting that Nora continues to play theater (and appearances are kept up), Torvald accuses her of play-acting when she tells him that he should not sacrifice his life for her:

Stop play-acting! [*Locks the front door.*] You are staying here to give an account of yourself. Do you understand what you have done? Answer me! Do you understand? (OI V 275; HIS VII 358)

His repetitious "Do you understand?", granting her no chance to respond, only strengthens the sense in which his demands gradually suck the air out of the room, thereby revealing the ugly side of his image of the home as a sphere of careless beauty.

Upon learning about Nora's fraud, Torvald leaves her with all the blame—yet fails to acknowledge her as somebody who has a capacity for being responsible. From his point of view, her love for him is irrelevant, and likewise her reasons. To Torvald, what matters is only how her fraud may stain his reputation.[56] This is what he desperately wishes to prevent by demanding a marriage in *Schein*.

Torvald's aesthetic consciousness represents a totalizing, static world-view. No arguments or emotional reactions Nora could muster can make him change his mind. Rather than listening, he pushes her away, accusing *her* of being disillusioned: "You are ill, Nora. You are delirious" (OI V 283; VII 372). Not even the fact that Nora is leaving him—which will, no doubt, represent a significant blow to his reputation—can make him question his understanding of their marriage. While he eventually admits to seeing her point of view, apparently accepting that their lives must indeed change, he still thinks that he is the one who will oversee the changes by re-educating his wife so that they can have a genuine life together (I return to this point later).

When she decides to leave, Nora is alone because the person she needs the most does not acknowledge her. She no longer desires the financial independence nor the naïve romantic unity of which she had been dreaming. Instead, she wants the freedom and love that grow out of the exchange between mutually recognizing subjects. Torvald is, if possible, even more isolated than before. He does not even realize that he needs others, least of all his wife. Nor does he understand that the passing of time brings changes, including changes to Nora's self-understanding and, as a consequence, to their relationship. When Krogstad returns the contract with Nora's forged signature, Torvald is massively relieved. Nora, on her side, takes no share in Torvald's joy. At this point, the Krogstad business is but a side-plot in her drama of selfhood. For her, the real problem is no longer the forgery but the fact that her marriage was never based on true recognition. By failing to recognize that she, like him, needs a companionship that goes beyond the framework of his aesthetic consciousness, Torvald has made himself irrelevant.

---

[56] Torvald depends on the recognition of others, but the other from who he craves recognition is not his wife, Nora, but an abstract, anonymous "they." If Nora is a puppet under the mastery of, first, her father and then her husband (OI V 280; HIS VII 366), then Torvald is a puppet whose movements are directed by a nameless small-town mentality. However, an anonymous, non-personalized other can offer no firm basis of recognition and hence no point of transition from the idea of freedom as self-sufficiency to the idea of freedom as realized in and through genuine human companionship. In this sense, Nora is right in her claim that he did not actually love her but merely loved the idea of being in love with her (OI V 280; HIS VII 366). It is worth noting that Nora here uses the plural you [*I*, in Ibsen's original], indicating that this not only applies to Torvald but also to her father. This is what has become increasingly clear to her throughout their conversation in the final act—if the term "conversation" can at all cover an exchange in which the parties systematically misunderstand each other.

When Nora walks out, she is thus not only leaving a husband and her children, but also a certain image of what it is to be human. She contributes to shaping the future, he remains stuck in the past. In this sense, Brandes is perhaps right in pointing out that Torvald is not mean. Caught in an aestheticizing picture whose frailty he fails to recognize, he is the sad inhabitant of a static home of dolls.[57]

Art and Education

While Torvald takes on the role of a self-admitted (domestic) aesthete, Nora herself is not a stranger to the aesthetic orientation. She willingly acts the larch bird, the squirrel, flirtatiously reveals the details of her costume for the masquerade ball, laughing, clapping her hands, and addresses the brutal financial reality that Torvald introduces—if they were to take up a loan and he suddenly dies, she will be unable to pay down the mortgage—as "ugly [stygt]" (OI V 202; HIS VII 215; trans. modified).[58] Her children are repeatedly described as delightful (dejlige). The same term is used to depict a life without financial worries (OI V 209; HIS VII 227) and the holiday decorations with which she occupies herself in order to forget about Krogstad's threats (OI V 230; HIS VII 269). Nora is determined to maintain her life as free of worries (sorgløst) and to retain the domestic cocoon that she has spun around herself.[59] Her aestheticizing attitude reaches its peak when she daydreams, vaudeville-style, of being the heroine who has saved her husband's life: first when he was sick and then when she, anticipating that Torvald will take the blame for her forgery, plans for her own suicide so as to relieve him of the burden.[60] Turning back to the discussion in the previous chapters, we could even suggest that Nora's romantic drama rotates around

---

[57] In The Master Builder, we find this metaphor in Mrs. Solness's static preservation of her dolls as a token of happier days.

[58] In Peer Gynt, we see Anitra described not only by bird motifs, but also as a plant. For a discussion of this point, see Aarseth, Dyret i Mennesket, 47.

[59] As she describes her life to Kristine: "No more worries [sorgløs]! Just think of being without a care in the world . . . being able to romp with the children, and making the house nice and attractive, and having things just as Torvald likes to have them! And then spring will soon be here, and blue skies" (OI V 216; HIS VII 241).

[60] Thus, when Nora realizes that Krogstad is going to tell Torvald about the loan, her reaction is precisely to worry that her beautiful dream will be debased: "That secret is all my pride and joy—why should he have to hear about it in this nasty, ugly way . . . hear about it from you" (OI V 226; HIS VII 260, trans. modified).

the lighthearted plot-structures that the young Ibsen, in drawing on historical material, had endeavored to leave behind.

Learning from Hegelian thought, we have seen that resistance to external
criticism is an intrinsic aspect of the aestheticizing outlook on life. How is
it, then, that in Ibsen's work, Nora, unlike Torvald, manages to liberate herself from this stance? This question lies behind and indirectly motivates the
criticism that has been launched against the Nora character, namely that she
is too naïve, too immature to stand forth as somebody who might plausibly
engage in the kind of thinking that, ultimately, leads to her decision to leave
her husband and children.

We find a version of this argument in Jay M. Bernstein's reading of *A Doll's
House*.[61] In his view, the problem is that Nora, while leaving everything in
order to find herself, is characterized as possessing a calm composure that
indicates that she has already gained the self she sets out to find. [62] If she
has not already undergone the transformation she desires,[63] such a sense of
herself would be hard to explain. Nora, so to speak, articulates her protest
against society before she has reached a platform from which such a protest
can be launched. Yet, as Bernstein argues, even though it represents, strictly
speaking, a dramatic lapse, this glimpse of Nora as transformed captures the
beauty of the play: "It is this ["that Nora's protest against society presupposes
the transfigured one she is about to quest after"] that transforms the chill of
the play's negativity into the warmth of affirmation, making Nora after all a
beautiful heroine, an heroic beauty to be emulated and admired."[64]

Bracketing the Adornian spirit in which Bernstein's reading is conducted—
and Adorno, we know, was a perceptive reader of Ibsen's work—it should
be noted that Koht already addresses this objection. Initially Koht pointed
out how Nora's sudden transformation had been viewed as a problem (this
is the argument we find in the English translation of his work).[65] In the later
(Norwegian) edition of his study, however, he defends Ibsen by pointing

---

[61] J. M. Bernstein, "Fragment, Fascination, Damaged Life: The Truth about Hedda Gabler," in *The
Actuality of Adorno: Critical Essays on Adorno and the Postmodern*, ed. Max Pensky (Albany: SUNY
Press, 1997), 167.

[62] Bernstein is referring to Nora's claim: "Never have I felt so calm and collected as I do tonight" (OI
V 283; HIS VII 373).

[63] As Nora later explains: "I must take steps to educate myself. You are not the man to help me
there. That's something I must do on my own. That's why I'm leaving you." And a few lines later, "If
I'm ever to reach any understanding of myself and the things around me, I must learn to stand alone.
That's why I can't stay here with you any longer" (OI V 281; HIS VII 368).

[64] Bernstein, "Fragment, Fascination, Damaged Life," 168.

[65] See Koht, *The Life of Ibsen*, vol. II, 153; *Henrik Ibsen*, vol. II, 107.

out that in being a chirping bird, for example, Nora is indeed play-acting to please her husband. Gifted actors will let this dimension of play-acting shine through in their performance. Thus, even early on in the play, there is more to Nora's character than her aestheticism—not just in terms of financial maturity, but also in terms of her potential as a dramatic character. Nora's aestheticism is but a mask that she wears when playing the naïve housewife.[66] As Koht ends up seeing it, this play within the play exemplifies Ibsen's theater-technical finesse.[67]

Koht is right to emphasize the complexity of the Nora character. However, this complexity is not only, as he indicates, a matter of finding the right actor, but also of seeing that Ibsen has left us with numerous clues with respect to Nora's personality and how it is deeper than we may initially think. This depth is not only a matter of economic maturity, but also of human growth more generally. We get this aspect of Nora into view by considering the dialogues with Kristine Linde, whom she has known before her days of marriage.[68] It is easy to underestimate the importance of the subplot of the Kristine Linde and Krogstad affair or brush it off as a gesture toward a lighter and more entertaining drama of intrigue. For while Nora, in her relationship to Torvald, is initially portrayed as a naïvely aesthetic character, Ibsen lets another side of her emerge through in her interaction with Kristine Linde. Without this side, Nora's transformation would perhaps be implausible. Against the background of her long-term friendship, however, it is not.

In the play, we learn that Kristine Linde and Krogstad long ago had been in love. However, their feelings were never acted upon because she was providing for her younger brothers and had to choose a man of means. Now her husband has died, leaving neither children nor money. Nora finds that Kristine should be proud to have taken care of her mother and brothers (OI V 212–213; HIS VII 234). Further, her conversations with Kristine help Nora articulate her own needs. They prepare her for what will come. Upon leaving Torvald, this is how she sums up her situation: "I must set about *getting* experience, Torvald" (OI V 282; HIS VII 369). Getting experience, further, is

---

[66] Koht, *Henrik Ibsen*, vol. II, 106.

[67] Koht, *Henrik Ibsen*, vol. II, 105–106.

[68] A similar dramaturgical concept emerges in *Hedda Gabler*, in which Mrs. Elvsted, formerly Mrs. Rysing, with whom Hedda had gone to school, testifies to Hedda's mean character (she recalls Hedda pulling her hair; OI VII 190; HIS IX 46). Realizing that Mrs. Elvsted was Tesman's old flame, Hedda has already characterized her as annoying (*irriterende*, OI VII 184; HIS IX 36). In anticipation of the discussion in Chapter 7, it should also be noted that just like Ejlert addresses Hedda with her maiden name, so does Tesman address Mrs. Elvsted as Mrs. Rysing (OI VII 184–188; HIS IX 36–43).

described as a duty toward herself (OI V 282; VII 370). It is a matter of testing out the knowledge that has been handed down to her, figuring out, as she puts it, "whether it's right for me" (OI V 283; HIS VII 371). And once we see that Nora is in this sense thinking maturely, we can accept that her dissatisfaction with her marriage is not the reason, per se, for her departure. When Nora articulates her pain and predicament, she centers on her duties toward herself.

Nora's desire to figure out what is right for her made Ibsen's contemporaries see her as a Kierkegaardian—a Kierkegaardian in a skirt, as they condescendingly put it.[69] However, in taking leave of her aesthetic consciousness, Nora appeals to experience and education.[70] Without denying the possible Kierkegaardian influence on the work (or on Ibsen's oeuvre more broadly), this appeal to experience and education is better explained with reference to Hegel.

Writing in the wake of the *Sturm und Drang* era, Hegel sees *Bildung*, the education in culture and history, as essential to philosophical activity. The goal is not only to produce *Bildung*, but also to conceptually capture the process of *Bildung* and, in one and the same move, to educate and produce knowledge about the process of education itself, i.e., the process through which the subject takes responsibility for itself and its outlook on the world. This educational aspect of Hegel's work informed Heiberg's program in Copenhagen—both in terms of his philosophical contribution and his work as dramaturge.[71] In a letter to the King, Ibsen, in 1860, had emphasized the educational aspect of drama. As he here puts it, the point is not simply that the dramatic arts have an educational function, but that the educational function is more essential to drama than to any other artform (letter of August 6, 1860, HIS XII 140). The general Hegelian tone of Ibsen's self-description in this letter will

[69] Erik Bøgh, review in *Dagens Nyheder* (København 24. desember 1879, nr. 348, Tolvte Aargang), http://ibsen.nb.no/id/11234213.0.
[70] Nora also reflects on religion. Julie Holledge emphasizes how doubt enters Nora's mind at this point. In my reading, however, Nora's transformation is not simply motivated (negatively) by doubt and a loss of religious footing, but also (positively) by her gradually acquiring agency through her work—and her understanding, through the conversations with Kristine, of the importance of this work. Similarly, her agency is not only, as Holledge indicates, sexual, but also based on her growing self-reflection. For Holledge's point, see her "Pastor Hansen's Confirmation Class: Religion, Freedom, and the Female Body in *Et dukkehjem*," in *Ibsen Studies*, vol. 10, no. 1 (2010): 3–16. The notion of Nora's sexualized agency features prominently in Bergman's production of *A Doll's House* at Dramaten, in which Nora, in Act One, is basically exchanging sexual favors for money, thus casting a grim light over the Helmer marriage from the very opening of the play.
[71] For this aspect of Heiberg's work, see Thomas Fauth Hansen, "The Expression of Infinity: Reflections on Heiberg's View of Contemporary Culture," in *Johan Ludvig Heiberg: Philosopher, Littérateur, Dramaturge, and Political Thinker*, 449–471.

not escape the reader. He has earned his position, as he puts it, by studying the principles, system, and history of dramatic art and literature (letter of August 6, 1860, HIS XII 139).

In this context, a number of points prove relevant. First, in Hegel's dialectics, education (*Bildung*) is a comprehensive notion covering both experience and education in culture. Being a process of self-transformation, it is self-driven and self-directed. The process, Hegel points out, can be painful; it requires that the subject does not stay in one place, that it leaves behind that which (it) is in order to acquire the distance needed for reflection. As the individual obtains a better self-understanding, so her space of thought and action increases. Hegel's description of this process must be given in full:

> Spirit has broken with the world it has hitherto inhabited and imagined, and is of a mind to submerge it in the past, and in the labour of its own transformation. Spirit is indeed never at rest but always engaged in moving forward. But just as the first breath drawn by a child after its long, quiet nourishment breaks the gradualness of merely quantitative growth—there is a qualitative leap, and the child is born—so likewise the Spirit in its formation matures slowly and quietly into its new shape, dissolving bit by bit the structure of its previous world, whose tottering state is only hinted at by isolated symptoms. (PS 6; HW III 18)

For Hegel, the realization that spirit is in a process of *Bildung* is an intellectual landmark (PS 6; HW III 18) and it is impossible, at this point, for philosophy to return to its earlier, more naïve forms.

Hegel's concept of *Bildung* accounts, at one and the same time, for spirit's progress through history and for individual education. Nora's path, too, is one of education.[72] Once she has realized her own predicament, she cannot stay in her marriage. She has to move on—and do so on her own. When Torvald responds to the return of the forged signature with his infamous "I am saved!", Nora realizes that her life must be reassessed. Her new mindset is expressed through a need to change from party costume to an ordinary dress

---

[72] This was also the case for the women philosophers, including Staël, who had turned to Rousseau's *Emile*. These philosophers critiqued Rousseau's views on the education of women, but also sought to make constructive use of his insights. See Mary Seidman Trouille, *Sexual Politics in the Enlightenment: Women Writers Read Rousseau* (Buffalo: SUNY Press, 1997). In Norway, Hulda Garborg would later publish her *Rosseau og hans tanker i nutiden* (Kristiania: Gyldendal, 1909).

(OI V 279; HIS VII 363).[73] Nora now sees the world differently, but once the world presents itself to her in this new way, she is already a new person. This new self must be appropriated. Torvald, however, cannot help. Nora needs to figure out her life herself; she needs, as Ibsen puts it, to take steps to educate *herself* ("Jeg må se at opdrage *mig selv*," OI V 281; HIS VII 368, emphasis added). Nora breaks out of the beautiful illusion her life has been in order to gain experience and perspective; via this self-education, she hopes to become more truly herself.

Hegel had emphasized that true education requires an element of alienation. Education is only possible to the extent that a subject liberates itself from its naïvely held beliefs. For Hegel, understanding requires distance and spirit must lose itself in order to gain itself more clearly. In this sense, we can speak of knowledge of that which was already known, of being truly familiar with that which we thought we knew. As Hegel sums up his observations:

> Quite generally, the familiar, just because it is familiar, is not cognitively understood. The commonest way in which we deceive either ourselves or others about understanding is by assuming something as familiar, and accepting it on that account; with all its pros and cons, such knowing never gets anywhere, and it knows not why. Subject and object, God, Nature, Understanding, sensibility, and so on, are uncritically taken for granted as familiar, established as valid, and made into fixed points for starting and stopping. (PS 18; HW III 35)

Das Bekannte überhaupt is darum, weil es bekannt ist, nicht erkannt—in all its untranslatable word-play, Hegel's phrasing could have stood as a motto for Nora's self-discovery. For Nora, what was familiar turns out to be unknown. What she thought was her life turns out to be a doll's existence.[74] What she thought was hers, in reality, belonged to somebody else. In Nora's voice: "our house has never been anything but a play-room. I have been your doll wife, just as at home I was Daddy's doll child. And the children in turn have been my dolls" (OI V 280–281; HIS VII 366–367). Upon seeing that her house is no home for her—upon realizing that she needs to be educated in order

---

[73] The Oxford translation adds another layer of meaning, rendering "yes, I've put on something else [Ja, Torvald, nu har jeg klædt mig om]" as "Yes, I have changed"; the PI is truer to the original: "Yes, Torvald, I've changed clothes now," 181.

[74] Moi helpfully draws the parallel to Staël and her notion of dolls and mannequins. See *Henrik Ibsen and the Birth of Modernism*, 235–236.

to *have* a home—Nora sees no other alternative than to leave. In this sense, Nora follows, with a Hegelian phrasing, a path of doubt and despair, although in the hope that there may be a future mode of existence that she will be able to fully inhabit and call her own.

Finally, with respect to Ibsen's play, it is worth noting how, for Hegel, *Bildung* is undertaken in the spirit of freedom. At stake is not abstract freedom, but freedom gained through a process of appropriation. Hegel importantly characterizes this as a process of work and philosophy, seeking to grasp the logic of this process, as the work of the concept (PS 43; HW III 65).

This scheme of Hegelian thought may help us shed light on the development of Nora's character. In setting out to find herself, she needs to figure out if that which she has believed in—the normative parameters of her existence—is really hers. Further, this process has already been prepared for by her secret work to pay her debt and her reflections, in the conversations with Kristine, on what that work meant to her. When Torvald sees her lack of financial responsibility as a sign of her essential, female character—"Nora, Nora, you are a woman!" (in the original, Torvald's line is infused with a Latinized verb that draws attention to his essentializing mindset: "Nora, Nora du est en kvinde!," OI V 203; HIS VII 216)—the audience will already know that it is through her work that Nora, behind his back, has begun to feel like a full human being (OI V 216; HIS VII 240). For Torvald, work is a means to a careless existence and, as a means to an end, it is a male matter. For Nora, by contrast, work is a question of taking responsibility for herself and those that she loves, and thus a genuinely human and humanizing activity. When Torvald reminds Nora that she is first and foremost a wife and a mother, she responds: "That I don't believe any more. I believe that first and foremost, I am *a human being,* just as much as you are—or at least I'm going to try to be" (OI V 282; HIS VII 370, trans. modified and emphasis added: Ibsen writes a human being [*et menneske*], and the McFarlane translation's "individual" thus renders Nora's claim rather toothless. Again the PI gets this right, 184).

When Nora is starting anew, returning to the place where she grew up, she is therefore returning home in more than one sense of the word: "Tomorrow I'm going home—to what used to be my home, I mean. It will be easier for me to find something to do there" (OI V 282; HIS VII 369). She is taking nothing with her, we learn—"I don't want anything of yours, either now or later" (OI V 281; HIS VII 369)—as her self-actualization has to be her own work. This is what Nora's wish to educate herself implies. The wonderful, to which she refers in the closing line, suggests that both she and Torvald would be in need of such education and only this could have brought them out of their aestheticized existence.

In this sense, *A Doll's House* does indeed put into play a constellation of Hegelian insights. To suggest this much is not, obviously, to deny that Hegel harbored misogynistic sentiments.[75] The point, rather, is that Hegel's work also entertains a model of experience (and *Bildung*) that points in a direction that transcends his views on the family.

Breaking Free of Aestheticism

The discussion of *Peer Gynt* (Chapter 2) touched on Hegel's claims about the end of art and the possibility that Ibsen, half a century after Hegel's lectures on fine art, points the way toward a new kind of art—art after the end of great art, as we could put it. I would like to conclude my analysis of Ibsen's Hegelian variations with a discussion of how Ibsen can be said to realize the idea of art after the end of great art—or, if one likes, drama after romantic drama. These reflections have been prepared for in that we saw, in the previous section, how Nora, through a process of work and education, moves from lighthearted play-acting to the serious game of achieving an authentic self. The question, then, is to what extent this new sense of self might be the harbinger of a new kind of art and drama that Hegel, with his idealist framework, could not have anticipated.

In the aesthetic lectures, Hegel defines art in terms of a harmony between form and content. As he puts it, "[t]he centre of art is a unification . . . of the content with its entirely adequate shape" (LFA 427; HW XIV 13). This unification, in turn, is a way in which the absolute finds a sensuous expression. Great art obtains its most adequate expression in the classical period: classical art shows us, as he puts it, "what true art is in its essential nature" (LFA 427; HW XIV 13). With Christianity, religion gets inward and more abstract. (In Ibsen's earlier work, it was Christianity that had made Emperor Julian experience a cleavage between spirit and its world, and long for the ancient religion that knew no opposition between truth and beauty.) The

---

[75] At this point, Hegel distinguishes himself from the Jena romantics and Staël, whose own *Bildungsroman, Corinne,* entails ample reflections on the way society prevents a woman from entering on a path of *Bildung. Corinne* was published the same year as Hegel's *Phenomenology of Spirit.*

development then continues on to Medieval and later modern art, including modern drama. In modern drama, the turn toward inwardness is reflected in character types that, like Hamlet, are pensive and whose actions are not expressive of their inner selves. In the early Nineteenth Century, Hegel points out, it is philosophy that will cater to the highest ideals while art turns to the domain of the ordinary. Art is still an expression of human life and concerns, but we now face a situation in which "aims are broadly and variously particularized and in such detail that what is truly substantial can often glimmer through them in only a very dim way" (LFA 1223; HW XV 556).

This is what Hegel thinks takes place with Goethe, Schiller, and Kotzebue.[76] At this point, there is no clear distinction between tragedy and comedy. Further, the new drama can no longer offer an adequate sensuous presentation of the absolute. We face a predicament in which art "no longer unites itself with anything objective and particularized" (LFA 1236; HW XV 572). For Hegel, this indicates the end of great art and its historical development. Yet, Hegel insists that we will still make and enjoy art.[77] Art will remain valuable and a source of pleasure and self-understanding. It is, as he puts it, "the best compensation for hard work in the world and the bitter labour for knowledge" (LFA 1237; HW XV 573).

Returning to Ibsen and Scandinavian Hegelianism, we can imagine playwrights of Ibsen's generation wondering about the future of art after great art. Nora's slamming of the gate, her leaving behind, among other things, an aestheticized existence, suggests the need for a less high-flung and less idealistic (to borrow Moi's term) kind of art, but still an art that, as Hegel has pointed out, matters tremendously.[78]

---

[76] For helpful readings of Hegel and modern art (in particular literature and drama), see Moland, *Hegel's Aesthetics*, Chapter 10, and Benjamin Rutter, *Hegel on the Modern Arts* (Cambridge: Cambridge University Press, 2010), Chapter 5.

[77] Art is, as he puts it in his discussion of painting, expressive "of what the human being is as human being [Mensch], what the human spirit and character is, what human being and *this* human being is" (LFA 887; HW XV 130–131, trans. modified).

[78] From this point of view, it is interesting that *A Doll's House*, at least on Salomé's reading, ends on a promising note: "If the unattainable and the uncertain is implied by the idea of 'wondrous,' it also contains unlimited possibilities and perspectives. If it is a battle and no victory that Nora is about to encounter, she is ready with a youthful, strong, and golden armor. If she parts in pain, it is not mere sorrowful and patient acceptance of a pain that comes from the loss of ideals but a contention and striving for a new ideal. She is imbued with refreshing boldness which bodes promise and beginning—the ending remains open." Or, beyond Salomé, we can suggest that the ending is itself a beginning. That is, we could imagine that the ending is not simply a question of Nora's emancipation but also indicates the celebration of a new vision of art, albeit one that grows out of and completes the artistic promise of Ibsen's early work. For Salomé's reading, see *Ibsen's Heroines*, 56; *Henrik Ibsens Frauen-Gestalten*, 43.

Ibsen did not work out this new kind of art single-handedly. Even though he claims not to have been particularly familiar with French literature, realism and naturalism (both featuring a parade of female heroines) had already gained a foothold through the works of Honoré de Balzac, Gustave Flaubert, and others.[79] As Zola had remarked, "there is more poetry in the little apartment of a bourgeois than in all the empty, worm-eaten palaces of history"[80] While these movements had, to some extent, been prepared for even earlier by Diderot, Lessing, and Herder, Ibsen brings these trends into the nineteenth-century theater and creates a drama whose poetic logic relies on its explorations of the lives that people lead and the gaps they experience between their lives and their dreams. As a result, art turns its back on purportedly timeless aesthetic ideals. Ibsen produces a drama that takes seriously the contingency and fragility—the unavoidable historicity—of modern existence.

To grasp this thought fully, however, we need to move beyond Hegel and extend our focus to Nietzsche's philosophy of history, theater, and life.

[79] For a claim about Ibsen's relative ignorance of French literature, see Meyer, *Ibsen*, 487. For a discussion of Ibsen's borrowing, in the context of *A Doll's House*, from French theater, see Thomas F. Van Laan, "The Ending of *A Doll's House* and Augier's *Maître Guérin*," in *Comparative Drama*, vol. 17, no. 4 (1983–84): 297–317. In the larger context of the reception of realist literature, it is worth keeping in mind, though, that Eleanor Marx-Aveling not only translated Ibsen but also Flaubert's *Madame Bovary* (Gustave Flaubert, *Madame Bovary*, trans. Eleanor Marx-Aveling [London: Wordsworth Editions, 1987]).

[80] Émile Zola, "Naturalism in the Theater," trans. Albert Bermel, in *A Sourcebook on Naturalist Theatre*, ed. Christopher Innes (London: Routledge, 2000), 49; *Le Naturalisme au Theatre. Les Theories et Les Exemples*. http://www.gutenberg.org/files/13866/13866-h/13866-h.htm (Accessed June 2018). Ibsen, however, writes a "domestic drama" and historical at that, yet does so in a way that demonstrates that the palaces of history can be approached in ways that make them less "worm-eaten." Unlike Ibsen, the slightly younger August Strindberg explicitly discusses this point. For a relevant discussion of Strindberg (and tragedy in a Scandinavian context), see Leonardo F. Lisi, "The Art of Doubt: Form, Genre, History in *Miss Julie*," in *The International Strindberg: New Critical Essays*, ed. Anna Westerståhl Stenport (Evanston: Northwestern University Press, 2012), 249–276.

5

Tragedy and Tradition (*Ghosts*)

Presented as "a Domestic Drama [et familjedrama] in Three Acts," *Ghosts* was even more provocative than *A Doll's House*. In *Ghosts*, we encounter the disillusioned Mrs. Helene Alving. Unlike Nora Helmer, Mrs. Alving decides to stay in a dysfunctional marriage and gradually comes to realize the costs of her decision. Her son, Oswald, is a painter whose philosophy of creativity and life-affirmation stands in stark contrast to his rapidly deteriorating health. While the play's morality—or, it was argued, lack of such—was initially attacked by the critics, including critics of a Hegelian disposition, readers have later sought to defend the play by emphasizing its Sophoclean tenets. It is, after all, a play that features a quasi-Oedipal triangle and that is structured around the main character's belated guilt, knowledge, and self-understanding.

If Ibsen draws on Greek tragedy, one may ask how this engagement is best understood. With the budding Nietzscheanism in Scandinavia, a new and radical understanding of Greek antiquity is brought to the table, one that fundamentally shatters the idealistic approach to which Hegel was still indebted. Is *Ghosts* part of this movement?

Nietzsche interprets Greek tragedy as an artform that, faced with almost unbearable human suffering, is still able to affirm life. In Nietzsche's view, this capacity for affirmation is at the heart not only of classical culture, but also of artistic creation more broadly. What is of interest to him is not the notion of the characters' guilt and self-discovery, but the transgressive musicality of the tragedy, above all the tragic chorus. In its *ur*-form, the chorus creates a rhythmic-musical unity between performers and audiences and gives rise to a celebratory experience of life as transcending individual suffering.

Nietzsche's philosophy of tragedy would influence generations of artists, including those of Ibsen's circles. Budding representatives of realism, naturalism, and what we have come to speak of as Nordic modernism soon turn to Nietzsche's work.[1] Here they find a novel and provocative approach to art in general and tragedy more specifically. To them, Nietzsche's work represents a

---

[1] For a study of Nordic art and modernism, see Arnold Weinstein, *Northern Arts: The Breakthrough of Scandinavian Literature and Art, from Ibsen to Bergman* (Princeton: Princeton University Press,

The Drama of History. Kristin Gjesdal, Oxford University Press (2021). © Oxford University Press.
DOI: 10.1093/oso/9780190070762.001.0001.

new will to unmask and critique the tradition. It offers a discussion of what is alive and what is just ghostly—and of the way in which we have come to lock the expressions of the past (e.g., tragedy) into static and idealized patterns of understanding. Finally, Nietzsche's discussion of tragedy calls for an art that goes beyond the Hegelian call for a sensuous shining of the ideal, allowing a transgressive experience that, ultimately, escapes the boundaries of reason.[2] Yet, for Nietzsche, philosophy is needed; philosophy helps us moderns to articulate what was lost when we let go of the life-affirming force of culture and to clarify and take a stance on the norms that have come to structure modern society.

Published a short decade prior to *Ghosts*, Nietzsche's *The Birth of Tragedy* can help us understand how Ibsen appropriates and transforms traditional forms of tragedy and, ultimately, the values of tradition more broadly. Against the reading of *Ghosts* as an ethical or cognitive drama of a Sophoclean bent, I suggest that Ibsen, in this work, twists the classical demands for the unity of characters, space, and time in a way that facilitates a proto-Nietzschean overcoming of the distance between the work and its audience. As such, he challenges a Hegelian focus on individual characters, their worldviews, and their clashes of horizons. In transcending a Hegelian framework, though, Ibsen does not completely let go of art's capacity to provoke and stimulate reflection. In my reading, Mrs. Alving, with her newly enlightened attitudes, presents the audience with a call to take on the kind of reflective-educational process that she herself embarked on, albeit too late in her case to change the course of her actions. With this turn, Ibsen both draws on *and* goes beyond the mythological-romantic model that Nietzsche, in the 1870s, had defended. He produces a work that is unapologetically modern.

However, before we proceed to explore this point in more detail, we need to ask how it was possible, in nineteenth-century Scandinavia, to transition so easily from a Hegelian to a Nietzschean framework of thought.

2008). For the reception of Nietzsche's philosophy in Norway, see Harald Beyer, *Nietzsche og Norden*, 2 vols. (Bergen: Grieg Forlag, 1958–1959).

[2] This thought would be of particular importance for Nietzsche's modernist reception in the theater (e.g., Artaud) and in dance (e.g., Isadora Duncan and Martha Graham). For an account of Nietzsche's legacy in dance, see Kimerer L. LaMothe, *Nietzsche's Dancers: Isadora Duncan, Martha Graham, and the Revaluation of Christian Values* (London: Palgrave Macmillan, 2006), 107–151 (Duncan) and 152–219 (Graham). The metaphor of the dancer figures prominently throughout Nietzsche's work. For a helpful collection of Nietzsche's remarks on dance, see Straßner, *Flöte und Pistole*, 97–103.

From Hegel to Nietzsche

In an 1899 commentary to *Aristocratic Radicalism*—and following his correspondence with Nietzsche ten years earlier—Brandes makes it clear that, in his writing and thinking, he has been influenced by two German philosophers: Hegel and Nietzsche. "Twice in my life I had been the spokesman of German Ideas," he writes, "in my youth Hegel's and in my mature years Nietzsche's."[3] While his critics had accused him of an intellectual U-turn, Brandes does not see it this way. Prior to its academic reception—which happened fairly late and only after Brandes's lectures—Nietzsche's work emerged in relative continuity with the Hegelianism with which Brandes was accustomed: it offered another way of thinking through the (arch-Hegelian) topics of culture, art, history, and education, and it did indeed spring out of the same discussion of philosophy and drama that had informed Hegel's work. However, to the philosophical critic, whose claims about a new beginning in European literature would challenge what he perceived as a placid status quo, it now seems the promises of Hegel's idealism can only be redeemed by going beyond it. Nietzsche's philosophy offers precisely such a possibility.

Brandes's position is not unreasonable. In fact, a similar approach to Nietzsche is sometimes pursued in contemporary scholarship. Without denying fundamental differences in style and worldview, Daniel Breazeale, Stephen Houlgate, and others have reminded later readers of the significant, and often overlooked, points of continuity between Hegel and Nietzsche.[4] Judging from Brandes's essay, these points of continuity must have been even more palpable when Nietzsche started publishing in the 1870s.[5]

[3] Georg Brandes, *Friedrich Nietzsche*, trans. A. G. Chater (New York: Macmillan Company, 1914), 60.

[4] As Houlgate puts it: "Not only are Hegel and Nietzsche both critics of 'reality-behind-appearance' dualism or 'other-worldly' consciousness; they are both critics (at least in intent) of *all* conceptual oppositions or *Gegensätze*. This belief in conceptual oppositions, which—almost invariably for Nietzsche, and frequently for Hegel—manifests itself in the belief in a world 'beyond' our ordinary experience, but which is not necessarily reducible to that belief, is identified by both these philosophers as 'metaphysical.'" Houlgate, *Hegel, Nietzsche and the Criticism of Metaphysics*, 22. For discussions of the intellectual overlaps between Hegel and Nietzsche, see also Daniel Breazeale, "The Hegel-Nietzsche Problem," *Nietzsche-Studien*, no. 4 (1975): 146–164; Heinz Röttges, *Nietzsche und die Dialektik der Aufklärung* (Berlin: de Gruyter, 1972); Reinier Franciscus Beerling, "Hegel und Nietzsche," *Hegel-Studien*, no. 1–2 (1961): 229–246.

[5] Later, in his letters to Brandes, Nietzsche speaks of his dislike of dialectics, perhaps even of reason itself (December 2, 1887). Brandes, *Friedrich Nietzsche*, 64; Nietzsche, Brief an Georg Brandes, http://www.nietzschesource.org/#eKGWB/BVN-1887,960 (Accessed July 2019).

Like Hegel, the early Nietzsche is skeptical of lighthearted and decorative aestheticism. They both demonstrate a systematic concern for classical tragedy. And again, like Hegel, Nietzsche takes this artform to be key to the understanding of art as such. Both Hegel and Nietzsche would criticize the subjectivism of Kant and romantic philosophy, and question ahistorical approaches to art. And whereas Hegel, in the 1820s, had lectured on the history of great art all the way to its supposed ending in romantic comedy, Nietzsche, a few decades later, had begun his path as a philosopher-philologist by asking whether art can still offer the kind of unifying, existential experience that it had given the Ancient Greeks.

As he starts his philosophical trajectory with an essay on tragedy ("On the Concept of Fate in Tragedy"), Brandes's writing evidences the relative continuity between Hegelianism and Nietzscheanism in nineteenth-century Scandinavia. Brandes's Nietzsche lectures from the 1880s were legendary. Indeed, these lectures were the first ever dedicated to Nietzsche's work.[6] Not long after, the Swedish poet Ola Hansson, who was actively contributing to German literature at the time, would publish a book on Nietzsche. From then on, Nietzsche's philosophy would get the undivided attention of Scandinavian intellectuals. But even before Brandes and Hansson, their fellow Scandinavians had taken an interest in Nietzsche. Some of this interest had been generated by Karl Hillebrand (who, for a short period of time, had been Heinrich Heine's secretary), especially his efforts to disseminate ideas from *Untimely Meditations*.[7]

Hillebrand's essays were known to Bjørnson, Ibsen's friend and fellow poet. During a prolonged stay in Tyrol, Bjørnson, some ten years before Brandes's reception, wrote back to Ibsen's circles in Norway with references to Hillebrand's work, especially his review of Nietzsche's meditation on history.[8]

---

[6] Brandes, in this period, would also lecture on Ibsen, including Ibsen's reception in Germany.

[7] *Untimely Meditations* is a collection of the first four essays in a series that Nietzsche had envisioned. The essays, each published separately between 1873 and 1876, are *David Strauss, the Confessor and the Writer*, *On the Uses and Disadvantages of History for Life*, *Schopenhauer as Educator*, and *Richard Wagner in Bayreuth*. Hillebrand reviews Nietzsche's essay on David Friedrich Strauß, with whose work Ibsen was already familiar from his preparatory reading for *Emperor and Galilean*. For Hillebrand's review, see Hauke Reich, *Rezensionen und Reaktionen zu Nietzsches Werken 1872–1889* (Berlin: Walter de Gruyter, 2013), 292–303.

[8] Beyer, *Nietzsche og Norden*, 56. Bjørnson's reference is worth noting since, in the wake of World War II, there were widespread attempts retrospectively to minimize Nietzsche's influence on Norwegian nineteenth-century culture, especially on Bjørnson. An example of this can be found in Francis Bull, "Bjørnson kontra Nietzsche," *Samtiden*, 1947, ed. Jac. S. Worm-Müller (Oslo: Aschehoug, 1947), 160–169.

In Nietzsche's work, several of the topics from Ibsen's early period are highlighted: tragedy and drama, history and historicity, and the future of art and culture. Hence, it should come as no surprise that this philosopher would catch the interest of intellectuals and artists in Ibsen's circles—even if (or precisely because) Nietzsche's work would challenge the Hegelian foundations that had dominated the stage in Copenhagen and beyond.[9]

The Ghosts of the Past

In writing *Ghosts*, Ibsen knew that it would be a controversial drama. As he confides to his publisher, "*Ghosts* will alarm some circles, but this is the way it must be. Were this not the case, it would not have been necessary to write the piece" (letter of November 23, 1881; HIS XIV 97). Indeed, in his review of *Ghosts*, the Norwegian poet Arne Garborg suggests that a story of this kind may be suitable for a novel. But a plot for a play, he bluntly states, it is not.[10] Ibsen's new work is too bleak and its moral is questionable. This was also the concern when the play was turned down by Christiania Theater, though Ibsen's supporters quickly pointed out that the internal, institutional politics of the theater might have motivated the decision.[11] Ibsen's vindicators, however, came to his rescue by bringing in a set of more principled aesthetic questions. As Bjørnson saw it, the criticism of *Ghosts* was grounded in a number of misunderstandings, including the supposition that art should be uplifting and pleasant, and that the characters' opinions should be expressive of the author's.[12]

Ultimately, the play premiered in Chicago. It was staged in Ibsen's original for an audience of Scandinavian immigrants. By now, Ibsen's audience knew not to expect "a poetry of delightful fragrance." Instead, they were exposed to a tour de force of dramatic realism: grit, misery, sickness, and death. Nothing, it seems, was spared them.[13]

---

[9] Further, we see in this period a closer contact between Georg Brandes and Henrik Ibsen, and Ibsen is becoming increasingly aware of his German-language audiences.

[10] Garborg claims that the play is simply an exposé followed by a disaster, thus qualifying as "a terrible novel," but not as dramatic material. http://ibsen.nb.no/id/446.0 (Accessed June 2019).

[11] See anonymous comment in *Dagbladet*, December 22, 1881. http://ibsen.nb.no/id/56315.0 (Accessed July 2, 2019).

[12] Bjørnson, Commentary in *Dagbladet*, December 22, 1881. http://ibsen.nb.no/id/56318.0 (Accessed July 2, 2019).

[13] A reviewer in Chicago was familiar not only with Ibsen but also with Bjørnson's work. Interestingly, the reviewer takes the opportunity to turn Bjørnson's old criticism of Ibsen (as discussed in Chapter 1) against him. Bjørnson's characters, he argued, do not resemble real people; the farmers

In approaching *Ghosts*, both critics and admirers have focused on Mrs. Alving, the play's main character and the only one who, except for the very opening scene, is present throughout the entire three acts. It is, above all, Mrs. Alving's hopes and fears that make up the dramatic core of this work. As the curtains part, Mrs. Alving's son Oswald, an aspiring painter, has just returned from Paris to celebrate the opening of an orphanage that his mother has built in order to honor the memory of his deceased father—or so, at least, is the official version of the story. For through Mrs. Alving's conversation with Manders, the pastor and family friend, we get a less flattering picture of Mr. Alving. Mr. Alving might well be remembered for his vitality, but he is not, for that reason, a model citizen, husband, and father.[14] Indeed, at some point, his excesses were such that Mrs. Alving decided to send the young Oswald away so as to spare him the trauma of a family on the brink of disintegration.

As the play unfolds, we learn that not only did Mr. Alving drink too much, but he also, at some point, forced his son to smoke his pipe.

OSWALD. I distinctly remember he sat me on his knee and gave me the pipe to smoke. "Smoke lad," he said, "go on, lad, smoke!" And I smoked as hard as I could, till I felt I was going quite pale and great beads of sweat stood out on my forehead. Then he roared with laughter . . . (OI V 367; HIS VII 421)

In Ibsen's work, this episode is more than a tasteless prank. It is, for the Alvings, a fatal mistake and, as such, a key to the ghost motif. Oswald is now sick with syphilis. This is what he has discovered in Paris and what has prompted his return to his mother's house. In line with the medical thinking of the day, he was thought to have contracted the disease by smoking his father's pipe.[15] As his health deteriorates, Oswald experiences an increasing

do not appear to be of flesh and blood. Ibsen, by contrast, achieved precisely such an effect. While distinguishing Ibsen from the outspoken political direction of Zola, the reviewer pitched him as a historically oriented rebel who is ready to overthrow old ideas in the hope that something new and radical will emerge from the rubble of history. See anonymous article on *Ghost* in *Skandinaven* (Chicago), May 25–27, 1882. https://www.nb.no/forskning/ibsen (Accessed July 5, 2019).

[14] Among the numerous references to Mr. Alving's zest for life, some reveal a genuinely joyful spirit, others a reckless lifestyle. See for example OI V 367; HIS VII 441 (the Pastor's comment) and OI V 412; HIS VII 506 (the discussion between Oswald and his mother, describing his vitality: "Det var som et søndagsvejr bare at se på ham)."

[15] Again we see the topic of the father's sin in Ibsen's work. In *A Doll's House*, Dr. Rank had asked "Why should I suffer for another man's sins? What justice is there in that? Somewhere, somehow, every single family must be suffering some such cruel retribution" (OI V 245; HIS VII 298). This topic, in vogue at the time, had Ibsen's audiences worry about a turn in his work to "the poetry of the

fear of dying, but also of losing the joy of life that fuels his creativity. In Act Two, his artistic testament—and fear of losing his art if he returns to his mother's house—is dramatized as follows:

MRS. ALVING. [. . .] Oswald . . . what was that you were saying about the joy of life?

OSWALD. Yes, Mother, the joy of life. . . . You don't see much of that around this place. I never feel it here.

MRS. ALVING. Not even when you are with me?

OSWALD. Never when I'm at home. But you don't understand.

MRS. ALVING. Yes, I do . . . I'm beginning to understand . . . now.

OSWALD. That . . . and the joy of work, too. Well, they are the same thing, in fact. But people here don't know anything about that either.

MRS. ALVING. Perhaps you are right. Oswald, tell me more about this.

OSWALD. Well, all that I mean is that people here are brought up to believe that work is a curse, and a sort of punishment for their sins; and that life is some kind of miserable affair, which the sooner we are done with the better for everyone.

MRS. ALVING. A vale of tears, I know. And we do our damnedest to make it that.

OSWALD. But people elsewhere simply won't have that. Nobody really believes in ideas of that sort any more. In other countries they think it's tremendous fun just to be alive at all. Mother, have you noticed how everything I've ever painted has turned to this joy of life. Always, and without exception, this joy of life. Light and sunshine and a holiday spirit [søndagsluft]. (OI V 402–403; HIS VII 489–490)

Oswald's fear of losing his joy of life can, it turns out, only be dampened by his erotic, but also practical, interest in Regine, the maid and daughter of the local carpenter, Jakob Engstrand. Regine, he envisions, can care for him when he gets worse and even has the strength to help him end his life if it becomes unbearable. However, as Mrs. Alving is soon to reveal, Regine is not simply the maid in the house. She is indeed the offspring of Mr. Alving's illicit affair with Regine's mother, at the time a maid with the Alvings. Regine's mother was swiftly married away to Engstrand, who stepped up to take

hospital." For this point, see Koht, *Ibsen* II 116–117. For a discussion of the reference to syphilis in *Ghosts*, see Per Vesterhus, "Hvordan ble Osvald syk?" *Tidsskrift for Den norske Legeforening*, no. 13 (2007): 1814–1816.

paternal responsibility. A decent sum of money was involved in this transaction. In truth, Regine is therefore not only the family maid, but also Oswald's biological half-sister.

Within this pentagon of characters—Mrs. Alving and Oswald, Jakob Engstrand and his (step-)daughter Regine, and Pastor Manders—the drama unfolds around Mrs. Alving's gradual acknowledgment of the unpleasant truths about her marriage (built on lies and deception), her son's upbringing (brought up by foster parents so as to be spared his father's reckless lifestyle), and Regine's life in the household (maid, daughter, Oswald's half-sister, *and* his possible lover). To further complicate the situation, this acknowledgment is, in part, triggered by her reflection on her past feelings for Pastor Manders. As a newlywed, Mrs. Alving fled her unhappy marriage and sought refuge with the Pastor who, in a spirit of clerical duty, overcame his feelings for her and sent her back to her lawful spouse and to an existence that, from Mrs. Alving's point of view, involved a constant effort to patch up her husband's faltering façade. When Pastor Manders realizes the truth about the Alving marriage, the conversation echoes the final dialogue of *A Doll's House*:

MANDERS. I feel quite dazed. Am I to believe that your entire married life . . . all those years together with your husband . . . were nothing but a patched-up abyss [en overdækket afgrund!; the translator's "façade" is too weak].
MRS. ALVING. Precisely that. Now you know. (OI V 375; HIS VII 435, trans. modified)

What appeared to be solid ground barely patches over a void. What appeared to be familiar is, in truth, alien. The polished surface of the Alving home masks layers of pain and injustice.

The price to pay for Mrs. Alving's obedience has been considerable—for her family and for herself. As Mrs. Alving reflects: "They'd taught me various things about duty and suchlike, and I'd simply gone on believing them. Everything seemed to come down to duty in the end—*my* duty and *his* duty and . . . I'm afraid I must have made the house unbearable for your poor father, Oswald" (OI V 413; HIS VII 509). In an act of self-sacrifice, Mrs. Alving takes responsibility for having stunted her husband's life-affirming character in an effort to create the image of a decent home for her son. Her efforts were in vain. Even after his death, Mr. Alving continues to haunt his son and wife. Hence, when the orphanage—which, following the Pastor's advice, has been left in God's hands and is therefore uninsured—burns down, this is, to the Alvings, almost a relief.

The metaphor of the ghosts is first introduced when Mrs. Alving catches Oswald and Regine in a flirtatious conversation. Mrs. Alving has shared with Manders her desire to spend Alving's dowry on the orphanage so as to purge her house of his ghost and be able to "feel as though that man had never lived in this house [and] there'll be nobody else here but my son and his mother." The two are interrupted by Regine's sharp whisper "Oswald! Are you mad? Let me go!" Mrs. Alving immediately responds "Ghosts! The two in the conservatory [her husband and Regine's mother] . . . come back to haunt us" (OI V 378; HIS VII 120).[16] In spite of her efforts to save her son, Mrs. Alving cannot escape the past. There is a painful, incestuous twist to Oswald's feelings for Regine, but also to the intimacy Mrs. Alving expects from Oswald. From this point, the domestic tragedy of A Doll's House is taken several steps further. What for Nora was a superficial, static, and aestheticizing existence is for Mrs. Alving a state of bottomless despair. While Nora had somewhere to go (she returns to the town where she grew up), Mrs. Alving is stuck with her dying son and a growing sense of helplessness. The idea of a domestic drama now obtains a significantly more claustrophobic and uncanny undertone. The darkness of Ibsen's Ghosts is pictorially represented when Munch, in his commission for Max Reinhard's 1906 opening play at the Kammerspiele in Berlin, portrays mother and son as being, in effect, undistinguishable (see color plate 6).

Challenging the Drama of Cognition

In order to get beyond the aesthetic and moral shock of Ghosts, Ibsen's audiences turned to the now familiar strategy of framing the play within the tradition. That is, they referenced a part of the tradition that Ibsen, with his new, contemporary drama, left behind: that of classical tragedy. In such a reading, Ghosts mirrors the belated self-knowledge, the gradual awakening, and the sense of guilt that characterizes Sophocles' Oedipus Rex.

---

[16] The horror of this scene is further strengthened by its being introduced against the background of the Pastor's defense of traditional family values. Oswald, however, points out that many of his unmarried artist friends in Paris lived with their partners in more moral ways than "some of our model husbands and fathers" who "took themselves a trip to Paris to have a look round on the loose" (OI V 370; HIS VII 426).

Like a female Oedipus, Mrs. Alving owns up to the truths of her life, and, again like Oedipus, these truths are gained too late for her to change her course of action. Hence, against the claim that the play does not feature a properly dramatic subject matter, efforts have been made to demonstrate that, precisely in tackling topics such as incest, guilt, and catastrophe, Ibsen reaches back to the pillars of European theater.[17]

Focusing on Mrs. Alving's conversations with the Pastor, Brian Johnston, for one, views Mrs. Alving's moment of guilt-struck self-knowledge as key to the overall meaning of the play. In his reading, *Ghosts* is the tragedy of Mrs. Alving's realization of her failure to play along with her husband's joie de vivre. As Johnston sums up: "the dead military father, Alving, has been wronged by his wife Helene . . . Helene tries to allay the ghost of her husband once and for all with a fraudulent ritual: as she is making arrangements for this her son, Oswald, returns from abroad and soon will leave with his sister, Regine, against the whole world of pious untruth created by Mrs. Alving against the values represented by her husband."[18] From this point of view, *Ghosts* harks back to classical tragedy in that it stages Mrs. Alving's gradual process of (re)cognition. Mrs. Alving, further, is no victim, but a character whose moral flaws contributed to the downfall of her late husband (debauched as he died), Oswald (gradually succumbing to the syphilis his father passed on to him), Regine (living as a servant in her father's house and nourishing phantasies about Oswald taking her to Paris), Engstrand (being unaware of his daughter's true family, possibly also his wife's true love), and even Manders (who was unable to give in to his desires for Mrs. Alving). Like a female Oedipus, Mrs. Alving has not been wronged, but is, indeed, the very source of the misery that surrounds her.

Even if we bracket its conservative undertones, Johnston's interpretation is marred by problems. First, Ibsen himself presents *Ghosts* as a sequel to *A Doll's House*.[19] In light of Nora's departure from Torvald, the interpretation of Mrs. Alving as a remorseful, female Oedipus figure—a wife and mother who should have known, but failed to see—does not make full sense. Nora suffered gross misrecognition from her husband: she was ready to leave the falsehood

---

[17] Hence, Ibsen's maneuvering of history and tradition brings us back to the questions that had preoccupied Lessing and Herder, namely to what extent a return to classical tragedy demands a break with the tradition through which it is mediated.

[18] Johnston, *The Ibsen Cycle*, 194.

[19] For a discussion of this point, Francis Fergusson, *The Idea of a Theater: A Study of Ten Plays, The Art of Drama in Changing Perspective* (Princeton: Princeton University Press, 1968), 490.

of an aestheticized existence, and, as we saw in Chapter 4, nothing in this play suggests that Nora should have stayed in order to keep up the façade of the marriage. Rather, *A Doll's House* and *Ghosts* are works that explore the cost of bourgeois marriage, especially (but not exclusively) for the female half of the equation.[20] Second, it is an open question whether the timeframe that undergirds the moralist reading of *Ghosts* can be defended. Mr. Alving was not a fallen man *because* of his wife's feelings for the Pastor and her subsequent decision to accept a marriage in pretense. He was a fallen man even before they got married (OI V 381; HIS VII 123). Finally, when Mrs. Alving reflects on her "guilt," it is clear that her propensity to do her duty, thus also to quell her husband's excesses, follows from her succumbing to the traditional expectations of married life. Her real fault, as it were, is not that she stifled her husband's joy of life, but that she passively accepted the repressive idea of life that Pastor Manders had presented her with ("All this demanding to be happy in life, it's all part of this same wanton idea. What right do people have to happiness? No, we have our duty [pligt] to do, Mrs. Alving!" OI V 371; HIS VII 429).[21]

Thus, another interpretation of the play's Sophoclean echo is called for. In response to the reading sketched earlier, Joan Templeton has argued that "[t]he shape of the tragedy is Sophoclean only in the most general way: the crisis of the drama is the revelation of the dreadful truth about the past."[22] In Templeton's view, the play is not about Mrs. Alving's realization of her failing commitment to her marriage, but about her inability to listen to herself and take her own needs seriously. Hence the play does not primarily trace Mrs. Alving's discovery of her guilt vis-à-vis her husband and her son, but it portrays a subject who does not live according to the truths she possesses. As Templeton makes her point, "[in *Ghosts*] there is no vacillating protagonist searching for the truth, or denying some truth already evident to everyone

---

[20] Of interest here is Stanley Cavell's discussion of the moral perfectionism played out in *A Doll's House* in *Conditions Handsome and Unhandsome: The Constitution of Emersonian Perfectionism* (Chicago: University of Chicago Press, 1990), 108–111. See also Rainer Forst, "The Injustice of Justice: Normative Dialectics According to Ibsen, Cavell and Adorno," *Graduate Faculty Philosophy Journal*, vol. 28, no. 2 (2007): 39–51.

[21] Pastor Manders describes the call for happiness as a rebellious spirit (*opprørsånd*; this is lost in the McFarland and Arup translation). It is hard not to notice how this is a line akin to the spirit we will find, six years later, in Nietzsche's criticism of the ascetic priest and the ascetic ideal in *On the Genealogy of Morality*. While it may or may not be too much to suggest, as Van Laan does in "Ibsen and Nietzsche," that Ibsen might have influenced Nietzsche, the thematic overlaps strengthen the sense of there being, in this period, a set of shared concerns that are articulated in art and philosophy.

[22] Joan Templeton, "Of This Time, of This Place: Mrs. Alving's Ghosts and the Shape of the Tragedy," *PMLA*, vol. 101, no. 1 (1986): 64.

else, but a woman who berates herself over and over again for not telling the truth she, and she alone, already knows, condemning herself with great anguish for having obeyed other people's rules instead of her own mind and heart."[23]

It cannot be doubted that Mrs. Alving betrays herself. Yet I wonder to what extent this reading substantially improves on the interpretations Templeton seeks to challenge. Whereas Johnston's reading suffers from an unsupported focus on Mrs. Alving's alleged duties to her husband and her son, Templeton's reading centers on Mrs. Alving's (failing) orientation toward the truth of her life. While the insights uncovered are not the same (they may even be incompatible), both interpretations are geared toward the knowledge gained by the protagonist. In both readings, what situates *Ghosts* in the vicinity of classical tragedy is a Sophoclean orientation toward a tragic *truth-content*, a process of belated reflection on behalf of the protagonist. Such a reading, however, does not sit well with the philosophical reception of Greek tragedy in the period leading up to, and including, the publication of *Ghosts*.[24]

Retrieving the Greeks

Between Herder's writings on dramatic poetry and Hegel's lectures on fine art, philosophical aesthetics featured a debate about how best to understand the relationship between modern and classical art or, more precisely, between modern art and its historical conditions.[25] This discussion emerged, at least in part, from a break with the classicist aesthetics of imitation and its emphasis on ahistorical form (see Chapter 1). In the paradigm of classicist poetics, the question of modernity was not an issue. With Herder and

[23] Templeton, "Of This Time, of This Place," 60.

[24] For a reading that, from a historical point of view, defends a less cognitivist approach to tragedy, see for example Jean-Pierre Vernant and Pierre Vidal-Naquet, *Myth and Tragedy in Ancient Greece*, trans. Janet Lloyd (New York: Zone Books, 1988); *Myth et Tragédie en Grèce Ancienne* (Paris: Librairie Francois Maspero, 1972), Chapters 4 and 5.

[25] The implications of this point exceed the history of philosophy of drama. For to the extent that one is willing to acknowledge that the eighteenth-century debate on Greek tragedy involves a philosophy of history and culture, Kant's aesthetics, with its formalism and its turn to the beauty of nature, is not so much the beginning of modern aesthetics as a deviation from a well-established philosophy of art. Furthermore, Hegel's turn to philosophy of art—his claim that in adopting the expression "aesthetics" we all the same "exclude the beauty of nature"—is not, as he presents it, a bold, post-Kantian move, but, rather, a return to a pre-Kantian tradition. For Hegel's self-understanding, see LFA 1; HW XIII 13–14. I further clarify this point in my "Interpreting Hamlet: The Early German Reception," in *Shakespeare's Hamlet: Philosophical Perspectives*, ed. Tzachi Zamir (Oxford: Oxford University Press, 2018), 247–273.

the *Sturm und Drang*, by contrast, the concern with classical Greek art was transformed into a discussion of its historicity, and ultimately also of the modernity of contemporary drama.[26]

This is indeed a watershed in the philosophy of theater. Later discussions of Greek tragedy, Nietzsche's contribution included, must be understood against this background.[27] Only because there already existed a strong connection between philosophy of art, on the one hand, and classical tragedy, on the other, could Hegel, without further ado, declare that drama "must be regarded as the highest stage of poetry and of art generally" (LFA 1158; HW XV 474). Only in light of this connection, further, could Nietzsche, half a century after Hegel's lectures, set out to overturn the entire framework of post-Socratic philosophy by calling for a reinterpretation of Greek tragedy.[28] While Hegel had foregrounded the truth-content of art,[29] Nietzsche questions this orientation. With his emphasis on the myth-carrying and ecstatic power of tragedy, he is interested in how tragedy, and especially its musical components, creates an ecstatic experience; it "transfigure[s] a region where dissonance and the terrible image of the world fade away in chords of delight" (BT 115; KSA 154).[30]

The Birth of Tragedy is a treatise on the origin of Greek drama. Yet it is also, at least when read against the background of the tradition from Lessing and Herder to Hegel, about the possibility of a living modern theater and, by implication, a living modern art. If, as Nietzsche suggests, the demise of

[26] It is, however, fair to say that Herder never had a good grasp on French tragedy, nor on the classicist theoreticians; it seems like his criticism is geared toward their German acolytes, but even his discussion of German classicism is often exaggerated and polemical.

[27] Nietzsche deliberately places himself within the German discourse of theater, as it stretched back to Lessing and Herder. See BT 58, 73: KSA I 80, 99. See also David Kornhaber, *The Birth of Theater from the Spirit of Philosophy: Nietzsche and the Modern Drama* (Evanston: Northwestern University Press, 2016). In fact, Nietzsche's initial plans for *The Birth of Tragedy* had not only included ample discussions of the ancients but also of Shakespeare, whose work, we have seen, featured centrally in the German discussion of modern theater. For Nietzsche's interest in Shakespeare, see Duncan Large, "Nietzsche's Shakespearean Figures," in *Why Nietzsche Still? Reflections on Drama, Culture, and Politics*, ed. Alan D. Schrift (Berkeley: University of California Press, 2000), 47. See also Katie Brennan, "Nietzsche's Shakespeare: Musicality and Historicity in *The Birth of Tragedy*," *Memoria di Shakespeare*, vol. 1 (2014): 109–128, and "Nietzsche's Hamlet Puzzle: Life Affirmation in *The Birth of Tragedy*," in *The Routledge Companion to Shakespeare and Philosophy*, ed. Craig Bourne and Emily Caddick Bourne (London: Routledge, 2019), 398–408.

[28] Excepting his propensity to visionary dreams, Socrates, and with him later philosophy, appears to Nietzsche as a "negative force . . . [driving toward] the disintegration of Dionysiac tragedy" (BT 71; KSA I 96).

[29] For Hegel's discussion of truth in art, see for example LFA 8; HW XIII 21–22.

[30] Moi offers an interesting discussion of the presence of these Greek gods in *Emperor and Galilean*. See *Henrik Ibsen and the Birth of Modernism*, 196–197. In my view, what is of interest here is not the presence of these gods, per se, but rather Julian's reflections on the old culture's emphasis on life affirmation.

tragedy is the demise of myth (BT 110; KSA I 148), then philosophers need to raise the question whether we moderns can at all find a way to retrieve the (mythical) power of art. Tragedy is not characterized by its search for cognition of the didactic or reflective kind—this, rather, would be the "Socraticism of science."[31] For Nietzsche, tragedy evokes a Dionysiac experience so fundamental and existentially profound that the Greek actors had to shield themselves with masks: "the Apolline quality of the mask is the necessary result of gazing into the inner, terrible depths of nature—radiant patches, as it were, to heal a gaze seared by gruesome night" (BT 46; KSA I 65). Powerful as it is, this experience is not exclusive to the chorus, but is shared by chorus and audiences alike; in the experience of tragedy, chorus and audiences are united in affirmatively confronting the ultimate conditions of life.

In Nietzsche's interpretation, tragedy at its best offers a balance between Dionysiac forces, which abolish individuation and create an equilibrium between music, chorus, actors, and audience, and the Apollonian drive toward clarity and individuation. In his words, "the difficult relationship of the Apolline and the Dionysiac in tragedy truly could be symbolized by a bond of brotherhood between the two deities: Dionysus speaks the language of Apollo, but finally it is Apollo who speaks that of Dionysus. At which point the supreme goal of tragedy, and indeed of all art [*Kunst überhaupt*], is attained" (BT 104; KSA I 140). Nietzsche asks whether this kind of tragedy can be reborn in Germany—especially from Wagnerian opera.[32] But he also conveys the hope that we moderns will be able to produce a new kind of drama, one that can present us, in a way that suits our modern sensitivities, with insights of an equally groundbreaking character. This, he suggests (in a Schopenhauerian spirit), would involve a performance that unites actors and

---

[31] As Nietzsche argues, the Socratic spirit eventually gains the upper hand and transforms tragedy into an object of reflection, thus abandoning its existential-mythological nature and lifeline. Both Hegel and Nietzsche see Euripides in this way. See for example LFA 1228; HW XV 562 and BT 83–84; KSA I 113.

[32] I have in mind Nietzsche's infamous declaration that the great champions of art need "a mythical home . . . a bringing back of all things German!" As he elaborates: "And if the German should look around with faint heart for a leader to take him back to his long-lost home, whose paths and highways he hardly remembers, then let him but listen to the blissfully enticing call of the Dionysiac bird [referring, probably, to the bird leading Siegfried to Brünhilde] which is on the wing, hovering above his head, and which wants to show him the way" (BT 111; KSA I 149). However, as his correspondence with Brandes makes clear, Nietzsche is soon disillusioned with the Germans. He characterizes himself as "very German" (in quotation marks, letter of December 2, 1887), but also proclaims, in *Ecce Homo*, that nobody comes worse off than the Germans (letter of November 20, 1888). See Brandes, *Friedrich Nietzsche*, 64 and 94; Brief an Georg Brandes, http://www.nietzschesource.org/#eKGWB/BVN-1888,1151 and http://www.nietzschesource.org/#eKGWB/BVN-1888,1151 (Accessed July 2018).

audiences in an experience that transcends the everyday, eclipsing, if only in passing, the suffering that originates from individualized existence.

Although Nietzsche soon abandons his hope that Wagner's operas can facilitate such artistic relief, he nonetheless keeps open the possibility of an adequate, modern work of art, perhaps emerging hand in hand with a trans-formation of philosophy and life.[33] Thus he significantly ends his attempts at self-criticism, added to *The Birth of Tragedy* in 1886, with a reference to his own Zarathustra, who, in his ability to laugh at the truth, incarnates the Dionysiac spirit (BT 12; KSA I 22).

In sketching this Nietzschean framework, I am not suggesting that Ibsen is a Nietzschean dramatist in a strict meaning of the term. Just as it was the case with Hegel, the point is not to read Ibsen's work in terms of allusions or references to philosophical ideas. *Ghosts,* as I see it, is in no way a program-matic declaration of Nietzscheanism. The question, rather, is how Ibsen, for his own dramatic purposes, draws on and transforms the artistic framework that Nietzsche's philosophy facilitates. According to Nietzsche, classical Greek tragedy does not focus on the ethical self-knowledge or truthfulness of the characters.[34] Instead, it is the energetic dimension that allows for up-lifting life-affirmation, even in the face of tragic truth. At stake, therefore, is a focus on the theatrical *experience*.[35] From this point of view, an exclusive emphasis on Mrs. Alving's self-knowledge is too limited.

Beyond the Classical

If, in a Nietzschean spirit, we want to avoid a reading of *Ghosts* in terms of the characters' pursuit of self-knowledge, we must ask how Ibsen engages the experiential aspects of drama that Nietzsche had brought into philosophical focus. To address this issue, we need to look, in more detail, at how Ibsen restructures the tightly knit panoply of characters, the unity of time, and

[33] For a study of Nietzsche's life and work as literature, see Nehamas, *Life as Literature*, in particular 200–234.

[34] For Nietzsche's critique of morality, as it springs out of Socratic optimism, see for example BT 70–71; KSA I 95–96).

[35] Constanze Güthenke traces an orientation toward the hermeneutic (re)experience of the Greeks in the classicist (philological) tradition leading up to Nietzsche. See her *Studying Antiquity in Nineteenth-Century Germany: Classical Scholarship and the Language of Attachment, 1790–1920* (Cambridge: Cambridge University Press, 2020).

the unity of place—i.e., the key elements of the classicist model with which Nietzsche sought to break.

The creation of good dramatic characters, enhancing the plot, is central to classical poetics.[36] In *Ghosts*, a strongly developed gallery of characters structures the plot from the outset. At the center hover the parallel parent–child relationships of, on the one hand, Helene and Oswald Alving, and, on the other, of Jakob and Regine Engstrand. In spite of a notable difference in background and class—Mrs. Alving is the widow of the Captain and the description of her home suggests that she is well-off; Engstrand is a carpenter of limited means[37]—both parents have lost their former spouses and are seeking a belated acknowledgment from their offspring. Both Mrs. Alving's son and Engstrand's daughter grew up with foster parents (though, in Engstrand's case, he saved Regine's mother from disgrace). In both cases, the acknowledgment asked for would also involve a reconciliation of the difficult parent–child relationship around which the drama evolves.

For the Alvings as well as the Engstrands, the desire for reconciliation takes the form of home-making.[38] Mrs. Alving' wants to rid herself of Captain Alving's dowry by building the orphanage (the uninsured building that burns down in Act Two, making the Pastor exclaim "*this* is a burning punishment [*straffedommen*] on this house of iniquity" [OI V 405; VII 494, trans. modified]). Engstrand, for his part, plans to create a home for retired

[36] Aristotle had insisted on the need for the characters to be better than average. See Aristotle, *Poetics*, trans. Gerald F. Else (Ann Arbor: University of Michigan Press, 1970), 43–44. The question of characters (their status and their unity) is one of the points that is frequently discussed in the German eighteenth-century debate on Shakespeare—and that Voltaire already had brought to the foreground in his 1729 *Letters*. See Voltaire, *Philosophical Letters: Or, Letters Regarding the English Nation*, ed. John Leigh, trans. Prudence L. Steiner (Indianapolis: Hackett, 2007), 69–70; *Lettres philosophique, Les oeuvres complètes de Voltaire* (Geneve: Institut et Musee Voltaire, Geneve and University of Toronto Press, 1969), vol. 6B, 59. See also Herder, *Shakespeare*, 29–30 and 32; *Werke* II 508–509. For a helpful account of the way in which, in Aristotle's view, the characters ought to be "better than present humanity," see Stephen Halliwell, *Aristotle's Poetics* (Chicago: University of Chicago Press, 1998), 166.

[37] In the Norwegian original, this shines through the descriptions of Engstrand's physical character (OI V 291; HIS VII), his manners, and way of speaking, which are contrasted with his daughter Regine's attempts at covering up her class background with the use of sophisticated French phrases (expressing the hope, it turns out, that Oswald will take her to Paris). Upon realizing that Mr. Alving is her father, Regine bluntly declares: "I think you might have brought me up like a gentleman's daughter, Mrs. Alving. It would have suited me a bit better than this. [*Tosses her head.*] Still, what the hell . . . ! What difference does it make! [*With a bitter glance at the unopened bottle.*] I'll be drinking champagne with the best yet, you see if I'm not" (OI V 415; HIS VII 512).

[38] This topic is later explored in *The Master Builder*, as well as *When We Dead Awaken*. In both cases, Ibsen draws a distinction between a home (*hjem*) and a house (*hus*).

sailors—a project he wants to name after the deceased Captain.[39] Neither Oswald nor Regine invests much in these surrogate homes. Nor do they warm up to their parents' attempts at reconciliation.[40] In fact, Oswald and Regine appear to need their parents only to the extent that they can assist in the effort to escape from the family to which, in each case, they never fully belonged.[41] Regine has been fantasizing about Oswald taking her to Paris but, upon realizing that such travel plans are impeded by his illness, she quickly announces her departure: "If I'd known Oswald had something wrong with him . . . And anyway, now that there can never be anything serious between us . . . No, you don't catch me staying out here in the country, working myself to death looking after invalids" (OI V 414; HIS VII 511). Being turned down by Regine—who assures them that she has "got some of this joy of life as well" (OI V 414; HIS VII 511)—Oswald depends on his mother to end his life when the illness becomes unbearable.[42]

On the face of it, the stunted families of the Alvings and the Engstrands are orchestrated by Pastor Manders and his tiresome sense of etiquette. Pastor Manders's repeated references to an anonymous third person, the "one" or "the they ["man" in Ibsen's original]," echoes Torvald Helmer's care for his public image.[43] As God's representative on earth, Pastor Manders is pushing for confessions, allocating forgiveness, teaching parents how to parent and children how to be sons and daughters. Yet his authority is shallow and his values increasingly porous. Eventually, the Pastor proves irrelevant and leaves with Engstrand to work on the promised Captain Alving Home (OI V 410; HIS VII 503).

[39] The Pastor eventually gives his blessing to the home when Engstrand offers to take the blame for the fire that, it turns out, was caused by the Pastor's throwing a snuffed candle into a pile of wood shavings (OI V 407–408; HIS VII 498).

[40] When realizing that Engstrand is not her true father, Regine condescendingly denounces him as "that rotten old carpenter" (OI V 414; HIS VII 512).

[41] As Oswald comments: "Everything will burn. There'll be nothing left to remind people of Father. And here am I, burning down too" (OI V 411; HIS VII 504). The metaphor of burning also figures prominently in Hedda Gabler and The Master Builder.

[42] Oswald refers to Regine's forthrightness, telling his mother "Regine would have done it [i.e., assisted with his suicide]. Regine was so marvelously light-hearted. And she'd soon have got bored with looking after an invalid like me" (OI V 420; HIS VII 162).

[43] See, for example, Pastor Manders's insistence that although politically radical literature and magazines can be read, "one doesn't talk about it. . . . One doesn't have to account to all and sundry for what one reads and thinks in the privacy of one's own room [indenfor sine fire vægge]" (OI V 360; HIS VII 407). Likewise, Mrs. Alving responds that his assumption that it was good for her to stay in her marriage is "simply taking it for granted that popular opinion is right [så støtter De Dem sådan uden videre til den almindelige gængse mening]" (OI V 374; HIS VII 433). This topic—that of popular opinion—is already touched upon in A Doll's House, but gets systematically explored in An Enemy of the People, published a year after Ghosts.

As Pastor Manders fades, however, we see the emergence of the dead Captain Alving, the ghost. The remaining four (or five) characters gather around a center that, while no longer there, is nonetheless all-present. It is by exposing their relationship to the deceased Captain Alving that the characters go through a process of self-examination. Captain Alving, the dead character around whose legacy the drama revolves, still pulls at the strings of the living. Ibsen further explores this topic in *Rosmersholm, Hedda Gabler, The Master Builder*, and *Little Eyolf*. The acutely felt absence of the Captain adds an eerie feeling to the drama; it discloses a void that is not simply that of Mrs. Alving or Oswald, but one that no one is entirely protected against. The audience would have to be existentially tone-deaf not to take part in this shared experience: that of being descendants and family members, of living with losses and coming to terms with the past. In this sense, the deceased Captain Alving adds a dialectics of presence and absence that reaches beyond the fictional characters and includes the audience, whether implied or actual. The ghost is not only that of Helene and Oswald Alving but a dimension of human life we all have to live with.

This, it seems, is Ibsen's version of the classical assemblage of characters. In *Ghosts*, we encounter a character gallery as tight and simple as can be, yet in its simplicity, it harbors death, impurity, and shame.[44] Further, what drives the plot forward is not only the presence of the characters, but also the absence of the Captain. It only adds to the complexity of Ibsen's work that the metaphor of the ghost (especially Hamlet's ghost) had been a central element in Lessing and the *Sturm und Drang* philosophers' attempt to liberate themselves from the predominance of classicist aesthetics (see Chapter 1).

At a first glance, *Ghosts* adheres to the unity of place.[45] The play opens with a dialogue between Regine and her father in Mrs. Alving's sunroom (and the adjacent living room), which marks the entrance to the house and the transition from interior to exterior and vice versa. The indoor-outdoor space of the sunroom is a perfect backdrop for a drama about the hardship—or even impossibility—of being fully and completely at home (since the home is also the site of the *Ur*-drama of parents, children, and the troublesome, yet much needed, bonds of nurturing and care). There are references to Paris and a

[44] In his reading of *Rosmersholm*, Freud famously points out how Ibsen thematizes the incest taboo. See Sigmund Freud, "Some Character-Types Met with in Psycho-Analytic Work" (1916), *Penguin Freud Library*, vol. 14, *Art and Literature*, trans. James Strachey (London: Penguin, 1985), 308–316. Freud does not discuss *Ghosts* in his study.
[45] As Aristotle points out: "in the case of tragedy it is not possible to represent many different parts of the action as of the time they are performed but only the part on the stage." *Poetics*, 64.

nameless town that can only be reached by boat. Though we hear about the orphanage and the retirement home for the sailors, the preceding acts take place in the same location.[46]

In classical poetics, the unity of place was intended to create an orderly backdrop against which the tragic action could obtain contours and gravity. Throughout Ibsen's play, the sunroom offers such a unity, and the changing light reflects the increasingly gloomy mindsets of the characters and the dysfunctionality of their exchanges. Yet, the space does not only present a background to the action. It is indeed unclear whether the characters need a unified space to emerge from or if it is, rather, the characters that create a certain *locus* in the drama. Of special importance is, again, the role of the dead Captain. The very idea of a ghost—in Ibsen's original the word used is not "ghost (spøkelse)," but *genganger* (as in the German *Wiedergänger*)— presupposes a place to which the spirit of the dead can return so as to haunt the living. A *genganger* does not venture to explore new places. It is place-bound, revealing itself to whomever occupies the venue. In *Ghosts*, the unity of the place is thus no simple continuum against which the action is played out but, indeed, a condition for action to take place: without a location to haunt, there can be no *gengangere*. This is even more so as the dead Captain Alving's ever-stronger presence temporally corresponds to the passing of the day and the emerging darkness. Ghosts, we know, do not appear in broad daylight. And in the play, the fading day is expressive of a claustro-phobic atmosphere in which the four individuals (five, if we include Pastor Manders and the way his life was shaped by his unrecognized love for Mrs. Alving) passively emerge as products of a past no longer subject to change or reparation.[47]

As the play proceeds, the unhealthy relationships of the Captain get increasingly foregrounded. The past plays, as it were, a significant part in the drama; it consumes more and more space until there is no oxygen left for

---

[46] As the second act opens, we are presented with "*The same room. A heavy mist still lies over the landscape*" (OI V 379; HIS VII 443). Likewise Act Three opens with the following instructions: "*The room as before. All the doors are standing open*" (OI V 406; HIS VII 495).

[47] Needless to say, Oswald's illness is neither a matter of free will nor of a tragic flaw. This was pointed out in Peter Hansen's contemporary review of *Ghosts* and was read as a naturalist impulse that undermined the tragic format of the play. However, as far as the Oswald character goes, his imminent death does not occasion reflection to the same extent as Mrs. Alving's past. In this sense, Oswald's impending death drives the plot in that it contributes to Mrs. Alving's tragedy—and her tragedy is indeed a result of choices made (or not made) and a life only half lived. See Hansen's review in *Illustreret Tidende* i København 8. januar 1882, http://ibsen.nb.no/id/400.0 (Accessed July 1, 2019). For a discussion of Peter Hansen's review, see Ivo de Figueiredo, *Henrik Ibsen. Masken* (Oslo: Aschehoug, 2007), 235–236.

breathing, no future, and thus no possible ending save that of madness and death. The increasing sense of being closed in materializes, for instance, in the following exchange between Mrs. Alving and Oswald:

OSWALD. Don't leave me! Where are you going?
MRS. ALVING [*in the hall*]. To fetch the doctor, Oswald! Let me get out!
OSWALD [*also in the hall*]. You are not getting out. And nobody's getting in.
    (OI V 420; HIS VII 523)

Not only does Oswald want to bind his mother to his plan for assisted suicide. Moreover, Mrs. Alving's motherly love borders on the incestuous ("I haven't made you completely mine yet—I must still win you [jeg *har* dig ikke; du må vindes]" [OI V 416; HIS VII 158]). Soon, though, she is presented with the brutal truth that Oswald might become child-like and thus perversely again be hers: "struck down by this ghastly thing, lying there helpless, like an imbecile child, beyond all hope of recovery," as he puts it (OI V 420; HIS VII 522).

Upon realizing the truth about himself, Oedipus blinds himself, but keeps living. Caring for her syphilitic son, a similarly pitiful existence is awaiting Mrs. Alving, as she is doomed to administer the morphine that will end her son's life *and* to live with the knowledge that she helped her son end his life. In fact, Mrs. Alving only reaches her sick, parental goal of owning Oswald completely—of there being "nobody else here but my son and his mother" (OI V 378; HIS VII 441)—when he is no longer there. Her impossible battle is won the very moment all is lost.[48] At this point, her space, her home on the stage (to borrow Nicholas Green's metaphor), is no longer the one she had sought to build and protect. It is but an existential coffin—in an emphatic sense, a *non*-place.

Finally, the unity of time, another trademark of classical tragedy, is both carefully observed and transformed in *Ghosts*. Marked through changes in weather and light, the play lasts from morning and into the evening. Act Three is introduced with the following temporal clues: "*It is dark outside, apart from a faint glow in the background, left*" (OI V 406; HIS VII 148). Darkness sets the stage for the last act's enlightenment, the revelation of the lies through which Oswald and Regine, the son and daughter, have understood themselves. Oswald learns that his "father was a broken man before

---

[48] The topic of excessive parental love resounds in *John Gabriel Borkman*, where Erhard is forced to choose between his mother and his aunt (who raised him), both of whom demand his undivided love.

[he was] even born" (OI V 413; HIS VII 509), and Regine is presented with the truth that she "belonged here in this house . . . just as much as [Oswald]" (OI V 413; HIS VII 509). Moreover, the darkness is needed for the utterly crushing ending in which Oswald, having seen the truth about his father, his mother, and himself, realizes that he is about to drift into madness and asks his mother to give him the twelve morphine pills he has stored up (OI V 419; HIS VII 521), only to decline so rapidly that he, still perched in the sunroom and its evening dark, "sits motionless as before" and repeatedly mutters "The sun . . . The sun" (OI V 422; HIS VII 525). (This, as we saw in the Introduction, later gave rise to Edvard Munch's famous painting for the University of Oslo [see color plate 2]). It is a wry, but philosophically significant fact that he has demanded that his mother, while helping him end his life, remain "cheerful" (OI V 416; HIS VII 515).

In terms of its timespan, the harrowing hours that are played out in *Ghosts* are only meaningful against the background of lives already lived, or rather lives that are lived poorly. Further, Mrs. Alving's self-understanding is, at least in Act One, contrasted with Pastor Manders and his hollow references to the authority of the tradition (in the form of an anonymous "one" or "they").[49] To Mrs. Alving, all that is passed down appears to be potentially ghostly. Tradition is taken as true without really being examined and, as such, it gains a subconscious grip on us:

MRS. ALVING. Ghosts. When I heard Regine and Oswald in there, it was just like seeing ghosts. But then I'm inclined to think that we are all ghosts, Pastor Manders, every one of us. It's not just what we inherit from our mothers and fathers that haunts us. It's all kinds of old defunct theories, all sorts of old defunct beliefs, and things like that. It's not that they actually *live* on in us; they are simply lodged there, and we cannot get rid of them. I've only to pick up a newspaper and I seem to see ghosts gliding between the lines. Over the whole country there must be ghosts, as numerous as the sands of the sea. And here we are, all of us, abysmally afraid of the light. (OI V 384; HIS VII 453)

---

[49] Pastor Manders's references to a faceless "the they" peaks as he, having been quick to judge the fire in the orphanage a punishment on the Alvings, realizes that it was not God but he himself who started it. However, he only worries about his reputation and position. Responding to Engstrand's remark that "the papers are [not] going to let [him] off very lightly," the Pastor admits to his fears: "No, that's just what I am thinking. That's just about the worst part of the whole affair" (OI V 408; HIS VII 499).

Ghosts inhabit the time of the living, yet their existence is atemporal: they return to a world that is ever-different, yet they remain beyond time, an existence entombed. Hence the timeframe of *Ghosts* is the time of the drama, the time (lives) of its characters, *and* the spooky temporal mode of a past never redeemed, of histories petrified, and traditions deprived of life, yet clearly influencing the living.[50] To some extent, we have to wonder if this might not be the time in which we all live. When the curtains fall, the audience leaves the theater in the awareness that Mrs. Alving will have to live with the consequences of her decision and that they, too, will have to cope with the way in which the past shapes and gives structure to the horizon of the present. In this way, the traditional unity of time is challenged in Ibsen's drama.

Through his dramatic interventions, Ibsen brings to life an artform, that of ancient tragedy, that could otherwise be seen as dead and stifling. By leaning on *and* subverting a traditional demand for form and structure—the very same elements that, upon the premiere of *Ghosts*, were used to defend the play against its critics[51]—Ibsen grapples with the ghosts of his trade. Along Nietzschean lines, his drama, further, is one that revolves around the experiential synthesis of work and audience. In Ibsen's work there is no chorus and music that elevate performers and audiences into a higher unity. Nonetheless the play facilitates a merging of existential horizons in the confrontation with a truth no less shattering than the one Nietzsche ascribes to Greek tragedy.

Tradition in Question

Tragedy, Nietzsche claims, presents us with the ultimate conditions of human existence, but also with a life-affirming ability that, at the end of the day, remains at the heart of human culture. As such, tragedy provides existential sustenance, to borrow a phrase from Andrew Huddleston's recent study.[52]

---

[50] In fact, one could say that Mrs. Alving's "tragic flaw" is not a particular character trait or action but a series of actions that, passively guided by traditional expectations, leads to her present predicament. No gods are involved in her case: only the overwhelming influence of a past that remains unaddressed and unchallenged, thus threatening her agency at the deepest level. I thank Lydia Moland for this point.

[51] For a discussion of this point, see de Figueiredo, *Henrik Ibsen. Masken*, 234–240. See also Øystein Rottem, "'Den antike tragedie, gjenopstaaet paa moderne jord': et notat om skjebnesynet i Henrik Ibsens *Gengangere*," *Edda*, vol. 91, no. 4 (1991): 345–358.

[52] Andrew Huddleston, *Nietzsche on the Decadence and Flourishing of Culture* (Oxford: Oxford University Press, 2019).

Such sustenance, Nietzsche argues, is best expressed as an ability to celebrate life in the face of human suffering. In making this claim, though, Nietzsche faces a hermeneutic problem. His own culture, he fears, is no longer able to see the need for tragic affirmation. In its pragmatic orientation, modern culture fails to acknowledge that human beings have needs beyond those of profit and mastery of nature. For Nietzsche, these needs are not "optional" or "extra," but fundamental to human existence. From this point of view, his 1872 work offers a historical account of the birth of tragedy in music, but also endeavors to shake the reader out of a mindset that, in Nietzsche's view, has caused the marginalization of art in modern culture.

The Birth of Tragedy is not only a book about art, but also a call for the return to a culture in which art, and especially tragedy, can play a fundamental role. From this point of view, it serves a critical function. Nietzsche wants his readers to reflect on the existential possibilities their culture facilitates; he wants his readers to assess the extent to which their pursuits can serve to further life. Yet he worries about the effect of reflection on art. He traces the marginalization of art back to Socrates and the Socratic spirit. This spirit, however, emerges out of tragedy itself, in particular Euripides' work. With its increasing number of actors and an ever-stronger emphasis on the dialogue, tragedy, in Nietzsche's view, becomes too rational. Music plays a smaller role and the individual actors—their points of view, their reflections—are foregrounded. With Euripides, tragedy reaches a state in which it is barely itself. In Nietzsche's judgment, "Euripides brought the spectator on to stage and thus made him capable of judging drama for the first time" (BT 57; KSA I 78). Euripides, in Nietzsche's view, potentially objectivizes art and turns it into something that is assessed rather than experienced—an attitude that he, with a blatantly ahistorical gesture, addresses as "bourgeois mediocrity" (BT 56; KSA I 77). In this way, Socrates' rationalist credo enforces a larger, historical-philosophical trend, and Nietzsche even speaks of his own culture as being Socratic (BT 71; KSA I 97, see also "Sokrates und die Tragödie," KSA I 533–549).

Yet, in seeking to evoke reflection on modern culture, Nietzsche makes use of a Socratic strategy. His genealogy of tragedy is indeed a philosophical maieutic: By presenting the philosophical truth of tragedy, it also strives to create the right conditions for this truth to be heard, understood, and, yet again, be taken as fundamental to its own time.

With his realist drama, Ibsen faces a similar hermeneutic challenge. His work, too, needs to create the conditions for its own reception. That is,

Ibsen produces a contemporary drama, while also seeking to establish the conditions of possibility of its genuine reception. In this sense, his drama, like Nietzsche's work, is maieutic—and by returning to Munch's sketch of Ibsen, Nietzsche, and Socrates (see the Introduction), it could be suggested that Socrates indeed deserves a place in the picture.

Ibsen, though, tackles the hermeneutic challenge of establishing the conditions of reception for his own kind of drama in a distinctively non-Nietzschean way. He lets his characters openly reflect on their backgrounds, cultural conditions, and frameworks of understanding. One example of this is, to refer back to Chapter 4, Nora's questioning of her education. As a character, Nora plays up against, and thus demonstrates, the cultural biases that have limited her existential space. Her reference, in the final act's conversation with Helmer, to Pastor Hansen, is a case in point:

HELMER. [...] Haven't you an infallible guide in questions like these? Haven't you your religion?

NORA. Or, Torvald, I don't really know what religion is.

HELMER. What do you say!

NORA. All I know is what Pastor Hansen said when I was confirmed. He said religion was this, that and the other. When I am away from all this and on my own, I'll go into that, too. I want to find out whether what Pastor Hansen told me was right—or at least whether it is right for *me*. (OI V 281–283; HIS VII 371)

We encounter a similar situation in *Ghosts*. In this case, too, the clergy is present as a conservative force. Mrs. Alving—not Helene, which would be the equivalent to the imbalance in first and last names that features throughout *A Doll's House*[53]—is not only a wife, a mother, and a potential lover (to Pastor Manders), but also a reader. Indeed, as Bergman highlights in his last stage production,[54] we first encounter her as a reader. Further, when Monrad, the Hegelian, reviews *Ghosts*, one of the things that baffles him is, precisely, Helene Alving's reading of contemporary journals.[55] Indeed,

---

[53] In *Ghosts*, it is the younger generation, Regine and Oswald, which is addressed by first names.

[54] Törnqvist does not discuss this point, but covers the production in *The Serious Game*, 209–223. The accompanying DVD includes the opening of the play.

[55] In the original, Monrad's reflections are as follows: "Vi see her en fint og ædelt anlagt Kvinde, hos hvem man helst skulde antage, at en naturlig Sædelighedsfølelse vilde i det Længste gjøre Modstand mod alskens theoretiske Reflexioner, dog ved Læsning af de moderne Fritænker-Skrivter, hvis Lærdomme hun efterhaanden har tilegnet sig, tilsidst bragt saa vidt i moralsk Vilderede, at hun billiger baade den frie Kjærlighed og Blodskams-Forbindelser og Selvmord, kort sagt, Forbrydelser,

after the opening dialogue between Regine and Engstrand, we encounter Mrs. Alving's reading material before we encounter her, *and* we encounter it through the Pastor's dissatisfied response. As for the transition from the Regine–Engstrand exchange to the initial dialogue between Pastor Manders and Mrs. Alving, Ibsen's directions are as follows:

> REGINE *goes out, left.* PASTOR MANDERS *walks up and down the room a few times, stands at the back of the room for a moment with his hands clasped behind his back, looking out at the garden. Then he again comes back near the table, picks up a book and looks at the title page; he gives a start and looks at several more.* (OI V 357; HIS VII 402)

Ibsen emphasizes the Pastor's bewilderment, having him mutter "H'm! Indeed!" (OI V 357; HIS VII 402). The Pastor clearly does not like what he sees, and the audience, even before Mrs. Alving emerges, will know that she is an educated woman (she reads) and that she is independent-minded (what she reads is controversial). For an audience of a Nietzschean disposition, it is clear that Mrs. Alving shares the philosopher's suspicion toward priests and Christian clergy more broadly.[56] Mrs. Alving's reflections on guilt, repression, and the demands of a "proper" life—and her gradual taking over of Oswald's call for (artistic) life-affirmation—express a similar spirit.

Ibsen's polemical image of the Pastor has sometimes been explained biographically. The portrait of the narrow-minded clergy was supposed to revenge the fact that his son was not accepted to study in Norway without first taking the mandatory entrance exams that Ibsen deemed unnecessary.[57] However, the introduction to the relevant volume of *Henrik Ibsen's Writings*

som det sædelige Samfund betragter med den største Afsky og gjør Alt for at hindre og straffe." https://web.archive.org/web/20170630093223/http://ibsen.nb.no/id/11192753.0 (Accessed June 2019).

[56] As Nietzsche sees it, Christianity presents a worldview that distinctively contrasts with that of the Greeks. Its teaching is that of guilt and sin, not of affirmation. The teaching of priests had been critiqued, and contrasted to truth, since a letter of 1864 and later on we find the contrast, even in Greek culture, between what Nietzsche calls "the reading priests" and musical tragedy. (See eKGWB/BVN-1867, 540, "Brief AN Carl von Gersdorff, 06/04/1867.") In his essay on David Strauß, priests, again are thoroughly criticized. ("David Strauß, the Confessor and the Writer," in *Untimely Meditations*, ed. Daniel Breazeale, trans. R. J. Hollingdale [Cambridge: Cambridge University Press, 1999], 1–57; KGA I 157–143.) Later, in *The Genealogy of Morality*, we encounter a fully developed attack on the ascetic priests, a tracing of philosophy back to their world-denying attitudes, and a whole treatise (the third treatise) launching a critique of priestly life-denial. (*On the Genealogy of Morality*, trans. Maudemarie Clark and Alan J. Swensen [Indianapolis: Hackett, 1998], 82; KSA V 360.)

[57] Contributing to this is Ibsen's letter to his publisher, Hegel (October 25, 1880; HIS IX 63–64). See also Ibsen's letter to his brother-in-law March 9, 1881.

also mentions the possible influence of Hedwig Dohm (HIS VII/B 416). In her 1872 critique of the church's message to women, *Was die Pastoren von den Frauen Denken*, Dohm had used the metaphor of a ghost (*Gespenster*) that, in broad daylight, sought to control the living. The editors do not further expand on the importance of Dohm's work. But in the context of late nineteenth-century culture, the motif of a woman educating herself by way of controversial reading material represents a significant gesture.[58] Dohm's work offers a way to shed light on this.

Hedwig Dohm was a formidable writer and intellectual. She was part of a generation that had taken full benefit of the new and growing women readership that had emerged in the wake of the Enlightenment and early romantic salons.[59] She herself had written drama.[60] But she had also written perhaps the most powerful criticism there is of Nietzsche's philosophical treatment of women (and, by implication, of Salomé and Scandinavians such as Laura Marholm, who had defended Nietzsche). What distinguishes Dohm's essay is not just the humor and non-moralizing attitude with which she approaches Nietzsche's work. She clearly respects and borrows from Nietzsche—especially his will to question tradition and prejudices. Moreover, her critique of the pastors and their grip on women's lives is itself of a Nietzschean caliber. Yet she argues that, in his treatment of women, Nietzsche falls short of his critical spirit.[61] What is needed, she argues, is a will to take the Nietzschean critique beyond Nietzsche, and to do so precisely in order to question traditional ways to think about gender and family structure. It is, as she sees it, not only the pastors, but also the philosophers—including those who rage against the Church and traditional values—who need to be reeducated. Dohm, further, approaches the issue of gender equality by encouraging women, in a

---

[58] Ibsen's notes include the following reflection: "These women of the modern age, mistreated as daughters, as sisters, as wives, not educated in accordance with their talents, debarred from following their mission, depraved of their inheritance, embittered in mind—these are the ones who supply the mothers for the new generation. What will be the result?" (OI V 468, my trans.).

[59] For an account of the new women readership, as it emerges out of industrialization, and the abandoning of women to the home sphere, see Ursula I. Meyer (ed.), *Die Welt der Philosophin*. 3. Teilband. *Aufklärung und revolutionärer Aufbruch* (Aachen: ein-FACH Verlag, 1997), 11–71 and 195–267.

[60] For an overview of Hedwig Dohm's background and writing, see Birgit Mikus, *The Political Woman in Print: German Women's Writing 1845–1919* (Oxford: Peter Lang, 2014), 209–243.

[61] For Dohm's critique of Nietzsche, see "Nietzsche und die Frauen" in *Ausgewählte Texte*, ed. Nikola Müller and Isabel Rohner (Berlin: trafo, 2006), 124–136; "Nietzsche and Women," trans. Anna Ezekiel, in *Women Philosophers in the Long Nineteenth Century: The German Tradition*, ed. Dalia Nassar and Kristin Gjesdal (Oxford: Oxford University Press, forthcoming).

spirit later followed by Nora and Mrs. Alving, to "become who you are" (the Pindarian line that Nietzsche had endorsed).

In Mrs. Alving's self-discovery, her journals and books feature centrally and help her withstand the Pastor's pressure to have her conform to the existing, social norms:

PASTOR MANDERS. Good. Let's see then. . . . [*He goes over to the chair on which his satchel is lying, takes a sheaf of papers out of it, sits down at the opposite side of the table and looks for a clear space to put his papers down.*] First of all we have . . . [*Breaking off.*] Tell me, Mrs. Alving, how did *these* books get *here*?

MRS. ALVING. These books? They are books *I* am reading.

MANDERS. You read that sort of thing?

MRS. ALVING. Of course I do.

MANDERS. Do you think that sort of thing makes you feel any better, or any happier?

MRS. ALVING. I feel, as it were, more confident.

MANDERS. Strange. How?

MRS. ALVING. Well, I find it seems to explain and confirm a lot of the things I had been thinking myself. That's the strange thing, Pastor Manders . . . there's really nothing new in these books; there's nothing there but what most people think and believe already. It's just that most people either haven't really considered these things, or won't admit them.

MANDERS. Good God! Do you seriously believe that most people . . . ?

(OI V 359; HIS VII 404–405)

By reading, Mrs. Alving—whose ownership of the books is emphasized through Ibsen's use of italics throughout this exchange—does not feel that she is turned into something different. Rather, she becomes, to borrow Dohm's (Nietzschean-Pindarean) expression, herself. It is, she indicates, the very content of these books that makes it possible for her, as a woman, to confront the Pastor, whose moral righteousness permits him to snoop around in other people's books *and* judge books he has not himself read ("I have read sufficiently *about* these publications to disapprove of them," OI V 360; HIS VII 406, trans. modified). When Mrs. Alving does not budge, the Pastor encourages her to keep her reading private, i.e., to refrain from transforming the content of these books into a lesson that is applied beyond the walls of her home. Further, when Mrs. Alving, against the

Pastor's wish, sets out to become who she is, she wants to follow Oswald's philosophy of life-affirmation. Against stifling conventions and history gone stale, Mrs. Alving takes the side of the future. And it is precisely as a reader that she has put herself in this position—whether that be taken in the strongest sense (as causing her radical views) or in a weaker form (as supporting them).

In emphasizing Mrs. Alving as a modern reader—and, in this capacity, as someone who is ready to break with tradition and endorse the new—Ibsen frames the bleakness of the Alving tragedy in a more future-oriented spirit *and* a spirit that all the same draws on and goes beyond Nietzsche's philosophy. While Mrs. Alving's insights come too late for her to change the course of her own life and the events that have shaped it, the audience, having witnessed her process of agony and reflection, is invited to follow her critical pursuits. In presenting Mrs. Alving's belated transformation, *Ghosts*, in other words, can encourage a future transformation of the audience through books and reading. As opposed to what Monrad, the Hegelian, would argue, this is not a religious-didactical process (see HIS VII/ B 444–445 for a discussion of this point). Nor is it a question of self-knowledge, narrowly construed. Instead, Ibsen, through the character of Mrs. Alving, dissects conventionalist values and places a spotlight on the life-transforming force of art. If there is, as Ibsen had put it, no moral of the story, the play is nonetheless written to address the Mrs. Alvings of the world: readers and audiences who are ahead of their time and willing to question passively accepted dogma and tradition.

Modern Tragedy

Nietzsche discusses how tragedy and art can offer a source of life-affirmation. While he criticizes the reflective tendency of art—and of philosophy—he still produces a book that defends a new account of art *and* that seeks to encourage a kind of audience and readership that can appreciate tragedy (and philosophy) in the right way. Unlike Nietzsche, Ibsen does not purport to offer an account of art. Yet his work, too, invites reflection on a new kind of literature and a new kind of reader.

Some years after the publication of *The Birth of Tragedy*, Nietzsche rejects the Wagnerian-Schopenhauerian metaphysics of his earlier work. In a similar spirit, he criticizes its style. The work, as he puts it, is "from precocious, wet-behind-the-ears, personal experiences;" it is "badly written, clumsy, embarrassing"—in short, an "impossible book" (BT 5; KSA I 13). Yet, what bothers Nietzsche is not simply his youthful admiration for Wagner and Schopenhauer, but also the way he had approached Greek tragedy through the lens of modern art and philosophy. In his admiration of Wagner's music drama, he had catered, somewhat naïvely, to the possibility of an artform that reintroduces a Dionysiac element in modern culture (BT 11; KSA I 21). Nietzsche later fears that by approaching ancient Greek tragedy with modern (romantic) concerns, he had "*ruined* the grandiose *Greek problem*" (BT 10; KSA I 20). For romantic art, Nietzsche points out, is the "most un-Greek of all possible forms of art" (BT 10; KSA I 20).[62] At stake, for Nietzsche, is in other words not only a revised understanding of ancient Greek tragedy, but also of one's relationship to history.[63] The question, though, is whether this revised understanding is best articulated in philosophy or in art.

Ibsen's drama, too, addresses our relationship to history and tradition. He actively transforms and makes use of the forms of classical tragedy, thus rescuing them from a ghostly existence. Yet Ibsen's work—and this is particularly clear with Mrs. Alving's critical-enlightened reading—refuses to shelter mythology of the Nietzschean-Wagnerian kind. Indeed, to the extent that Ibsen's work can at all be said to present the audience with something resembling a chorus, so central to Nietzsche's reflections on the mythological aspects of tragedy, his version of a collective or collectivizing voice is the dried out, empty reference to "the they" that saturates the wretched Pastor Manders's appeal to tradition and convention. Instead, Ibsen, in *Ghosts*, explores our relationship to the past through a variety of individual viewpoints, positions taken, and life-choices made. Equally interesting, he explores the power of the past by way of the play's formal-dramatic dimensions, namely his take on the unity of characters, space, and time. The past, in this work, is represented by the dead Mr. Alving, but the past also permeates the world of the living— the characters in the play *and* the audience of the drama. For Mrs. Alving and Oswald, coming to grips with the past is an experience of existential terror

[62] In his correspondence with Brandes, though, Nietzsche claims that with his interest in music, he is not free of a romantic side: "I am afraid I am too much of a musician not to be romantic. Without music life, to me, would be a mistake" Letter of March 27, 1888. Brandes, *Friedrich Nietzsche*, 77; Brief an Georg Brandes http://www.nietzschesource.org/#eKGWB/BVN-1888,1009 (Accessed July 2018).

[63] As we have seen, this had been an aspect of Ibsen's drama from the very beginning. What makes *The Vikings at Helgeland* a historical play is not so much that it addresses history, but rather that it addresses a certain historical literature (the saga). What Ibsen centers on in this work is the protagonist's relationship to her past. The same can be said about *Catiline* and the characters of Furia and Catiline.

that undermines all didactic orientations.[64] Yet, along with the terrors she faces, Mrs. Alving, as a reader, glimpses the truth that Oswald had sought to live by: that of life-affirmation and joy. If this insight arrives too late for Mrs. Alving to change her life, it is not too late for Ibsen's audiences. Without adopting the mythological pathos of Nietzsche's philosophy, *Ghosts* discloses a space in which reflection on such values, past and present, can be had and new values can be generated. This topic will be further pursued in *An Enemy of the People*, a work that, while explicitly referencing education and educators, adds another layer to the Nietzschean dimension of Ibsen's drama.

[64] I thus resist George Steiner's reading of *Ghosts* and the cycle from *Pillars of Society* to *An Enemy of the People*, as being in the service of a "deliberate, intellectual purpose," namely those of the "pedagogue and reformer." It is, as I see it, this reading of the middle plays that forces Steiner to postulate an absolute break between Ibsen's realist period and his last symbolic plays. I briefly return to this point in my conclusion. For Steiner's reading, see George Steiner, *The Death of Tragedy* (New York: Knopf, 1961), 303–351, the quotes are from 290.

6

Teaching History (*An Enemy of the People*)

Ibsen touches on issues of education and educators in *Emperor and Galilean, Pillars of Society, A Doll's House,* and *Ghosts.* Written in the period between 1873 and 1881, each of these four plays centrally features the topic of learning: learning from history, from journals, from school, from art, from life, and, most importantly, learning from the intersections between these areas. It is as if Ibsen's drama demonstrates that only when these aspects of learning interrelate can we speak about education proper, and only with such education in view can we initiate a truly meaningful discussion of how history and tradition are best conveyed—whether in schools and universities or among readers and theater audiences. In Ibsen's plays, there is little patience for the existing educational institutions. Indeed, his characters indicate the need for a radical overhaul of the educational system, implying that such a move will facilitate far-reaching cultural change, including a more productive relationship to the past and tradition.

Ibsen's exploration of teaching and education culminates in *An Enemy of the People.* The play's main character, Dr. Stockmann, confronts his townspeople's unwillingness to consider facts and scientific discoveries and set aside short-sighted, selfish interests. He criticizes a public stuck in the ways of the past. The public, in his view, is incapable of independent thought. He thunders against groupthink and launches a series of hateful attacks on his fellow townspeople. On further reflection, though, he comes to ask how they have become so meek. At this point, he decides to join his daughter, Petra, as a schoolteacher.[1] While Mrs. Alving, in *Ghosts,* had been a self-educated reader, Petra is not only educated but also an educator. With his daughter, Dr. Stockmann stakes out a radical, educational reform—one that is designed to resist conformity and passive acceptance of the truths of the

---

[1] I do not agree with Van Laan's claim that "[i]n contrast to almost all the rest of Ibsen's last twelve plays, his major prose dramas of modern middle-class life, *An Enemy of the People* focuses our attention primarily upon a single character, scarcely asking us to feel any concern for the fate of anyone else." As I see it, the larger Stockmann family—including Stockmann's brother, wife, and daughter—significantly contribute to the play. See Thomas F. Van Laan, "Generic Complexity in Ibsen's *An Enemy of the People,*" *Comparative Drama,* vol. 20, no. 2 (1986): 99.

The Drama of History. Kristin Gjesdal, Oxford University Press (2021). © Oxford University Press.
DOI: 10.1093/oso/9780190070762.001.0001.

past. Dr. Stockmann and his daughter seek to educate children who are able to question the ruling consensus and are willing to confront the truth—even when it is inconvenient.

Like *The League of Youth*, *An Enemy of the People* was initially conceived of as a comedy (*lystspill*). After *Ghosts* had been banned in England and Germany,[2] Ibsen wanted this to be a play with a broader appeal (HIS VII/B 602). However, the broad appeal seems to rest with the one-dimensionality of the Stockmann character, the severity of his attacks, and the gap between his self-appointed moral righteousness and his increasingly battered outer appearance. The Doctor spares none; high and low—they are all subject to his scorn. In his rigidity, he is, no doubt, a comical figure.

While *An Enemy of the People* was initially a success, history later caught up with it.[3] Critics have worried about the political implications of Dr. Stockmann's contempt for the masses, a worry that is strengthened if we take into account the popularity of Ibsen's work in the National Socialist era.[4] The elitist sentiments that Ibsen has Dr. Stockmann air in *An Enemy of the People* have been associated with Nietzsche's celebration of the aristocratic individual. Among readers who approach the play in this way are Harald Noreng, Ivo de Figueiredo, and Atle Kittang.[5] Noreng and Kittang view Dr. Stockmann as a low and comical embodiment of Nietzschean thought and, as a consequence, *An Enemy of the People* as a work that ultimately mocks and transcends (rather than seriously engages with) Nietzschean ideas and concepts.[6] Figueiredo, on his side, sees Ibsen as a spokesman for potentially anti-democratic values and a Nietzschean advocacy of the "strong individual."[7] Given the Nietzschean commitments discussed in the previous chapter, both

[2] See Asbjørn Aarseth, *Peer Gynt and Ghosts: Text and Performance* (London: Macmillan Education, 1989), 99.

[3] Unlike the situation with *Ghosts*, several theaters were interested in *An Enemy of the People*. The play received positive reviews, including Marcus Jacob Monrad's article in *Morgenbladet* (January 14, 1883). Atle Kittang discusses the reception of the play in *Ibsens heroisme. Frå Brand til Når vi døde vågner* (Oslo: Gyldendal, 2002), 129. In the 1950s, the play reached further popularity with Arthur Miller's adaptation. For a discussion of the recent reception of *An Enemy of the People*, see Van Laan, "Generic Complexity in Ibsen's *An Enemy of the People*," 95–103.

[4] See Steven F. Sage, *Ibsen and Hitler: The Playwright, the Plagiarist, and the Plot for the Third Reich* (New York: Carroll & Graf Publishers, 2006), 3–5 and 310–311. See also Ferguson, *Henrik Ibsen*, 280–282.

[5] We find an earlier version of this argument in Anathon Aall, "Ibsen og Nietzsche," *Samtiden*, vol. 17, no. 3 (1906): 147–163.

[6] See Harald Noreng, "En folkefiende—helt eller klovn?" in *Ibsen på festspillscenen*, ed. Harald Noreng (Bergen, J.W. Eide Forlag, 1969), 15–27. See also Kittang, *Ibsens heroisme*, e.g., 167, 177.

[7] Figueiredo claims, for example, that "aristocratic radicalism is a quite plausible formulation [langt på vei en plausibel formidling] of the main points in Nietzsche's philosophy." Ivo de Figueiredo, *Henrik Ibsen. Masken*, 474 (my trans.). See also Kittang, *Ibsen's Heroisme*, 170.

of these approaches are limiting in that they fail to ask whether Nietzsche's work—and its reception in Scandinavian nineteenth-century culture—can be reduced to a plain (or even simplistic) idea of elitism. While it is obvious that Nietzsche's philosophy has an elitist dimension, we should also take into account how his early work contains profound reflections on education. In conveying a commitment to a broader humanity (which is different from conventional humanism), this part of Nietzsche's work, while far from unproblematic, still points beyond a narrow or plain conception of elitism.[8] Moreover, for Nietzsche, education is intrinsically linked up with the way we relate to history. It is via education—and the work of individual educators—that we can free ourselves from the oppressive aspects of tradition (with Ibsen: the ghosts of the past) and make productive use of history to form a vision for the future.

In this spirit, the present chapter seeks to explicate, with reference to *An Enemy of the People*, how Ibsen relates to the Nietzschean commitment to *Bildung* in history and the human flourishing it seeks to enable. It shows how Ibsen takes up a largely Nietzschean ideal of education, but also demonstrates how he, beyond Nietzsche's early contribution, views modern, realist drama as central to the realization of this ideal.

Individual Greed, Placid Consensus

Ibsen started working on *An Enemy of the People* just a year after *A Doll's House* had been published (letter of March 22, 1881; HIS XIV 76). The play, however, was set aside in order to write *Ghosts* (letter of November 23, 1881; HIS XIV 96). While Ibsen had initially envisioned four acts, he ended up with five. Unlike *Ghosts*, a work that draws on and expands the classical unity of time and place, *An Enemy of the People* is situated in a number of different locations: Dr. Stockmann's living room, the newspaper office, the hall of the public meeting, and Dr. Stockmann's study. The venue is an unspecified town on the southern coast of Norway. There are eleven named characters and a large group of townspeople that is reminiscent of the mass gatherings in the early, historical works. The play premiered at the Christiania Theater in 1883.

---

[8] For a recent account of these aspects of Nietzsche's work, see Huddleston, *Nietzsche on the Decadence and Flourishing of Culture*. For a discussion of Nietzsche on education, see also Joshua Billings, forthcoming in "Nietzsche's Philology of the Present," *New Literary History*.

At the opening of *An Enemy of the People,* Dr. Stockmann is about to make a discovery that will shake his coastal hometown to its core. The baths that support the town's economy appear to be contaminated by residues from local tanneries and pose a risk to the convalescents. As Stockmann sums it up, "[t]he whole establishment is a whited poisoned sepulchre" (OI VI 38; HIS VII 559). The sick that come to be cured are in reality getting sicker.[9] Sensing the threat to the town's financial foundation, his brother Peter, the Mayor of the town, tries to stop Dr. Stockmann from going public with his findings. When Dr. Stockmann refuses to listen, the Mayor turns popular opinion against him by questioning his brother's motivation, if not also his sanity. When the Mayor engages in a dialogue with the newspaper printer, Aslaksen, who is about to realize how much it would cost to add a new pipe system to the Baths, their conversation develops as follows:

ASLAKSEN. [. . .] What would people like us live on in the meantime?

MAYOR. I regret to say that is an extremely difficult question to answer, Mr. Aslaksen. But what do you expect us to do? Do you think anybody is coming here if you get people going round making up these stories about the water being polluted, and about the place being a cesspool, and the whole town . . .

ASLAKSEN. Do you think the whole thing might just be imagination?

MAYOR. With the best will in the world, I cannot come to any other conclusion. (OI VI 78; HIS VII 559)

Unable to convince his peers of the pollution, Dr. Stockmann calls a town hall meeting. The audience, however, is reluctant to let him speak. The increasingly frustrated Doctor cannot be stopped. The play reaches its dramatic peak when Dr. Stockmann, utterly disillusioned and in a state of increasing paranoia, makes a last-minute change to his speech. Having practically been denied the right to speak at his own meeting, he no longer feels bound to talk about the contaminated water. Instead, he wants to address an

---

[9] The symbolic significance of the baths should not be overlooked. In *A Doll's House,* Nora betrays her middle-class background (and her insensitivity to the hardships of others) by suggesting that her less well-off friend Kristine Linde should have solved her problems not by tiresome work but by convalescing at a bath. OI V 211 conveys this point, but buries the parallel to the later play by translating "a bath (*et bad*)" as "a little holiday at some quiet little resort." The new PI uses "spa" in both *A Doll's House* and *An Enemy of the People.* In *An Enemy of the People,* the reference to the baths carries additional weight if we take into account the Roman baths and their importance for public life. I thank Marit Grøtta for this point.

even deeper problem: that of a contaminated public. As Dr. Stockmann puts it, "the revelation I am going to make to you is incomparably bigger than this petty business about the water-supply being polluted and the Baths standing over a cesspool" (OI VI 93; HIS VII 665). He has, he continues, made "the tremendous discovery . . . that all our *spiritual* sources are polluted and that our whole civic community is built over a cesspool of lies" (OI VI 93; HIS VII 665).

Dr. Stockmann turns against the people with a tirade about its leaders and their preference for docile consensus over critical debate:

> All I mean is I got wind of the colossal botch-up our so-called leaders had managed to make of things down at the Baths. If there's anything I just can't stand at any price—it's leaders! I've just about had enough of them. They are just like a lot of goats in a young forest—there's damage everywhere they go. Any decent man and they just get in his way, they're under his feet wherever he turns. If I had my way I'd like to see them exterminated like any other pest [skadedyr]. (OI VI 95; HIS VII 668)

The Doctor, however, does not end here. The people have fallen prey to passive groupthink. They must take their share of responsibility—and of Dr. Stockmann's scorn: "The worst enemy of truth and freedom in our society," he claims, "is the compact majority. Yes, the damned, compact, liberal majority" (OI VI 96; HIS VII 670). At this point, an impromptu vote is held and Dr. Stockmann—with his views about the contaminated water and the contaminated public—is declared an enemy of the people (OI VI 102–104; HIS VII 681). The Doctor loses his apartment lease and his position at the Baths. His family is ostracized and his young children dismissed from school.[10] Stockmann, though, is unrelenting and insists that "the strongest man in the world is the man who stands the most alone" (OI VI 126; HIS VII 727, trans. modified). Further, his idea of the strong, dissenting individual is presented against the background of quasi-Darwinian reflections on "the difference between pedigree and cross-bred animals" and a call to compare "a mongrel [. . .] with a poodle whose pedigree goes back many generations, who has been properly fed and has grown up among quiet voices and soft

---

[10] Yet his family gathers around him. In this way, the Stockmanns stand in stark contrast to the dysfunctional families we encounter in *Pillars of Society, Ghosts,* and other plays.

music" (OI VI 99; HIS VII 676). It is no wonder that lines such as these have caused discomfort among Ibsen's twentieth-century readers.

Discomfort is, indeed, a warranted response—and it may well be a response that Ibsen had called for. Hence it should not lead us to dismiss the play out of hand, but rather have us ask what interpretative strategies are available. We should ask, for a start, how Ibsen's plays present the decay of public life—a topic that had been of interest to him since at least *Emperor and Galilean*. Doing so, it is helpful to keep in mind the explicit political framework Ibsen had sketched in *Pillars of Society*, a work that overlaps, in characters and rhetorical buildup, with *An Enemy of the People*. That is, before we even encounter the moral pillars that lend the play its title, we meet their zealous defender, Adjunct Rørlund, comfortably seated with the wives of the well-off.[11] The Adjunct reemerges in *An Enemy of the People*.

In *Pillars of Society*, the Adjunct is a defender of traditional values. He rails against the "hollowness and decay" of society and the "scum of humanity" and praises Consul Bernick's commitment to his family and his will to front a team of self-appointed guardians of morality in their small coastal town. As the play unfolds, the audience learns that the representatives of the social upper class (and self-appointed moral guardians) are, in truth, immoral. While spearheading the plans for a new railway line, Bernick has secretly purchased land around the planned tracks, which could later be sold to the railway company for personal profit. But his thirst for profit does not end with that. He also allows his barely patched-up ship to set out to sea, speculating that a lucrative insurance payment can be collected if the ship goes down.

Pillars of Society culminates as the eager Adjunct Rørlund organizes a parade to celebrate the public spirit of Bernick and his peers. Amid the Adjunct's praise of Bernick's "selflessness [*uegennyttighet*]" (OI V 118; HIS VII 193) and the lauding cries of "Consul Bernick! The Pillars of Society! Hurrah! hurrah! hurrah!" (OI V 120; HIS VII 197), Bernick realizes that his son may be on board the ill-fitted ship. He breaks down and moves to confess his misdoings, admitting that "until today I have not by any means been

---

[11] In Ibsen's stage instructions:
> *Within the conservatory, a group of ladies is seated round a table. At the middle of the table sits* MRS. BERNICK. *On her left sit* MRS. HOLT *and her daughter, then* MRS. RUMMEL *and* MISS RUMMEL. *On* MRS. BERNICK'S *right sit* MRS. LYNGE, MISS MARTHA BERNICK *and* DINA DORF. *All the ladies are busy sewing. The table is piled high with bits of material, cut out and partly made-up, and with other articles of clothing. Further back, at a little table on which stand two pots plants and a glass of fruit juice, sits* RØRLUND, *a schoolteacher; he is reading aloud from a book with gilt edges, but the audience is only able to catch an occasional word.* (OI V 23; HIS VII 11)

a disinterested man. Even if I have not always striven for monetary gain, it is nevertheless clear to me now that a lust for power, a craving for influence and for position has been the driving force behind most of my actions" (OI V 121; HIS VII 198). As the curtains close, his son has safely returned. Yet, we do not know if the townspeople will forgive the Consul for his misdeeds. All we know is that the people, having willingly let themselves be led astray by a group of greedy capitalists posing as disinterested benefactors and guardians of old-time civility, will have to face serious deliberations about public life and standards.

In a Scandinavian context, the question of public goods and private interests—and of tradition as providing narratives by which the *status quo* is justified—had been at the center of the reception of Nietzsche's work. This is especially true of Georg Brandes's Nietzscheanism.[12] In the debates that followed his *Aristocratic Radicalism*,[13] Brandes indeed references Ibsen's Dr. Stockmann character.[14] Moreover, he situates Nietzsche within a broader context of history, art, culture, and criticism (including Schiller, Goethe, and Flaubert). Nietzsche's critics, he claims, misunderstand him. They fail to see that in a modern mass society, the majority can be easily duped. No society is good if it does not allow individuals to stand out from the crowd and question the commonly accepted values or the way things appear to be.[15] Such individuals, in turn, are not necessarily met with enthusiasm and acceptance. Yet, in breaking with the traditional paths of self-understanding and justification—in making them explicit and turning them into something that one can take a stance on—they serve an educational function.

Nietzsche's analysis of the intersection between groupthink, power, tradition, and education sits at the center of his work. This is clear in *On the Genealogy of Morality*, published five years after *An Enemy of the People*, but also in his work in the early 1870s, most importantly *Untimely Meditations*. For Nietzsche, human action is never disinterested, but based

[12] Even a vocal critic such as Harald Høffding, Brandes's opponent and a Kierkegaardian of sorts, would admit to Nietzsche's importance in this area. See Harald Høffding, "Demokratisk radikalisme," in *Fr. Nietzsche. Tre Essays*, by Georg Brandes and Harald Høffding (Aarhus: Akademisk Boghandel, 1972), 67. Høffding admits to Nietzsche's greatness—only that this, in Høffding's view, is not really a *philosophical* greatness but an artistic one (ibid., 75).

[13] See Georg Brandes, "Aristokratisk radikalisme," in *Fr. Nietzsche. Tre Essays*; partly translated in *Friedrich Nietzsche: An Essay on Aristocratic Radicalism*, trans. A. G. Chater (London: William Heinemann, 1915).

[14] Georg Brandes, "Det Store Menneske, Kulturens Kilde," in *Fr. Nietzsche. Tre Essays*, 80.

[15] Brandes, "Det Store Menneske," 98–100.

upon a scheme of values, be they articulated or not.[16] Nietzsche worries that, in his time, economic values have gotten the upper hand. These values have usurped those of history-making and culture. As presented in his early work, the task of questioning the dominant (unexamined) values, including narrow bourgeois selfishness, is left with the few "true *men, those who are no longer animal, the philosophers, artists, and saints*" (UM 159; KSA I 380, the emphasis is Nietzsche's). Their call, in turn, is contrasted with "the egoism of the money-makers [that] hold sway over almost everything on earth" (UM 150; KSA I 368). The individuals who are indeed able to question passively accepted values are characterized as the physicians—and recall, at this point, that Ibsen made Stockmann a medical doctor—of mankind (UM 133, 149; KSA I 345, 366).[17] Their goal is to help us break free of placid consensus, work to mend a broken society, and create a genuinely historical life-form: one in which old truths can be questioned and the new can emerge.

The Death of Public Life

In *An Enemy of the People*, Dr. Stockmann faces a situation not unlike the one we find in *Pillars of Society*. Traditional values and public credibility are being misused in order to disguise personal greed.[18] The plot revolves around a surge of cynicism, hypocrisy, and shortsightedness. The problem of selfishness—or, alternatively, the probing of the conditions for thinking and acting directed toward a public good—undergoes at least three stages of articulation. In Act One, the audience encounters the responses to

[16] In *On the Genealogy of Morality*, Nietzsche puts it as follows: "One has taken the *value* of these 'values' as given, as a fact, as beyond all calling-into-question." Nietzsche, *On the Genealogy of Morality*, 5; KSA V 20.

[17] The comparison of the physician and the philosopher stretches back to the Stoics and can also be found in Rousseau, Herder, and the nineteenth-century discourse of *Bildung*. For a discussion of the tradition of *Bildung* in nineteenth-century philosophy, see my "Bildung," in *The Oxford Handbook of German Philosophy in the Nineteenth Century*, 695–719.

[18] Ibsen does not appear to distinguish between morality and politics. Both these areas are, it seems, threatened if personal interest is put before a concern for the common good. In line with this, Berenick's confessions do not emphasize his betrayal of his family, friends, and former lover, but precisely that he, in conducting public business, failed to put private interest aside. While I appreciate Erik Østerud's suggestion that Ibsen's work should be read as part of a broader discussion of the public sphere, I deviate from his Habermasian aims and terminology. Furthermore, while Østerud provides a thorough analysis of the changing political life in Norway, he does not discuss how the play frames the issue of personal (economical) gain. See Erik Østerud, *Det borgerlige subjekt. Ibsen i teorihistorisk belysning* (Oslo: Novus forlag, 1981), Chapter 17.

Dr. Stockmann's findings. While he is absorbed in his scientific pondering (and not without a dose of self-congratulatory fanfare), just about everyone else is seeking to profit from his discovery that the Baths are polluted. In Acts Two and Three, Dr. Stockmann encounters the cynicism of his brother and friends, and the difficulty of carving out, in the midst of selfish (monetary) interests, a space for solidarity with the sick. Finally, at the town hall meeting in Act Four, Dr. Stockmann shifts his focus from the particular reactions to the water issue to a concern about a general lack of a critical public in his township. Each of these phases sheds light on his inflammatory speech and must be analyzed in more detail.

In Act One, Dr. Stockmann and his family appear oblivious to the financial motives that guide their peers. Yet it is clear that Dr. Stockmann himself is not free of selfish interests, though these are not pecuniary, but bound up with recognition from the scientific community and the public at large. Finding that the Baths, the "artery" of the town, are but a "cesspool" (OI VI 37–38; HIS VII 558–559),[19] he euphorically presents himself as a "lucky treasure hunter [heldig skattegraver]" and quasi-modestly puts aside his daydreaming of being celebrated as the town's true savior (OI VI 40–41; HIS VII 564, trans. modified).[20] At this point, Dr. Stockmann's only worry is that his brother, the Mayor, will resent the fact that he did not himself discover that the Baths were polluted (OI VI 42–43; HIS VII 568).[21]

The reactions from his peers, though, are less naïve. They all respond to Dr. Stockmann's findings by seeking to capitalize on it. Morten Kiil, his father-in-law, seizes the opportunity to avenge an earlier public humiliation (OI VI 44; HIS VII 571). The printers and editors of the local newspaper eye an opportunity to fast-track social revolution (OI VI 50–51 and 64; HIS VII 583 and 610). Aslaksen, representing the homeowners in town, welcomes the opportunity to present his group as dedicated to truth and science (OI VI 49; HIS VII 581).[22] Dr. Stockmann is out of touch with reality. In sharing

[19] In the secondary literature, it has been pointed out that Ibsen might have had the problem of cholera in mind. It is worth noting the perceived relation, at the time, between the spread of cholera and the expanding Western capitalism, stemming, in part, from the fact that cholera was brought back from colonies overseas. For a discussion of this point, see Timothy Carlos Matos, "Choleric Fictions: Epidemiology, Medical Authority, and An Enemy of the People," *Modern Drama*, vol. 51, no. 3 (2008): 353–368 (357 in particular).

[20] Again, this notion of a public celebration is anticipated in *Pillars of Society*.

[21] This, it turns out, is especially important because the discovery confirms a worry Dr. Stockmann had aired, to no avail, when the plans for the Baths were initially discussed (OI VI 40; HIS VII 563).

[22] Aslaksen also plays a role in *The League of Youth*, another play with an explicit political tone. For a discussion of this point, see Kittang, *Ibsen's Heroisme*, 157.

his findings with the Mayor, Dr. Stockmann declares himself proud to stand "shoulder to shoulder in the brotherhood of [his] fellow citizens" (OI VI 53; HIS VII 587). He is confident that his discovery will put an end to a predicament in which the water worsens the condition of "those poor invalids who come to us in good faith and pay good money hoping to get their health back!" (OI VI 54; HIS VII 591).

In Act Two, the Mayor's response to his brother's findings puts a speedy end to Dr. Stockmann's confidence that his discovery will be received as a service to the town. The townspeople, it turns out, hold no commitment to the sick, but only care about economic interests that will be threatened if the Doctor goes public with his findings. From this point of view, the Mayor is not a game-changer, but simply a person who has what it takes to admit openly to the unspoken selfishness that also guide Kiil, the newspaper printer and editors, and the society of homeowners. While the Mayor displays an exaggerated concern for his own health (he refuses to eat late and touch alcohol, and connects health issues with economic interests in a most blatant way ["I stick to my tea and bread and butter. It's better for one's health in the long run . . . as well as being more economical," OI VI 24; HIS VII 553]), he announces his hope for "lots of convalescents [brav mange syge] to help give the place a reputation" (OI VI 25; HIS VII 535). This, further, is what he quite shamelessly celebrates as the "civic pride" of the town ("en rigtig god borgerånd," OI VI 25; HIS VII 534). Even before the issue of the contaminated water is brought up, the Mayor has forged a bond between health and a prospering economy—a bond that Dr. Stockmann will question at the town hall meeting.

At this point, we witness a fatal collision between the brothers.[23] To disguise the truth about the damaging effect of the Baths is, for Dr. Stockmann, "an absolute crime against the public and against society" (OI VI 55; HIS VII 593). The Mayor, for his part, insists that it is in the interest of the town that the report is being withheld (OI VI 56; HIS VII 593). Neither of the brothers speaks in his own name. They both view their position as representing the interests of a larger, unidentified "we." Dr. Stockmann insists that the public extends beyond the town and, at the end of the day, includes humanity (i.e.,

---

[23] Ibsen goes out of his way to show that Dr. Stockmann and his family remain unaffected by economical motives. In Act Five, Dr. Stockmann dismisses the profitable option that presents itself when, in the midst of the water battle, his father-in-law has invested in the Baths. His father-in-law hopes for a significant gain if Dr. Stockmann will admit that he was wrong about the contaminated water. As an incentive, he offers to give Dr. Stockmann the stocks. Dr. Stockmann, though at this point he has lost everything, refuses to be bought.

it includes the sick who flock to the Baths only to get sicker). For the Mayor, a healthy public life is only possible if he and the town are granted short-term financial security. In fact, his monetary orientation is so entrenched that his only way of trying to convince his brother not to publish his findings is by repeated reference to the financial well-being of his own (the Doctor's) family. At this point, we not only encounter a confrontation between two brothers, but also a collision between two different conceptions of what it takes to sustain a healthy public life: a commitment to human flourishing, on the one hand, and a desire to secure a financial platform, on the other. From the point of view of the Doctor, the Mayor's orientation toward financial concerns—*and* his willingness to exploit the passivity of the community and suppress the truth—is inhumane. From the point of view of the Mayor, by contrast, the Doctor's commitment to truth-telling is so extreme that he qualifies as an enemy of the (town's) people. Neither of them appears to realize that different conceptions of society are at stake. Dr. Stockmann cannot, for the life of him, understand how, in wishing to defend the public's right to know, he is branded its enemy (an enemy of the public at this point [*samfundsfiende*, with its slight difference from a *folkefiende*], OI VI 61–62; HIS VII 603). His brother, by contrast, cannot understand why Dr. Stockmann remains wedded to his truths.

The problem the Doctor faces is not only the contaminated water but also a public that refuses to think beyond selfish interest and shortsighted fiscal gain. Alternatively, the challenge he confronts—the challenge we, the audience, confront—is how to balance two models of public life. Rendering this in quasi-Hegelian terms, it could be argued that this is the clash of horizons around which *An Enemy of the People* is structured.[24]

Finally, with the town hall meeting in Act Four, tragedy verges on farce, but a farce of the most excruciatingly painful kind. The tragedy of the new bourgeois life, owning up to its own priorities (or grossly failing to do so), has no room for grandeur. That, it seems, can only exist when the protagonists represent positions that embody genuine values. The Mayor's stance—to suppress the truth and possibly allow the sick to get sicker if only the economy thrives—is impossible to justify in such terms. Guided by the economic elite, the people refuse to hear what the Doctor has to say. Moreover—and this is what threatens to make Dr. Stockmann lose his mind—they refuse to

[24] For a discussion of the tight, almost classical structure of *An Enemy of the People*, see Kittang, *Ibsens Heroisme*, 129.

think for themselves. When a despairing Dr. Stockmann proposes that the water issue is reflective of a larger societal contamination, the audience at the meeting turns into a threatening mob.[25]

How, then, should we interpret Dr. Stockmann's infamous speech—his condemnation of the passive public—if the topic of public life is viewed as crucial to the dramatic and philosophical nerve of *An Enemy of the People*?

First, it is clear that in refusing to let the Doctor express his worries (in the newspaper and at the meeting), the public does not simply deny him a fair hearing. Rather, in its anxiety to preserve its financial interests and its deference to authority, the public ruins its habitat and life-support: public life itself. In the play, it is not evident that the Doctor is right (i.e., that the Baths *are* in fact contaminated). Dr. Stockmann, moreover, is too fanatic and one-dimensional to come off as a plausible savior of the town.[26] What is evident, though, is that he should be given a chance to present his scientific findings so that people can make up their minds and proceed, if needed, to investigate the water issue and discuss a possible solution. While at this point it would be too much to claim that truth is quelled, it can certainly be claimed that truthfulness and knowledge are put in jeopardy.

Second, Ibsen, in the town hall scene, exposes the motivation for the townspeople's refusal to listen to science. It is not so much that they reject Stockmann's orientation toward truth, but, rather, that they meekly follow their leaders. They take the established truth to remain beyond questioning and do not see that traditional ways, while convenient for the leaders, will not necessarily bode for a healthy future for the people. Ultimately, what is being threatened is the very capacity for critical thinking.

In *An Enemy of the People*, public life is not destroyed in a tragic battle for values, but, rather, in passive complacency. The self-appointed hero is a fanatical doctor bitterly remarking, as his trousers are torn and he has been subjected to physical attack, that one should never wear one's best clothes when rooting for revolution.[27] Public life dies so discretely that the

[25] Again, the parallels to Nietzsche are remarkable. In Nietzsche's wording: "If, however, a man should arise who really gave the impression of intending to apply the scalpel of truth to all things, including the body of the state, then the state would, since it affirms its own existence before all else, be justified in expelling such a man and treating him as *an enemy*" (UM 185; KSA 414–415, emphasis added).

[26] Here I agree with Noreng and Kittang: Ibsen's treatment of his protagonist is, indeed, comical. However, in my view, this does not make his demise less tragic—quite to the contrary.

[27] As Dr. Stockmann explains to his wife: "You should never have your best trousers on when you turn out to fight for freedom and truth. Well, it's not that I care that much about the trousers—you

audience (and the audience of the town hall meeting) hardly notices the loss.[28]

Though we may disapprove of his condescending attitude, this interpretation provides a framework within which we can at least begin to understand Dr. Stockmann's frustrations.[29] He is frustrated because his peers fail to see that their values have been usurped. The play, however, does not end with Dr. Stockmann's speech in Act Four. It continues, in Act Five, to offer a new perspective on his predicament *and* on the credibility (or, rather, lack of such) of the people. Toward the end of the play, we see the Doctor develop the ability to distinguish between the people and the ways in which they have let their outlook be co-opted by the authorities. In order to understand the dramatic function of Act Five—how it sheds new light on Dr. Stockmann—it might be helpful, yet again, to refer to Nietzsche's philosophy.[30]

Being Human

In the early 1870s, Nietzsche had been concerned about the development of modern mass society. In his *Untimely Meditations* and other places, he writes about the passivity of the people and celebrates critical (or even oppositional) thinking. For him, critical thinking does not represent a break with history (this would be a naïve approach), but a way of relating to history in a more productive manner. Nietzsche's language anticipates that of Ibsen's Dr. Stockmann. As he writes, "When the great thinker despises mankind, he despises its laziness [ihre Faulheit]: for it is on account of their laziness that

can always put a stich in them for me. But what gets me is the idea of that mob going for me as though they were my equals [ligemænd]—*that's* what I can't stomach, damn it!" (OI VI 107; HIS VII 691).

[28] I disagree with Franco Moretti, who praises Ibsen as "[t]he only writer who looks the bourgeois in the face, and asks: So, finally, what have you brought into the world?" yet deems *An Enemy of the People* Ibsen's only mediocre play. In my reading, *An Enemy of the People* explores, precisely, the possibility of a public life under the conditions of the new bourgeoisie. As such, it is far from a mediocre play. For Moretti's remarks, see *The Bourgeois,* 175 and 170 (see also 187).

[29] Erik Østerud's interpretation takes into account the transition to a system of party politics in Norway and emphasizes how this, at the time, was seen as a concession to private interests (and a leaving behind of the ideal of the politician as a person of judgment, rather than somebody defending a particular set of beliefs, values, or interests). See Østerud, *Det borgerlige subjekt,* 69–70.

[30] Needless to say, my focus on Nietzsche does not exclude alternative or additional sources of influence, one of which is likely to be John Stuart Mill's *Utilitarianism,* which Brandes had translated and later given to Ibsen. See Einar Ingvald Haugen, *Ibsen's Drama: Author to Audience* (Minneapolis: University of Minnesota Press, 1979), 46. In his turn to Nietzsche, Brandes emphasizes the continuity with Mill.

men seem like factory products, things of no consequence and unworthy to be associated with or instructed" (UM 127; KSA I 338).

In *The Birth of Tragedy*, Nietzsche had claimed to detect a cultural crisis. Being based on science and instrumental rationality, and being divorced from all questions of value, modern culture has begun "to turn and flee from its own consequences." Art, Nietzsche continues,

> exhibits this general crisis: in vain do the artists imitate all the great productive periods and natures, in vain is the whole of "world literature" piled up around modern man for his solace, in vain is he placed amongst all the artistic styles and artists of all times, so that he may give them names—as Adam gave names to the beasts; despite all this, he remains eternally hungry, a "critic" without desire or energy, Alexandrian man who is basically a librarian and proof-reader, sacrificing his sight miserably to book-dust and errors. (BT 88; KSA I 119–120)

Nietzsche describes how a waning historical culture either provides nothing but amusement (he identifies this with the culture of opera, BT 89–95; KSA I 120–129) or becomes an occasion for scholarly work. Such a view of culture entails no commitment to genuine truth and meaning. It is in this context that the ancient Greeks emerge as the "supreme teachers" (BT 95; KSA I 129). Their culture—or, rather, their relation to history as mediated through culture—offers a perspective from which we can assess the challenges of modern life.

As we saw in Chapter 5, Nietzsche is particularly worried about the death of tragedy and the drying up of tragic culture. However, he is also concerned with our modern inability to appreciate the greatness of tragedy during its golden age. At this point—from the point of view of the historian and philosopher—Nietzsche connects his philosophy of tragedy with his concerns about history and education. We moderns, he fears, have passed tragedy over to the "cultured historiographers," who approach it as a source of distant historical admiration (BT 96; KSA I 130). As a result, we miss not just the educational dimension of the Greek festivals, but also the opportunity to gain education in and through the experience of art more broadly.[31] In fact, as Nietzsche sees it, "[t]here is no other period in art in

---

[31] Richard Schacht traces Nietzsche's interest in education back to *The Birth of Tragedy*, proposing that "Nietzsche regarded the Greeks' artists as their educators in the most important sense, cultivating their sensibility and transforming both their sense of themselves and their sense of their world in such a way that they were unsurpassed in their life-affirmation." Richard Schacht, "A Nietzschean

which so-called education and true art have confronted each other with such feelings of estrangement and aversion as the one we now see before our very eyes" (BT 97; KSA I 130). Needed is not only a new art, but also a new way of thinking about the experience of art and about education in a broad sense.[32]

In emphasizing the musical power of Greek tragedy, Nietzsche calls for a reevaluation of art and, equally importantly, for a new way of relating to the past and, through it, the present. That is, as part of his study of tragic culture, he also questions how history is being passed down to us. From this point of view, it should not be surprising that Nietzsche transitions from *The Birth of Tragedy* to a lecture series on the modern university. In *Untimely Meditations*, he then develops his critique of the poverty of modern historical existence through a discussion of teachers and educators.

Schopenhauer as Educator is the third of the *Untimely Meditations*. Here Nietzsche analyzes the predicament of modern culture and asks why it is so difficult to change. On his analysis, most of us "hide . . . behind customs and opinions [Sitten und Meinungen]" (UM 127; KSA I 337). Ours, further, is "an era which sees its salvation in public opinion" (UM 128; KSA I 338).[33] Thus, human beings must be brought to a confrontation with themselves. In his words: "The man who does not wish to belong to the mass needs only to cease taking himself easily; let him follow his conscience, which calls to him: 'Be your self [Sei du selbst]! All that you are now doing, thinking, desiring, is not you yourself'" (UM 127; KSA I 338). Humanity, for Nietzsche, is a potential inherent in us all, but its actualization demands an effort that very few are prepared to pursue. Hence the "man who does not wish to belong to the mass" must demonstrate, through his actions, what humanity can be. Jeffrey Church summarizes the Nietzschean position by suggesting that "[i]n devoting ourselves to humanity, we claim for ourselves the right to posit a self-standing ideal. We show to an indifferent universe that we ourselves can create an ideal that endures the passing away of all things in nature, that we can transcend natural desire and devote our lives to this ideal, and that this

Education: Zarathustra/*Zarathustra* as Educator," in *Philosophers on Education: New Historical Perspectives*, edited by Amélie Oksenberg Rorty (London: Routledge, 1998), 319.

[32] Hence, to refer back to the discussion in Chapter 5, an educational art need not be cognitively oriented or didactical.

[33] As discussed in Chapter 5, this topic is also foregrounded in Mrs. Alving's discussions with Pastor Manders in *Ghosts*.

transcendence constitutes the realization of our contradictory ends, our wholeness and perfection."[34]

It is in this spirit that Nietzsche turns to Schopenhauer—not only as a philosopher (whose work had featured centrally in *The Birth of Tragedy*) but also as an exemplary teacher. According to Nietzsche, Schopenhauer was committed to the truly human (UM 137; KSA I 351). Just as Schopenhauer had discovered his philosophical calling in the encounter with Kant, so Nietzsche looks to Schopenhauer to free his potential as philosopher. In this context, the point is not so much the contents of his philosophy as his status as an exemplar. In Nietzsche's enthusiastic formulation, Schopenhauer should be "the leader who leads us from the depths of sceptical gloom or criticizing renunciation up to the heights of tragic contemplation, to the nocturnal sky and its stars extended endlessly above us, and who was himself the first to take his path. His greatness lies in having set up before him a picture of life as a whole, in order to interpret it as a whole" (UM 141; KSA I 356).

The crisis of modern culture, in Nietzsche's view, can only be addressed through the teachings of such exemplars, as they set forth a positive transcendence of the status quo. An exemplar, however, does not convey a form of life for passive appropriation. He or she offers inspiration, thereby helping others to realize their potential. According to Nietzsche, each of us carries in ourselves "a productive uniqueness . . . as the core of [our] being" (UM 143; KSA I 359). However, the realization of this productive uniqueness, as Nietzsche sees it, is counter-acted by laziness, a lack of courage to realize one's true being and thus, more fully and completely, be human. Philosophers and educators have failed to aspire to self-realization of this kind, and, for this reason, they have also failed to raise independent minds (UM 155; KSA I 374). What Nietzsche advocates, in other words, is a freeing of the will to realize an existential project, which, in turn, will contribute to the realization of the human. In Nietzsche's language at the time, this is a matter of forgetting oneself in truth. At stake is a call to self-reliance. This, for Nietzsche, is true wisdom, contrasted with the "lukewarm or frosty mode in which scholars usually accomplish their daily work" (UM 173; KSA I 399). Such a view of self-transformation is at the heart of Nietzsche's philosophy in the years following *The Birth of Tragedy*.

[34] Jeffrey Church, *Nietzsche's Culture of Humanity: Beyond Aristocracy and Democracy in the Early Period* (Cambridge: Cambridge University Press, 2015), 61.

It is as part of this program that Nietzsche distinguishes between the pedantry of the modern scholar and what he calls a genuine teacher of humankind. Such a teacher will address students independently of class and background. Against a system where "[t]he state never has any use for truth as such, but only for truth which is useful to it . . . , whether it be truth, half-truth or error" (UM 190; KSA I 422), Nietzsche promotes a "heroism of truthfulness" (UM 155; KSA I 374). This heroism, however, does not lead to one set of privileged truths, but prepares us for an ongoing *quest* for truth—and a recognition that this quest for truth must evolve through history and cultural exchange.[35] Education, art, truth, and historical existence are, in other words, intrinsically related for Nietzsche. It is no wonder, then, that for Nietzsche, "your educators can be only your liberators" (UM 129; KSA I 341)[36] and that education, in order to achieve this goal, needs to be dramatically rethought.

Educational Commitments

The overlap between Nietzsche's thinking and the outlook of Ibsen's Dr. Stockmann is most obvious at the point when the Doctor rails against public culture. Nietzsche, too, speaks about a need for "the removal of all the weeds, rubble and vermin that want to attack the tender buds of the plant" (UM 130; KSA I 341). However, given Nietzsche's interest in liberal (or, rather, liberating) education—and his coupling of history, art, truth, and critique—we cannot stop here. For, as we have seen, the aim of Nietzsche's criticism of the placid masses is to liberate a broader human potential. Is this true of Dr. Stockmann as well? Might he, in his status as an enemy of the people (in its complacency), be viewed as a champion of the human? In responding to this question, I will focus on how the notion of individual responsibility structures the last act and how, as Dr. Stockmann presents it, it is related to a search for humanity, truth, and education, on the one hand,

---

[35] In his fourth *Untimely Meditation*, Nietzsche connects this with a sense of the tragic, which is identified with the *Schein* of experiencing an ennobling through the encounter with "something holy that endlessly outweighs all [of man's] struggle and his distress" (UM 213; KSA I 453). Unlike Jeffrey Church, I do not see this as a tribute to a Herderian-Kantian legacy, but as an aspect of Nietzsche's work that goes beyond his Enlightenment commitments. In my view, the metaphysical aspect of Nietzsche's philosophy of culture runs along with—is sometimes supported by, at other times in conflict with—a commitment to humanity.

[36] Again, this aspect of Nietzsche's philosophy will be important to Brandes, who offers a free rendering of these lines in *Aristokratisk radikalisme*, 13.

and an adequate conception of how the ways of the past must give way to the hopes for the future, on the other.

In *An Enemy of the People*, Ibsen explores a number of threats to individual responsibility, including, as we have seen, naïve deference to authority and groupthink. The commitment to individual responsibility—or, rather, the absence of such a commitment—figures prominently throughout the final act of the play. Among the townspeople, there is a distinct lack of willingness to own up to their choices and take responsibility for the values they, actively or passively, adhere to. With the exception of Dr. Stockmann's friend, Captain Horster, who remains elevated above the behavior of his peers, the townspeople sheepishly comply with the authorities. On their view, being a good citizen involves, first and foremost, a willingness to subordinate oneself. Along these lines, Peter, earlier in the play, positions himself as Dr. Stockmann's superior and accuses him of never having been able to submit to authority and being guilty of a "chronic disposition to take things into your own hands" (OI VI 30; HIS VII 545).

In Ibsen's work, the unwillingness to assume personal responsibility is rendered in terms of a submission to the They or the One (*man*, in Ibsen's original). The landlord terminates Dr. Stockmann's lease because "he daren't do anything else . . . because of the others . . . public opinion . . . [he is] not his own master . . . [and] dare not risk putting certain people's backs up" (OI VI 107; HIS VII 690). Then there are the anonymous hate letters (OI VI 109; HIS VII 694). Dr. Stockmann's daughter, Petra, loses her teaching post because her supervisors do not want to upset a faceless group of parents. Captain Horster, who had lent Dr. Stockmann the venue for the meeting, is made redundant because his superiors do not dare to keep him (OI VI 111; HIS VII 698). Namelessness reigns in the form of missing signatures and meek references to what "one" does and does not do. Stockmann broke with these expectations and is therefore excommunicated by, precisely, the nameless majority.

Finally, the individual responsibility that the townspeople recognize is related to financial opportunities. Act Five makes this point clear. When Morten Kiil, Dr. Stockmann's father-in-law, offers to give him (Dr. Stockmann) the recently purchased stocks (if he withdraws his findings), he opens a possibility of financial security for Dr. Stockmann and his family.[37] Having

---

[37] Additionally, Dr. Stockmann's consent would clear the accusations against the tannery owners, Kiil being among them. As Kiil approaches Dr. Stockmann, he remarks that "every bit of the money is tied up now in the Baths. And I just want to see now if you are completely and absolutely stark raving

learned of Kiil's purchases, the Mayor turns Dr. Stockmann's own ammuni-
tion against him: He, too, is driven by personal advantage and seems to have
plotted cleverly with his father-in-law.[38] At this point, the newspaper editors
can make sense of what appears to be Dr. Stockmann's strategy and offer,
against a share in his gain, to do damage-control on his reputation (OI VI
120–121; HIS VII 717).[39] Once it is suspected that Dr. Stockmann's motivation is selfish, his actions finally appear intelligible. While the Doctor's commitment to individual responsibility gives rise to nocturnal stone-throwing
and anonymous hate-mail, selfish, monetary interest can at least be understood. Dr. Stockmann, however, chases everyone out and sends Kiil a three-
fold rejection of his offer: no, no, no (OI VI 122; HIS VII 720).

For Dr. Stockmann, the expectation that he should put private (financial)
interest above his commitment to truth represents nothing short of a threat
to his humanity. When faced with the objection that he should carefully
consider the financial predicament of his family, Dr. Stockmann promptly
responds: "They've threatened me with all sorts of things; to deprive me of
my basic human rights. . . . They tried to degrade me, to rob me of my self-
respect, tried to force me to put personal advantage before my most sacred
convictions" (OI VI 67; HIS VII 614). While Dr. Stockmann, in his initial response, seems unduly upset, the later developments—his refusal to put personal advantage over truth and the people of his town turning into a faceless
lynch mob—abundantly demonstrate that his accusations, though lacking in
sensitivity and rhetorical finesse, were not entirely off-mark. Indeed, there *is*
an abyss between, on the one hand, the willingness to stand up, even at the
cost of bankruptcy, for the truths in which one believes, and, on the other, the
thoughtless comfort of an anonymous majority.

How, then, does this shed light on Dr. Stockmann's speech in Act Four?
When he, in his hateful townhall rant, talks about the "common people," he
is not referring to a class denominator but to the mindset of the anonymous
"they." As he puts it: "The sort of common people I'm talking about are not

mad, Dr. Stockmann. If you are still going to have it that creepy, crawly things are coming from my
works, you might as well be flaying Katherine alive, for all the difference it makes—*and* Petra, *and*
the boys as well. But then no decent father would do that—not unless he was a madman" (OI VI 117;
HIS VII 710).

[38] In the words of the Mayor, "These violent, ruthless attacks you have made—all in the name of
truth—against the leading men of the town [. . .] Just your part of the bargain in exchange for being
included in that vindictive old man's will" (OI VI 115; HIS VII 706).

[39] Ibsen's presentation of journalists here echoes Nietzsche's criticism. For a discussion of
Nietzsche's criticism, see Church, *Nietzsche's Culture of Humanity*, 186–187.

found simply among the lower classes; they are crawling and swarming all round us—right up to the highest social level." He even offers the towns-people an example—their own Mayor: "You've only got to look at that nice, pretty Mayor of yours. My brother Peter is as mass-minded a person as any-thing you'll find on two legs [. . .] and that's not because he's descended, like me, from some awful old Pomeranian pirate or something—because that's what we are [. . .] but because he thinks what his superiors thinks and believes what his superiors believe" (OI VI 100; HIS VII 678).

In his speech in Act Four, Dr. Stockmann clearly goes too far and is un-likely to receive much sympathy from the audience—neither the audience in the town hall meeting nor the audience of Ibsen's play.[40] He uses a language of extinction and claims to love his town so much that he is willing to destroy it rather than see it prosper on a lie (OI VI 102; HIS VII 681). However, in Act Five the behavior of the townspeople serves to make his point about a lack of responsibility a lot more plausible. It makes us see that Dr. Stockmann may well be right that the real problem facing the town is not only external de-struction (from water poisoning or a weak economy), but also the slow dete-rioration of public life. Further, it is worth paying close attention to the order of events in Acts Four and Five. Dr. Stockmann cannot prove the points that he makes about the threats to public life. It is the people that will have to prove or disprove the truth-value of his speech. From a dramatic point of view, this has to happen *after* the town hall meeting in Act Four. In this re-spect, Act Five is of fundamental importance to our understanding of the play and the Stockmann character.

As we transition from Act Four to Act Five, it becomes even clearer that Dr. Stockmann's tirade does not only address the townspeople, but also what he takes to be the very conditions of a well-functioning public life. Thus, the main problem with Dr. Stockmann's speech is not his talk of "higher" and "lower" animals (though this, too, is troubling), but, rather, that it ends up undermining the public space he seeks to protect. He fails to embody his own values. He fails, in short, to demonstrate the virtues he is calling for. His is not only the flaw of contempt, but also that of a gap between theory and practice, learning and life. To the extent that the townspeople, through their actions,

---

[40] At this point, Thomas Ostermeier, in his Schaubühne production, shrewdly fuses the theater au-dience and the audience at the town hall meeting, so that the audience at the performance is, by asso-ciation, guilty of the kind of denial and mass-mindedness that characterizes the audience at the town hall meeting (i.e., in Ibsen's play). Similarly, in his 1964 version of *Hedda Gabler*, Ingmar Bergman merges audience and stage, albeit in terms of lighting. See Mikael Timm, *Lusten och dämonerna. Boken om Bergman* (Stockholm: Norstedts, 2008), 368.

verify his points about the compact majority, it is up to Dr. Stockmann to mend the contradiction into which he has tangled himself. At this point, Dr. Stockmann is no longer a comical figure. He emerges as a fallen man— yet, in a Nietzschean spirit, with the potential to rise to his ideals and, thereby, also to greatness. How, if at all, can Dr. Stockmann compensate for a predicament in which he himself, with his condescending attitude, contributes to the closing of public space? The answer Ibsen gestures at is simple and can be rendered in a word: education.

Just like Nietzsche had seen education as an antidote to placid consensus, Ibsen has education—and the role of the educator—feature prominently in *An Enemy of the People*. In this context, three points are worth making.

First, Dr. Stockmann's identity as an educator gains depth and distinctness when contrasted with Adjunct Rørlund. In *Pillars of Society*, the very use of his title ("adjunct") has an air of pedantry about it (in the Norwegian original, his lines are prompted by his academic title and last name, which are lost in McFarlane's translation).[41] If Adjunct Rørlund does not possess much pecuniary capital, he is loaded with self-proclaimed moral worth. In *Pillars of Society*, Adjunct Rørlund is a guardian of the town and its traditional self-understanding. In a language that stylistically (though not, as we shall see, in content) anticipates Dr. Stockmann's speech at the town hall meeting, Adjunct Rørlund complains about there being "some tares among the wheat" that have to be "weeded out." In his view, "the thing that counts is to keep society pure" (OI V 25; HIS VII 15). The metaphor of purging is further developed when he, toward the end of *Pillars of Society*, speaks about "elements of corruptions from without" that the town should seek to "get rid of" (OI V 119; HIS VII 195). In the words of the Adjunct, moral uprightness, social status, and financial safety are seamlessly bound together. While socializing with, or rather, morally educating, the wives of the elite, he contrasts the destitute life of the lower classes with "a good and pure home, where family life is seen in its fairest form" (OI V 27; HIS VII 17). And upon declaring his love to Dina, whose (lower) class standing makes him reluctant to marry her, he pompously establishes that "[w]hen a man is called to serve as a moral pillar of the society in which he lives [. . .] one cannot be too careful" (OI V 38; HIS VII 40). In this way, Adjunct Rørlund embodies the false teacher type that Nietzsche, a few years earlier, had mocked as a

---

[41] Likewise, in Michael Meyer's translation, which renders him Dr. Roerlund. See Henrik Ibsen, *Pillars of Society*, trans. Michael Meyer, *Plays*, vol. IV (London: Methuen, 1980).

"mere clattering thought-and-calculating-machine" (UM 140; KSA I 355). The ideals that Adjunct Rørlund preaches—the will to independence and responsibility, the individual as a productive citizen (OI V 119; HIS VII 195)—are thoroughly undermined by his own cowardice, flattery, and selfishness. We find the Adjunct similarly spineless in *An Enemy of the People*. When Dr. Stockmann's sons, after the town hall meeting, are dismissed from school, the teacher behind the dismissal is none other than Rørlund (OI VI 124; HIS VII 724).

When Dr. Stockmann decides to turn to teaching, his vision could not have been more different from Adjunct Rørlund's. Echoing Nietzsche's insistence on the teacher-physician, Dr. Stockmann prescribes the remedies of independent thought. Dr. Stockmann does not wish to educate the young to a given set of truths or dogma. He sets out to cultivate "the independence of mind" (HIS VI 124; HIS VII 723) and make "decent and independent men" out of the children (OI VI 125; HIS VII 725). His students, further, will be the children of the dispossessed. Real poverty, as he sees it, is not that of economic deprivation, but a lack of ability to think for oneself. In this way, the final act redeems the motifs aired when Dr. Stockmann genealogically traces both himself and his brother, the Mayor, back to a wretched pirate, thereby suggesting that the same gene pool could give rise to two such different individuals. At the end of the day, it is nurture, not nature, that makes a difference, and as Dr. Stockmann now sees it, such educational nurturing is his true calling as a doctor.

Second, it must be noted that, in a certain sense, Dr. Stockmann has already demonstrated his credentials in the field of education. He has raised three children who seem independent and wise beyond their years.[42] With her upright spirit, Petra incarnates Dr. Stockmann's accomplishments as a father and educator. She proves herself on a number of occasions. Being an educated woman, she has been asked to translate from English an article for the local newspaper. However, when she realizes that its content, while certainly an easy sell, is ideologically tainted, she turns down the job (OI VI 71–74; HIS VII 624–628). Her real feat, in this context, is not her knowledge of English, but her moral compass and courage. The editor's warning that she should not be so "outspoken" when her father cannot manage without his (the editor's) help is met with a scornful sigh (OI VI 74; HIS VII 628).

---

[42] In the context of Ibsen's play, it is interesting to see Nietzsche suggest that the true teacher addresses his student like "a son being instructed by his father" (UM 134; KSA I 347).

Petra represents a generation of women that is difficult to imagine being stuck playing bird games with a Helmer or, like Mrs. Alving, leading a life of covering up her husband's misdeeds. Nor, for that matter, could one easily envision Petra Stockmann taking on the servile and philistine teacher role of Adjunct Rørlund.[43] Quite to the contrary, the two, Petra and Rørlund, are explicitly contrasted at the beginning of the play when her brother reports, in response to Petra's eager investment in her studies, that Rørlund views hard work as a punishment for sins (OI VI 35; HIS VII 553).

Petra is in favor of exposing her younger brothers to all sorts of views, atheism included, and reflects on how hypocrisy reigns in school and at home: "All this hypocrisy, both at home and at school. At home one mustn't say anything [about sensitive issues such as atheism]; and at school we have to stand there and lie to the children" (OI VI 36; HIS VII 555). When encouraged to explain her claim about lying, she refers to situations in which teachers have to represent ideals they do not themselves believe in (OI VI 36; HIS VII 555). Already in Act One, she dreams of opening her own school (OI VI 36; HIS VII 555).[44]

Third and finally, we ought to ask what kind of truth or truthfulness Dr. Stockmann and Petra promote. From Petra's remark (quoted earlier), it is clear that their new school will have little room for conventional wisdom. The goal, rather, is to challenge such wisdom and force it to expose itself. In doing so, Dr. Stockmann, much like Mrs. Alving, asks us to question the "doctrine inherited from [our] forefathers" (OI VI 98; HIS VII 674). While Dr. Stockmann specifies this doctrine as the identification of the people and the masses, the audience will at this point know that he is worried about the consequences of a tradition that is both stifling and passively adopted. For in his eyes, truth is far from eternal: "The life of a normally constituted truth is generally, say, about seventeen or eighteen years, at most twenty; rarely longer. But truths as elderly as that have always worn terribly thin. But it's only *then* that the majority will have anything to do with them" (OI VI 97; HIS VII 672). Truth itself is historical, but once the majority adopts a new truth, it is usually already old. Petra represents—she not only teaches, but

---

[43] Again, it is important in this context to note how women philosophers in this period cultivated an interest in new ideas of education (see Chapter 5).

[44] At this point, we also see a parallel, explicitly drawn by Nietzsche, between a loss of religion, on the one hand, and a new emphasis on education, on the other. The loss of absolute values and ideals (God) need not result in the loss of values *überhaupt*.

exemplifies—new truths or, more precisely, a new and critical attitude toward established truth. And this is what Dr. Stockmann now wants to be part of.[45]

Dr. Stockmann's emphasis on education is important for our understanding of the play. In spite of his talk of high and low animals, the Doctor, as he joins his daughter, sees humanity as a task or a commitment, though, as he admits, one that is often held back by poverty (OI VI 101; HIS VII 679). Education facilitates a will to inquiry and questioning of the status quo. This educational project does not make Dr. Stockmann's spiteful remarks about the masses any less uncomfortable. The point, rather, is that in order to understand the full complexity of Act Four, Dr. Stockmann's speech included, the context of interpretation should be expanded to the whole play: the way in which Ibsen, throughout Acts One through Three, builds toward the crescendo at the meeting in Act Four and then, in Act Five, lets the people, with their authoritarian character types, prove themselves in need of education. Hence, if Dr. Stockmann is an enemy of the people (and its *de facto* shortcomings), he still proves to be a defender of humanity, broadly conceived.

The Drama of Education

At this point, a reader could object that my discussion of Ibsen's affinity with Nietzsche does not really take into account how Nietzsche's philosophy, in the 1930s and beyond, was endorsed by the National Socialists and that Ibsen, as it were, would be guilty by association. However, we need to keep in mind that the National Socialist adoption of Nietzsche was, to a significant extent, enabled by a combination of his sister's aggressive editorship and a selective strategy of reading. Further, and equally important, the framework in which Ibsen encountered Nietzsche's thought was rather different from 1930s Germany. In the period leading up to the completion of *An Enemy of the People*, Nietzsche barely had a reception to speak of in Germany and the Scandinavian readership was left with the task of trying to figure out how Nietzsche's work could best be put to use. For Ibsen's generation, it is, in other words, an open question how Nietzsche should be read, and his work is interpreted by thinkers who defended democratic rights as well as by

---

[45] The contrast to Solness, the Master Builder, and his anxiety about the new is striking.

artists and intellectuals who were attracted to the idea of the exceptional in-dividual.[46] As a dramatist, Ibsen does not take a stance in this debate.[47]

In *An Enemy of the People*, Dr. Stockmann emphasizes how public life thrives on openness and new ideas. Yet he faces a predicament in which the pressures of the new economy, combined with public meekness and group-think, threaten politics and a dynamic public life. Is, then, public life, and with it political hope, about to petrify and die? Ibsen does not answer this question. We do not know how Dr. Stockmann's experimental school project develops and whether or not the townspeople will eventually take to his ideal of independent thought. What we do know is that Ibsen's play, *An Enemy of the People*, contributes to opening up such debates, doing what Stockmann fails to do at the meeting (which is, it should be noted, itself a kind of the-atrical performance, albeit a rather pathetic one). In this way, it is no longer up to the doctor *cum* teacher to educate and cure people—nor is it solely up to Ibsen's academically minded peers, as they debate the relevance of Nietzsche's philosophy in the context of Scandinavian culture. With Ibsen, such a task extends to the playwright. This kind of drama will offend and provoke. It will, understandably, be met with resistance. Yet, it is a drama that seeks to educate—not in the sense of furnishing the audience with a set of particular opinions, beliefs, or standpoints, but, rather, to keep individual and collective mindsets open and inquiring.

To the extent that Nietzsche discusses art after *The Birth of Tragedy*, he retains a broadly romantic approach. A work that, in Ibsen's fashion, scrutinizes problems and issues would be unacceptable to him. While phi-losophy, through Nietzsche's Zarathustra, retains a playful, artistic character,

[46] This is evidenced by the debate between Brandes and Harald Høfding, who pleaded for a move from aristocratic individualism to democratic radicalism. A few years later, there was a call, among Nietzsche-inspired intellectuals such as Irgens Hansen, for a turn, in the face of the tyranny of common opinions, from a focus on the people (*folket*) to a focus on education to individual respon-sibility. For a discussion of this aspect of the Nietzsche debate in Norway, see Beyer, *Nietzsche og Norden*, vol. 1, 93–101. See also Anatol Schneider, *Nietzscheanismus. Zur Geschichte eines Begriffs* (Würzburg: Königshausen und Neumann, 1997), 35–69.

[47] Yet Ola Hansson's moves between attacks on and endorsements of Ibsen's work follow the conjectures of his Nietzsche reading. See Beyer, *Nietzsche og Norden*, vol. 1, 116–117. For Hansson's account, see Ola Hansson, *Friedrich Nietzsche. Hans Personlighed og hans System*, trans. Arne Garborg (Christiania: Alb. Cammeyers forlag, 1890). For an account of Hansson, Brandes, and the debate between them, see Adrian Del Caro, "Reception and Impact: The First Decade of Nietzsche in Germany," *Orbis Litterarum* 37 (1982): 32–46. See also Michael J. Stern, *Nietzsche's Ocean, Strindberg's Open Sea* (Berlin: Nordeuropa-Institut der Humboldt-Universität, 2008), especially 74–93. Stern discusses the enlightenment commitments of Brandes's work and the inherent anti-Semitism of Hansson's response.

art does not for that reason get closer to a critical spirit. In spite of Brandes's efforts to have him appreciate Ibsen, Nietzsche remains unenthusiastic.[48]

Ibsen's work, however, questions the opposition between art and social engagement. While remaining engaged, his realist drama avoids didacticism.[49] In the spirit of the *Sturm und Drang* philosophy of drama, it does not preach truths, but questions prejudices. Moreover, this questioning does not only (or, most interestingly) take the form of character lines or utterances, but is presented through the acting out of the complicated relation between the characters' beliefs and ideals, on the one hand, and their action and practices, on the other. This point is made even clearer if we take into account Ibsen's own characterization of good and bad teachers and his (Nietzschean) emphasis on the relationship between teaching and life.

With his realist drama, Ibsen clearly goes beyond a romantic paradigm, if narrowly conceived. Yet, in relative continuity with his own roots in the *Sturm und Drang* movement, we must distinguish between didacticism (which Ibsen's drama avoids) and a larger dramatic capacity to question unexamined belief (which it endorses). Or otherwise put, Ibsen's drama—in a spirit that is Nietzschean, yet goes beyond the confines of Nietzschean philosophy— shows how our unexamined beliefs and the baggage we take over from tradition shape collective as well as individual lives. While Nietzsche himself failed to see the affinity between his own work and that of Ibsen's, Brandes had been aware of these parallels. Moreover, while Nietzsche is overall skeptical of realist art (but praises a philosopher and dramatist such as Lessing), Wilhelm Dilthey had acknowledged, early on, the kinship between realism, on the one hand, and the critical aspirations of the early philosophers of theater, on the other.[50]

After *An Enemy of the People*, Ibsen remains committed to a drama that addresses fundamental human and social questions without thereby being didactic or conclusive in its nature. We see this in *Hedda Gabler*. With *Hedda Gabler*, however, the comical elements that characterize *An Enemy of the*

---

[48] Nietzsche comments on Ibsen in five places: in three fragments from 1887/1888, Ibsen is criticized for his idealism. In a letter from 1888, he is mentioned as one of the names that Brandes has recommended. Finally, the following year, Nietzsche, as part of a generally misogynic reflection in *Ecce Homo*, characterizes Ibsen as an old virgin.

[49] I do not follow the reading, pursued by Bernard Dukore and others, that sees the Stockmann character as a direct spokesman for Ibsen's own views. See Dukore, *Money and Politics in Ibsen, Shaw, and Brecht*, 109.

[50] For a discussion of this point, see my "A Task Most Pressing: Dilthey's Philosophy of the Novel and His Rewriting of Modern Aesthetics," in *Interpreting Dilthey: Critical Essays*, ed. Eric S. Nelson (Cambridge: Cambridge University Press, 2019), 200–216.

People are (mostly) gone and we face the tragedy of an individual who is fundamentally out of sync with her time. As had been the case with *The Vikings at Helgeland*, the experience of history is front and center. Indeed, the drama of Hedda Gabler is played out against the lives and visions of two historians, whose relationship to the past could hardly be more different. Hence it is *Hedda Gabler* that, in the final chapter, will conclude my discussion of the relationship between history, life, and modern drama.

7

History and Existence (*Hedda Gabler*)

Hedda Gabler features the spoiled and increasingly desperate General's daughter, whose *Lebensmüde* drives her into a search for beauty and a destructive play with people and pistols that eventually leads to her suicide. Spectacularly incapable of understanding his wife, Hedda's husband, Jørgen Tesman, only contributes to her ennui. Her friend, Ejlert Løvborg, incarnates a different attitude: he has a grand vision of life and shares in Hedda's quest for beauty. Ultimately, Hedda is also let down by Løvborg, who shoots himself, though not with the kind of beauty Hedda had expected. Tesman and Løvborg are both historians by trade.[1] Yet, their mindsets are very different. Tesman is a pedant. Løvborg is wild and poetical. While Tesman cares about facts, Løvborg is in the business of meaning and value. Hedda, on her side, lives with these historians—and she lives with the past and with her family's history and its outdated ideals. In combining a focus on history, value, beauty, and life, *Hedda Gabler* emerges as a Nietzschean play.

A consensus line of reading traces the Nietzschean tenors of Ibsen's work to Hedda and her image of the Dionysiac Ejlert Løvborg, complete with vine leaves in his hair and easily associated with the perspectives developed in *The Birth of Tragedy* (see HIS IX/B 27). Such a reading, though, places a heavy burden on the interpreter. In Ibsen, the metaphor of vine leaves is present as early as 1865, that is, seven years before the publication of *The Birth of Tragedy*.[2] Vine leaves also figure in *Brand* and *Emperor and Galilean*. Further, as far as *Hedda Gabler* goes, the image of Løvborg with vine leaves in his hair is a relatively late manuscript addition and was not central to Ibsen's development of plot and characters.[3] Finally, unlike *Ghosts*, *Hedda Gabler* does not explicitly draw on classical tragic forms and motifs.

---

[1] For a general discussion of late nineteenth-century academic history in Norway, especially the contributions of Ernst Sars, see Narve Fulsås, *Historie og nasjon. Ernst Sars og striden om norsk kultur* (Oslo: Universitetsforlaget, 1999).

[2] Letter to Bjørnson (January 28, 1865). http://www.ibsen.uio.no/BREV_1844-1871ht%7CB18650128BB.xhtml (Accessed June 2019).

[3] See Hemmer, *Ibsen og Bjørnson*, 249.

The Drama of History. Kristin Gjesdal, Oxford University Press (2021). © Oxford University Press.
DOI: 10.1093/oso/9780190070762.001.0001.

Hence any effort to hinge the Nietzschean tenors of *Hedda Gabler* on the famous vine leaves must include an explanation of how Ibsen came to re-shape, in a new and distinctively Nietzschean way, an image that had already been circulating prior to *Hedda Gabler* and even prior to the publication of *The Birth of Tragedy*. While this hermeneutic challenge could in principle be met, a different concern proves more unwieldy. For even if it were the case that Ibsen, in *Hedda Gabler*, deliberately draws on Nietzsche's notion of the Dionysiac, the Dionysiac in Nietzsche's work is a force that cannot be experienced in its pure form. In tragedy, the Dionysiac is associated with the chorus and music and is, as such, opposed to the individuation of the actors on stage. As a result, it can hardly be associated with one particular character, such as Ejlert Løvborg. Thus, even if we were to meet one or both of the hermeneutical challenges outlined thus far, we would still end up with little more than a hypothesis that Ibsen, in *Hedda Gabler*, is freely (and misguidedly) drawing on Nietzsche, and the question, then, is what exactly has been gained by this exercise.

There is another strategy of interpretation available to readers of a philosophical or even Nietzschean inclination. For as we saw in Chapters 5 and 6, the Nietzschean tenets of Ibsen's drama transcend the philosopher's work on tragedy in the narrow sense. In particular, we find a turn toward the topics of history and education—concerns that were very much part of Ibsen's time *and* that connected the Scandinavian interest in Nietzsche's work to the earlier impulses of Hegelianism. The central presence of the two historians in *Hedda Gabler* may lead us to think of Nietzsche's *Untimely Meditations*, though not the discussion of Schopenhauer and education in the third essay, but this time the second essay, *On the Uses and Disadvantages of History for Life*. Here, Nietzsche analyzes different types of history and historians, thus bridging the topics that he had discussed in his early work with the approaches he pursues in later works such as *The Genealogy of Morality*.

In an important 1998 article, Asbjørn Aarseth traces allusions in *Hedda Gabler* to *On the Uses and Disadvantages of History for Life*.[4] Aarseth, however, does not develop his points beyond the observation that Tesman incarnates what Nietzsche calls the "antiquarian historian" and Løvborg the "critical historian." A parallel reading of *Hedda Gabler* and *Untimely*

[4] Asbjørn Aarseth, "Vital Romanticism in Ibsen's Late Plays," in *Strindberg, Ibsen and Bergman: Essays on Scandinavian Film and Drama*, ed. Harry Perridon (Maastricht: Shaker Publishing, 1998), 1–23. See also an earlier version of this argument in Michael W. Kaufman, "Nietzsche, Georg Brandes, and Ibsen's *Master Builder*," *Comparative Drama*, vol. 6 (1972): 169–186.

Meditations is, in my view, a good starting point—better than the emphasis on *The Birth of Tragedy* alone. Yet, Nietzsche intends his typology to characterize tendencies in historical thought—models for how we conceive of history—not individual historians. Further, as far as Ibsen's drama goes, a strong focus on Løvborg and Tesman risks pushing Hedda, the play's main character, into the background. Hence, if we, with reference to a work such as *Untimely Meditations*, are to spell out the Nietzschean reverberations in *Hedda Gabler*, a more promising place to start is the difference between scientific history and a history conducted in the service of life. Such a starting point, I hope, can help us get Hedda back into the picture, and, by way of her role in the play, secure a better grasp on the relationship between Nietzsche's philosophy of history and Ibsen's drama than we would get through a sheer matching of philosophical concepts and dramatic characters.

While *Hedda Gabler* includes two historians, the main character of the play is and remains Hedda Gabler—a character who, strictly speaking, no longer exists as she is now the newly wed Hedda Tesman. With her existential longings, her battles with nihilism, her struggles to be at home in the world, it is Hedda, rather than the historians, who intensely lives out (and spectacularly fails to realize) the notion that the ideals of history can support and sustain the present. Hedda is trapped in history, just as she is trapped in her domestic quarters—a grand villa now turned into an empty symbol of middle-class comfort and consumption. Staking her very life, Hedda, like the Nietzschean philosopher, refuses to let go of the thought that history is infused with existential meaning. The realization of this meaning, though, is more than what a single individual can take on. It requires a culture in which values can gain reality and matter to the way people lead their lives. Rather than a plain Nietzschean exposé of historical types and approaches, it is Hedda's battle with such ideas that gives *Hedda Gabler* its Nietzschean undertones.

It adds to the subtlety of Ibsen's drama that he lets this existential agony be acted out by a woman. Hedda's life—and, even more so, her death—demonstrates the costs of an existence so full of unrealized promises and desires. By approaching modern life through a series of iconic women characters, not a single one of whom escapes their tragic predicament, Ibsen clearly goes beyond the framework of Nietzsche's philosophy narrowly speaking. Ibsen's inquiry of modern life, as lived in and with history, reaches its full articulation as Hedda emerges as a heroine of dramatic modernity. Whereas Hjørdis, in *The Vikings at Helgeland*, displays a deep (and proto-modern) frustration at the subjectivization of values, Hedda faces a world of utter barrenness, one in which human life, as she sees it, can no longer be invested with meaning. From this point of view, the Nietzschean idea that history should further life risks sounding like a hollow philosophical dream.

Nietzschean Overtures

I would like to begin this chapter by briefly returning to Nietzsche's philosophy of tragedy, thus both building on and going beyond the discussion in Chapter 5. In *The Birth of Tragedy*, Nietzsche calls for a reawakening of ancient tragedy and the experience it afforded: a synthetic and synthesizing musical experience of a magnitude that obliterates the distance between chorus and spectators, sublating them into a higher, non-individualizing totality (see Chapter 5). As Nietzsche puts it, this is an experience in which individuation, associated with the image-laden Apolline, is transgressed and "we become one with the immeasurable, primordial delight in existence and receive an intimation, in Dionysiac ecstasy, that this delight is indestructible and eternal" (BT 81; KSA I 109). This point has made Jonas Barish—and with him Martin Puchner and others—speak of an anti-theatrical prejudice not only in Nietzsche's contribution, but also in philosophy more broadly.[5] Barish points out that the Dionysiac is marked by an absence of individual actors: it is about rhythm and music, not characters, lines, and dramatic structure.[6] It is, in short, about a dimension of tragedy that, he fears, cannot be carried on in modern theater or, worse still, is opposed to it.

[5] In fact, as Barish sees it, this prejudice is so widespread that it ultimately reaches theater itself, including Ibsen's drama. In Ibsen's drama, those who plainly act their roles are seen as villains and those who protest against it are the tragic heroes of their theater and their world. As Barish concludes his reflections on Ibsen, "[b]ondage consists in slavish fidelity to one's prescribed role, as with Pastor Manders, or in the cultivation of a self-image wholly at odds with observable reality, as with Hjalmar Ekdal. The theater thus serves implicitly as a standard of narrowness and artificiality, and the rejection of it as a sign of inner substance and power. The search for authenticity involves a denial of theater, because the theater itself is a denial of reality." Jonas Barish, *The Antitheatrical Prejudice* (Berkeley: University of California Press, 1981), 451.

[6] See Barish, *The Antitheatrical Prejudice*, 400–418. See also Martin Puchner, *The Drama of Ideas: Platonic Provocations in Theater and Philosophy* (Oxford: Oxford University Press, 2010), 141–142. For a different approach to this point, see Kornhaber, *The Birth of Theater from the Spirit of Philosophy*. For Kornhaber, Nietzsche, with his interest in stage performance (rather than drama as text), is indeed a philosopher of the theater. While I am in agreement with Kornhaber's placing of Nietzsche in the line of philosophy of theater from Lessing to Schiller, I do not follow his emphasis on Nietzsche's own contribution being primarily a philosophy of theater (rather than a philosophy of art and culture, more broadly). However, for the young Nietzsche, tragic culture must be approached, as Kornhaber points out, precisely by way of tragedy as performed (rather than read). In this sense, Nietzsche is, as he puts it, "the first performance theorist" (ibid., 50).

On the face of it, Barish's observation cannot be disputed: The Dionysiac allows for no individual characters. What can be disputed, though, is the notion that Nietzsche does not care about modern theater. In a way, the entire *Birth of Tragedy* is an attempt to think through the possibility of a contemporary artwork that can facilitate the kind of life-affirmation and elevating experience that, in Nietzsche's analysis, tragedy created in Attic culture. In this work, Nietzsche is interested in how tragedy, at its best, achieved a successful balance between the Apolline and the Dionysiac. Moreover, Barish assumes that Nietzsche's relevance to drama theory is limited to his claims about ancient tragedy. However, as we have seen in Chapter 6, the affinities between Nietzsche and nineteenth-century theater go beyond Nietzsche's work on tragedy.[7] Rather than limiting themselves to Nietzsche's reflections on art and theater, Ibsen and other nineteenth-century artists drew inspiration from his work more broadly.[8] Once we give up the assumption that either we solely focus on *The Birth of Tragedy* or Nietzsche's work is of no relevance for theater, we open for a more inclusive interpretation of Nietzsche's relationship to the performative arts. This, obviously, is not to say that *The Birth of Tragedy* is not important.[9] All it suggests is that Nietzsche's influence goes beyond this seminal work.

While Nietzsche was critical of the performing arts (especially opera), he had been engaged with acting and theater since his early youth.[10] Throughout the 1870s and 1880s, he routinely referred to Shakespeare, Goethe, Schiller, and Franz Grillparzer. *Untimely Meditations* include references to Aeschylus, Hölderlin, and Kleist. Brandes had made Nietzsche aware of Ibsen, but also of August Strindberg, with whom Nietzsche corresponded in the late 1880s.[11] Like many of his contemporaries, Nietzsche, at the time, sought to make sense of realism and naturalism in drama and literature more broadly. And even after he abandoned *The Birth of Tragedy*, he retained his interest in

[7] This applies whether one, like Julian Young, emphasizes the Schopenhauerian aspects of Nietzsche's metaphysics, or, like Béatrice Han-Pile, connects it with a return to pre-Socratic philosophy. See Julian Young, *Nietzsche's Philosophy of Art* (Cambridge: Cambridge University Press, 1994) and Béatrice Han-Pile, "Nietzsche's Metaphysics in the *Birth of Tragedy*," *The European Journal of Philosophy*, vol. 14, no. 3 (2006): 373–403.

[8] Hence it is symptomatic that Strindberg, throughout the years he turned to Nietzsche, had not read *The Birth of Tragedy*, but *Beyond Good and Evil*, *The Case of Wagner*, *Twilight of the Idols*, and *The Genealogy of Morality*. For this point, see Kornhaber, *The Birth of Theater*, 96–97.

[9] See, again, LaMothe, *Nietzsche's Dancers*.

[10] Large, "Nietzsche's Shakespearean Figures," 47.

[11] See Herman Scheffauer, "A Correspondence between Nietzsche and Strindberg," *The North American Review*, vol. 198 (1913):197–205. See also Kornhaber, *The Birth of Theater*, Chapter 4.

theater. A quote from the *Gay Science* evidences that ten years after the publication of his first book, Nietzsche, while having broken away from Wagner, was still interested in the experiences the theater provides or fails to provide. "At the theatre," he writes, "one is honest only as a mass; as an individual one lies, lies to oneself."[12] The metaphysical currents of *The Birth of Tragedy* long gone, Nietzsche had not given up the idea of a transformative experience of meaning that can challenge the notion of a disinterested, subjective-universal attitude as a key component in aesthetic experience.[13] In this sense, Nietzsche's critique of theater remains a part of his more comprehensive critique of modern culture.

As the young Nietzsche had argued, tragedy is ultimately celebratory. In the face of suffering, tragedy "speaks of over-brimming, indeed triumphant existence," or as he also puts it, a "fantastic superabundance of life" (BT 22; KSA I 35).[14] The affirmation of life remains a key component of his thought. Moreover, there exists in Nietzsche a parallel between drama and history. This parallel, as we have seen (Chapter 1), had already been explored by Lessing, Herder, and others. However, as Nietzsche sees it, history and art should be in the service of life. Just as a lack of genuine art and artistic experience leaves us with an unhealthy distinction between inner and outer—and, as a consequence, a lack of life-affirmative expression—so a lack of historical sense leaves us with an alienating distance between the self and its culture that ultimately prevents the active and critical use of history in shaping the future.[15]

In *Untimely Meditations*, Nietzsche deepens the notion of there being a parallel between modern history and modern art. In his view, modern agents do not genuinely care about history. Relatedly, they fail in the area of art: "as the youth races through history, so do we modern men race through art galleries and listen to concerts," he writes (UM 98; KSA I 299). He fears that culture is reduced to an aestheticizing afterthought; there is no longer an affirmative approach to art. Under such circumstances, we are deprived of a context in which our lives can find a larger (symbolic) meaning. Meaning,

---

[12] Nietzsche, *The Gay Science*; KSA III, Book Five, section 368.

[13] See also Nietzsche, *On the Genealogy of Morality*; KSA V, third treatise, section 6. Further discussion can be found in Nick Zangwill, "Nietzsche on Kant on Beauty and Disinterest," *History of Philosophy Quarterly*, vol. 30 (2013): 75–91.

[14] For a discussion of this point, see Bernard Reginster, *The Affirmation of Life: Nietzsche on Overcoming Nihilism* (Cambridge, MA: Harvard University Press, 2009). Reginster, however, pays little attention to *The Birth of Tragedy*. This, in my view, leaves him with an incomplete image of the development as well as the systematic versatility of Nietzsche's notion of life-affirmation.

[15] See Nietzsche's discussion in BT 96–97; KSA I 130–31.

after all, is a function of value, and art, for Nietzsche, is an activity in which value is created, appreciated, passed on, and kept alive. However, what worries Nietzsche even more than the hollowing out of culture, is the experience that we do not even *care* about the loss of meaning. He worries that the modern abandonment of art and history to specialists (art and history are no longer part of life) does not even generate a sense of alienation (*Befremdung*). Instead, we meekly comply with the status quo. At this point, we will, as Nietzsche puts it (in a tone that echoes in the lines of Ibsen's Stockmann), seek refuge in "an intentional stupidity [Stumpfsinn]" (UM 98; KSA I 299). Art and history are, in other words, closely connected in that they both relate to what Nietzsche views as the possibility of a life that is led with a surplus of celebratory energy, creativity, and expressivity. When this connection is severed, we are left not only with poorer art and history, but also with a poorer existence.

From this point of view, Nietzsche's concern for art and dramatic poetry cannot be reduced to an attempt to rekindle the spirit of early Greek tragedy (like Barish argues). Nor is it focused simply on realizing a particular musical-artistic program (such as Wagner's). Beyond the early 1870s, Nietzsche's artistic legacy is related to (or at least centrally includes) a more comprehensive effort to discuss the human life conditions that span across, but are not limited to, his philosophy of tragedy and philosophy of history and culture. Philosophy, history, art, and education all contribute to a continuum of human flourishing. What matters is no longer theater and drama in the narrow sense of the terms but, rather, historically mediated culture as a sphere of value in and through which human beings actualize themselves. After all, what had interested Nietzsche from the beginning was tragic *culture*, not a narrow notion of tragedy as a *genre*. In this sense, Barish's worry is partly warranted, though his point should not be related to a one-sided cultivation of the Dionysian forces, but to Nietzsche's broader, philosophical outlook. With this broader Nietzschean framework in mind, we turn to *Hedda Gabler*.

History and Historians

In some ways, *Hedda Gabler* was a success before it was even finished. Ibsen's manuscript was sent out early on to translators in England, France, and Germany. It premiered in Germany (Munich) and was staged in Finland,

Sweden, and Denmark before it was made available to a Norwegian theater audience.

Ibsen subtitles his work "A Drama [Skuespil] in Four Acts." As the play opens, Hedda and Jørgen Tesman have just returned from their honeymoon. It is soon made clear, though, that Jørgen has spent his days as a newlywed doing archival work for a study of Medieval Brabantian handicraft, a work that, he hopes, will land him a position at the local university.[16] However, in spite of his excitement at the topic of medieval Brabant, there can hardly be a more dull and narrow-minded historian than Ibsen's Jørgen Tesman. It is symptomatic that we first encounter Tesman through Aunt Julle's unintentionally comical portrait of her nephew's mindset: "Yes, collecting things and sorting them out . . . you've always been good at that" (OI VII 179; HIS IX 26). Hedda's patience with Tesman's scholarship is limited. Not without a touch of irony, she confides in Judge Brack, the cynical family friend:

BRACK. [. . .] And I was convinced you were having a wonderful time on the trip!

HEDDA. Oh, magnificent!

BRACK. But Tesman was always saying so in his letters.

HEDDA. Yes, he was! He's absolutely in his element if he's given leave to grub around in the libraries. And sit copying out ancient parchments . . . or whatever they are.

BRACK [a little maliciously]. After all, that is his particular raison d'être. Part of it, anyway.

HEDDA. Yes, that's it. So it was all very fine for him. . . . But for me! Oh no, my dear Brack. For me it was horribly tedious!

BRACK [sympathizing]. Was it really as bad as all that?

HEDDA. Oh yes, use your imagination . . . ! (OI VII 205; HIS 75–76)

Later, in Act Four, Tesman's self-description confirms his wife's initial characterization. In Tesman's own words: "putting other people's papers in order . . . that's just the sort of thing I'm good at" (OI VII 264; HIS IX 196).

---

[16] The reference to Brabant was no novelty in Ibsen's work and culture. In The Pretenders, we encounter a Master Sigard of Brabant. References to Brabant also figured in Rudolf Keyser's study of the history of the Norwegian Church under Catholicism (1856–1858). Further, we should keep in mind Richard Wagner's 1850 Lohengrin. See Rudolf Keyser, Den norske kirkes historie under katholicismen, https://babel.hathitrust.org/cgi/pt?id=wu.89097230825;view=1up;seq=1142 (Accessed June 2019). See also Roger Hollinrake, Nietzsche, Wagner, and the Philosophy of Pessimism (London: Georg Allen and Unwin Ltd, 1982).

There is, no doubt, a long way from Ibsen's free and artistic handling of history in his early work to the more pedestrian orientation of a Jørgen Tesman. And the audience is led to sympathize with Hedda's boredom. Ostermeier's 2005 production has Hedda, played by Katharina Schüttler, confined in a sleekly modern, home that seems increasingly claustrophobic as Julle and Tesman's expectations become clear to her (see color plate 7).

In contrast to Tesman, there is the free-spirited Ejlert Løvborg, whom Hedda, in her despairing moments, envisions with vine leaves in his hair (i.e., the feature that has been taken to signify his Dionysiac disposition). If Tesman studies a past long gone and of interest only to a specialized readership of academic historians, Løvborg, for his part, has written a popular world history and is about to publish a work on the present that, transcending his métier as historian, purports to foretell the future. Just as we get Tesman's academic credentials described by his aunt, so Løvborg's first success is conveyed by his work companion, Mrs. Elvsted: "Yes, [it is] a big new book, dealing with cultural development [Kulturgangen] . . . sort of altogether [sånn i det hele]. It's a fortnight ago, now [that it was published]. And then when it sold so many copies . . . and caused such an enormous stir" (OI VII 187; HIS IX 41).

In different ways, Tesman and Løvborg use Hedda for their historical-pedagogical endeavors. With his lecturing about the cultural value of the places they visit, Tesman pulverizes every veneer of a romantic honeymoon. As Hedda describes it to Brack, "you ought to have a try at it! Hearing about the history of civilization day in and day out" (OI VII 206; HIS IX 77). Hedda brutally undercuts her husband's didactic *entretiens* by stating, with a sweeping generalization, that "academics [fagmennesker] aren't a bit amusing as travelling-companions" (OI VII 206; HIS IX 77). Løvborg, by contrast, does not bore Hedda with historical exercises. When she was younger, he used to invite her to sit perched next to him on the couch in her father's study and secretively muse about a life free of social conventions and bourgeois etiquette (OI VII 222; HIX IX 109). Tesman's lecturing is unbearably dull—and so is the life Hedda envisions she will have with him. Løvborg's teaching, by contrast, is vital and invigorating and this, it seems, is carried over into their early friendship. Hedda testifies that there was "something beautiful, something attractive . . . something courageous to . . . this secret intimacy, this companionship that no one even dreamed of" (OI VII 222; HIS IX 108). And, what is more, Løvborg makes it clear that even though he wants to beat Tesman in the race for a position at the University, he has no desire to accept it (OI VII 218; HIS IX 101)—he does not, to borrow Hedda's phrase, want to be a *fagmenneske*. All he wants is the *agon*, the excitement of the competition.

Løvborg's ideals (and his hopes for a history so grand that it makes academia seem idle and petty-minded) face two threats: his alcohol consumption and his need to lean on the far more reasonable Mrs. Thea Elvsted. Once an object of Tesman's affection, Mrs. Elvsted has turned to Løvborg and is ready to "save" him and the book project that Hedda will later describe as their baby. Mrs. Elvsted's orderliness keeps Løvborg away from his Dionysiac excesses. As Løvborg, in Act Three, describes his relationship to her, this is not undividedly positive news: "She's broken my courage, and my defiance [Det er livsmodet og livstrodsen, som hun har knækket i mig]" (OI VII 248; HIS IX 162). Torn between excess and dullness, Løvborg, at the end of the day, is unable to live as he preaches. And unless he stays true to the spirit of his ideas, his words have no value. This, at least, is how Hedda views it. It is, among other things, with this in mind that she first coaxes Løvborg to attend the fatal party (with the risk that he will return to his drinking [Act Two]) and later dares him to fearlessly take his life (Act Three). Once more, it is clear that Hedda longs for a connection between history, life, and value. The point is not only that Hedda practically asks Løvborg to commit suicide, but that she, like him, sees him as a failure if he cannot stick to his own ideals and care enough about them to get his work written and published without the assistance of the more dry- (and sober-)minded Mrs. Elvsted. For Hedda, grand visions are only worthwhile if they translate into life; history is only worthwhile if it informs the present and the future.

A similar intersection between history and life features centrally in Nietzsche. Nietzsche, we know, was trained as a classicist.[17] Not only had he written the extravagant *The Birth of Tragedy*. He had also produced more traditional studies of Greek culture and poetry.[18] Further, the debate that ensued in the wake of *The Birth of Tragedy* had raised fundamental questions about the methods and goals of historical work. Nietzsche's ardent critic, Ulrich von Wilamowitz-Moellendorff, had accused him (Nietzsche) of being neither historical nor philosophical.[19] Shortly after, and possibly as a response

[17] For a discussion of the importance of Nietzsche's training, see for instance Anthony K. Jensen, *Nietzsche's Philosophy of History* (Cambridge: Cambridge University Press, 2013), 7–57.

[18] Jensen discusses this point in *Nietzsche's Philosophy of History*, 3, 75, 80.

[19] See Ulrich von Wilamowitz-Moellendorff, "Zukunftsphilologie," in Reich (ed.), *Rezensionen und Reaktionen*, 56–77. It is but the irony of history that Wilamowitz-Moellendorff should, in turn, be accused of approaching Greek tragedy through the lens of Ibsen's contemporary drama. See William M. Calder III, "The Riddle of Wilamowitz's *Phaidrabild*," in *Greek, Roman, and Byzantine Studies*, vol. 20 (1979): 219–236. I thank Constanze Güthenke for this reference.

to this debate, Nietzsche offered his typology of historians in the second untimely meditation.

In the second meditation, *On the Uses and Disadvantages of History for Life*, Nietzsche surveys three historical prototypes. He first portrays the efforts of *monumental* history, which is driven by admiration for the great deeds of the past and a sense that the past can serve as an ideal or inspiration in the present.[20] Then there is *antiquarian* history, which "preserves and reveres" (UM 72; KSA I 265). Antiquarian history gives future generations a knowledge of the past understood as finished, objectivized, and a subject of scientific inquiry. Finally, there is *critical* history, which approaches the past as a continuous educational development (UM 76; KSA I 269).

In *Hedda Gabler*, Ibsen gives Løvborg's manuscript the title "The Philosophy of a Future Culture" (HIS IX/B 27). In pointing out the relevance of *Untimely Meditations* for our understanding of *Hedda Gabler*, Aarseth associates Tesman with the antiquarian and Løvborg with the critical historian: "Jørgen Tesman with his interest in old periodicals and domestic crafts can be seen as a caricature of the antiquarian. Ejlert Løvborg is apparently less empirically oriented, but highly creative in his historical imagination and with his remarkable interest in the social forces of culture and the future course of civilization, his contribution seems to be more in line with the type Nietzsche calls the critical historian."[21]

While Nietzsche's philosophy—and, indeed, *Untimely Meditations*—provides a hermeneutic foil for *Hedda Gabler*, his historical typology is hardly the most promising place to start. Nietzsche operates with three kinds of historical approaches. Ibsen, on Aarseth's reading, only has two. And though Tesman might well fit with the antiquarian model, it is unclear, to say the least, whether Løvborg's historical work would best be characterized as critical (as Aarseth suggests) or as monumental. More important, however, is the fact that for Nietzsche, this division is not all that fundamental. Quite to the contrary, he makes it clear that all three kinds of history are needed. As he puts it, "[t]hese [the monumental, antiquarian, and critical] are the services history is capable of performing for life; every man and every nation requires, in accordance with its goals, energies and needs, a certain kind of

---

[20] The monumental historian argues "[t]hat the great moments in the struggle of the human individual constitute a chain, that this chain unites mankind across the millennia like a range of human mountain peaks, that the summit of such a long-ago moment shall be for me still living, bright and great—that is the fundamental idea of the faith in humanity which finds expression in the demand for a *monumental* history" (UM 68; KSA I 259).

[21] Aarseth, "Vital Romanticism," 8.

knowledge of the past, now in the form of monumental, now of antiquarian, now of critical history" (UM 77; KSA I 271). Hence the real question is not which of the three approaches a historian chooses, but whether or not one's cultivation of history is indeed in the service of life. If the bonds between history and life are severed (and, as a consequence, history no longer serves as a reservoir of meaning), then culture becomes aestheticized and history reduced to an objectivizing science.

Once Nietzsche has made it clear that all the three kinds of history are needed, he continues by stating that life "does not require. . . . a host of pure thinkers who only look on at life, of knowledge-thirsty individuals whom knowledge alone will satisfy and to whom the accumulation of knowledge is itself the goal" (UM 77; KSA I 271). For Nietzsche, the more fundamental distinction is that between history as narrowly scientific and history as it remains alive and conveys value. Such a reading is confirmed by Nietzsche's connecting of history, in a broader sense, with education. As he puts it, "I trust that *youth* has led me aright when it now *compels me to protest at the historical education of modern man* and when I demand that man should above all learn to live and should employ history only in *the service of the life he has learned to live*" (UM 116; KSA I 324). This, it seems, is the real difference between Tesman and Løvborg. For Løvborg, history is potentially in the service of life—at least it would be, if his life were sorted. Tesman's life is "sorted," but history is decoupled from it. This is what makes Tesman's lecturing so boring for Hedda.

For Tesman, history is an object to be analyzed dryly and without passion; history should be dissected and classified—each object and each event in its place. This place, in turn, is always in the past. History is not studied with the needs of the present in mind. For Løvborg, by contrast, history relates to the present and even the future. History, for Løvborg, can therefore not be about "collecting things and sorting them out," as Aunt Julle had put it. It is, rather, a subject that matters existentially; historical understanding is directly relevant for how one should live.[22]

The point, on Nietzsche's model, is not that one has to choose between these two approaches, but that they offer different conceptual tools through which we can approach our relationship to the past. The relationship between the past and the present is, indeed, a topic with which Ibsen,

---

[22] Hedda's conversation with Løvborg has a palpably erotic side to it. Løvborg, further, is the only one to call her by her maiden name—just as Tesman will later addresses Mrs. Elvsted as Ms. Rysing.

in the 1860s, had been most concerned. It was fundamental to the historical plays that made up the bulk of his early work. Further, from within *Hedda Gabler*, the history–life connection is entirely central to a full appreciation of the character of Hedda, the play's protagonist. That is, by turning away from Nietzsche's historical classifications to his theory of the larger purpose of historical work, we also get Hedda back in view.

For Hedda, the past is neither a theoretical nor an academic object. Her relationship to the past is, emphatically, a question of her self-understanding. In marrying Tesman, Hedda sees her identity reduced to empty phrases (as in Aunt Julle's proud comments about Hedda's class background). It is framed and displayed as mere decorum in the form of her father's portrait on the wall (OI VII 171; HIS IX 11).[23] Moreover, it does not matter to Hedda that she now inhabits the Lady Falk Villa. The villa, with its grand past, is still an empty shell. Stretching himself financially, Tesman had bought the villa for Hedda's sake. However, in her exchange with Brack, Hedda has a different story to tell. It is worth quoting at length:

HEDDA [*looking straight ahead*]. [. . .] I don't really know why I should be . . . happy. Or perhaps you might be able to tell me?

BRACK. Yes . . . among other things, because you've got just the home [hjem] you wanted.

HEDDA [*looks up and laughs*]. Do you also believe that fairy story [ønskehistorien]?

BRACK. Why, isn't there anything in it?

HEDDA. Oh yes . . . there's something in it.

BRACK. Well?

HEDDA. There's this much in it, that I used Tesman as an escort to take me home from the evening parties last summer . . .

BRACK. Ah, regrettably. . . I had to go quite a different way.

HEDDA. True enough, you were going a rather different way, last summer.

BRACK [*laughs*]. Touché, my lady! Well . . . but you and Tesman, then . . . ?

HEDDA. Yes, well then we came past this house one evening. And Tesman, poor fellow, was floundered and dithering. Because he couldn't think of anything to talk about. So I felt sorry for the poor erudite man . . .

---

[23] In *Lady Inger*, we encounter an early example of Ibsen's penchant for family portraits: Lady Inger turns the portraits around upon feeling crushed by her past and the traditions that saturate the walls of her home.

BRACK [*smiles sceptically*]. Did you? Hm . . .

HEDDA. Yes, by your leave sir, I did. And then . . . to help him along a bit . . .
I happened to say, just on the impulse, that I'd like to live here in this villa.

BRACK. No more than that?

HEDDA. Not that particular evening.

BRACK. But afterwards, then?

HEDDA. Ah yes. My impulsiveness had its consequences, my dear Mr. Brack.

BRACK. Unfortunately . . . impulsiveness does that only too frequently, my lady.

HEDDA. Thank you! But in this ardour for Lady Falk's villa Jørgen Tesman and I met in mutual understanding, you see! It brought on engagement and marriage and honeymoon and the whole lot. Ah well, Mr. Brack . . . as one makes one's bed one must lie on it . . . I almost said.

BRACK. But this is delicious! And perhaps you didn't really care about the place at all?

HEDDA. No, God knows I did not. (OI VII 210–211; HIS IX 85–88)

Without a living historical context, the villa, with all that it symbolizes, is devoid of meaning. The "smell of lavender and pot-pourri in all the rooms" is, for Hedda, a nauseating manifestation of the petit-bourgeois ambition that Aunt Julle brings with her (OI VII 210–211; HIS IX 85–88). Brack may be able to offer Hedda a break from her boredom, yet, what Hedda really craves—what she seeks in Løvborg—is a way to reconnect history (legacy) and life, a way to make life *meaningful*. She needs him to demonstrate, in real life (rather than by way of academic credentials), that the past matters, that there is indeed a way to connect history and existence. For Hedda, what sets Løvborg apart is not the object studied (Medieval Brabantian crafts or world history), but the *attitude* with which he approaches his work. In Tesman's case, the object of research only matters dramatically because it reflects his dry disposition. It is obviously relevant that Ibsen, with *Emperor and Galilean*, had himself written what he called a world-historical drama and thus approached history with an attitude that differs from that of a *fagmenneske*. Yet the fate bestowed on Løvborg indicates, quite sensibly, that a merely existential history is also not a solution.

In this sense, we have reasons to assume, with Aarseth, that Nietzsche's theatrical legacy includes his reflections on history in *Untimely Meditations*.

Going beyond Aaarseth's claim, however, we should grant that the resonances from *Untimely Meditations* do not boil down to a mapping of different historical-academic types onto dramatic characters, but, more profoundly, address philosophical-existential alternatives: different approaches to history, life, and the connection between them. From this point of view, *all* one-sided historical approaches, be they categorized as antiquarian, monumental, or critical, fall short. The same applies to the contrasts between merely academic and sheer life-infused history: they both provide extreme positions, departure points for reflection rather than genuine philosophical-existential alternatives.

That said, the standard focus on Hedda's image of Løvborg and his (Dionysiac) vine leaves has the advantage of establishing a link between Ibsen's drama and the part of Nietzsche's work that deals specifically with tragedy. Thus, we ought to ask if there is, with respect to the Nietzschean resonances in *Hedda Gabler*, a way to combine a broader focus on history and life, on the one hand, with an emphasis on tragedy, on the other. At this point, it is helpful to keep in mind how Nietzsche both breaks away from *and* places himself within the discussion of stagecraft and repertoires in late eighteenth- and nineteenth-century European philosophy.

History, Tragedy, Existence

In the reception of Nietzsche's work, it is often overlooked how he situates *The Birth of Tragedy* within the context of German philosophy of theater. What is unique about this tradition is that the approach to drama (and the role of the theater within a new world of middle-class audiences and vernacular languages) goes hand in hand with a discussion of history and, even more so, the historicity of human existence, especially in its modern form. As the classicist paradigm lost its grip and European drama started to express genuinely modern ideals and forms, Lessing, Herder, A. W. Schlegel, and Hegel had insisted that drama is a point from within which one may explore culture and history more broadly.[24] For these philosophers, history is not viewed in narrowly epistemological terms. Rather, a philosophical understanding of

---

[24] This, as we have seen, is particularly clear in the case of Shakespeare, who was regarded, from the 1750s onward, as the first modern playwright. Hettner's *Das moderne Drama* funnels the discussion of historical drama, making up the first third of the work, through a discussion of Shakespeare.

human historicity forces us to transcend a narrow construction of academic disciplines and subfields and open for a larger, collaborative enterprise that includes philosophers as well as artists.[25]

At this point, we begin to get a more complete view of the interaction between Ibsen's drama and Nietzsche's philosophy. Rather than exemplify a philosophical position, a work such as *Hedda Gabler* presents a set of different philosophical and existential possibilities without seeking to erect a hierarchy, develop a teleology, or reach a clear conclusion about their fit. Ibsen is part of a literary culture that, for almost a century and a half, had been drawing on philosophical thinking, and the philosophy in question had itself been informed by art, in particular by drama. As drama gains a modern coinage, stage-setting, music, and characters disclose the successes and failures in our existential maneuvering *and* the progress and failures we make in trying to understand and conceptualize our historical life.

In their one-sided approaches to history, Tesman and Løvborg barely make it beyond the comical, if not outright farcical. They emerge as caricatures whose actions the audience can easily anticipate—only to obtain a sense of comical release when their expectations are not only met, but indeed exceeded. In spite of the apparent differences between them, they are both the kind of scholars who isolate their historical interests and fail, in terms of academic *orientation* (Tesman) or personal strength (Løvborg), to connect life and scholarly work. Tesman suffers from a shortage of life, Løvborg from a shortage of discipline. Further, they both act out a conceptual *position*. With Hedda, it is different. She responds to a *Lebensgefühl*. Hence, the picture of the two historians must be completed by bringing in the main character, who takes the work from the (mostly) farcical to the tragic, although the tragic, for Ibsen, is never without a connection to the comical.[26]

He emphasizes that even historical drama must be contemporary and that the best historical drama reflects its own time (as well as the time of the plot). See Hettner, *Das moderne Drama*, 59–60.

[25] Thus, in Nietzsche's work, we find references to the art of philosophizing and the creative philosopher. For a discussion of Nietzsche's notion of philosophy as art, see Aaron Ridley's *Nietzsche on Art* (London: Routledge, 2007), 89–112.

[26] For a recent study of Ibsen's humor, see Ståle Dingstad, *Den smilende Ibsen. Henrik Ibsens forfatterskap—stykkevis og delt* (Oslo: Centre for Ibsen Studies, 2013). Dingstad, though, does not draw parallels between Ibsen's humor and Nietzsche's call for a philosophy (and art) of affirmation. Nor for that sake is it often mentioned in the secondary literature how the Hegelian call for late comedy served to legitimize the Scandinavian interest in the comedy and the vaudeville.

With her high-end material demands and mean-spirited comments, Hedda might emerge as a rather spoiled young woman. Nowhere is this more evident than when she, driven by jealousy and disappointment, burns Løvborg's unpublished manuscript, which Tesman rescued when Løvborg left it behind after a night of heavy drinking. Having sent Løvborg off with one of the dueling pistols she inherited from her father, Hedda has a moment to herself:

[HEDDA *listens at the door for a moment. Then she goes to the desk and takes out the package with the manuscript, peeps inside the wrappers for a moment, takes some of the leaves half way out and looks at them. Then she takes it all over to the armchair by the stove and sits down. After a while she opens the stove door, and unwraps the package.*]

HEDDA [*throws one of the folded sheets into the fire and whispers to herself*]. Now I'm burning your child, Thea! With your curly hair! [*Throws a few more sheets into the stove.*] Your child and Ejlert Løvborg's. [*Throws in the rest*]. I'm burning . . . burning your child [Nu brænder,— nu brænder jeg barnet]. (OI VII 250; HIS IX 167)

Hedda's motives may, at first, seem petty. Yet, as so often with Hedda Gabler, her reluctant speech and lingering give her lines another layer of meaning. Not only does she burn the manuscripts, but it is clear that she, too, is burning. The bond between Mrs. Elvsted and Løvborg may have caused her jealousy, but it is also a reminder of Løvborg's failure to consistently and freely pursue his vision of a synthesis of history and life. It is the fact that he needs Mrs. Elvsted to keep him on track—that his vision did not carry enough weight to keep him going—that destroys the beauty for which Hedda longs.

In Ibsen's play, it is Hedda, more than anyone else, who shelters desires beyond the ordinary.[27] In *A Doll's House*, Ibsen had let Nora long for a miracle, a true union with her husband. Hedda's dreams, by contrast, go far beyond her

---

[27] I would like to draw attention to a feature of the Scandinavian reception that is of importance to the discussion of Nietzsche's dramatic legacy, generally speaking, and Ibsen's work, in particular. For once Nietzsche's work is better known in Scandinavia—and Nietzsche does indeed acknowledge the importance of this reception in several places, including *Ecce Homo*—many of his readers would quickly distance themselves from his negative views on women (for this point, see Beyer, *Nietzsche i Norden*, 59–61). In fact, August Strindberg stands out in that he actively endorses this dimension of Nietzsche's thought in a period when feminism was gaining a foothold in Scandinavia. This point is especially worth noting if we keep in mind Ibsen's strong female protagonists, including Nora Helmer and Hedda Gabler.

marriage.[28] In fact, she is hardly interested in her marriage and indicates, as we have seen, that she practically got married out of sheer boredom. When Løvborg speaks of her love for Tesman, she brushes him off with "Love? That's good! [Kjærlighet! Nej, nu er De god!]" (OI VII 221; HIS IX 106). Caring only about his academic advancement, the recognition of his peers, and the comforts of the home, Tesman cannot give Hedda what she needs.[29]

Tesman realizes that Hedda's outlook on life is different and that he should offer her more than just a petit bourgeois life ("I couldn't possibly have expected her to put up with a plain petit bourgeois environment [rent småborgelige omgivelser]," OI VII 197; HIS IX 61, trans. modified). For Tesman, Hedda thus represents a way out of such an environment, an ascent to a freer life. And yet he relies on a full-time position and a regular salary—tokens of the petite bourgeoisie—in order to offer her the kind of life she previously would take for granted. In this way, Tesman's plans remain constrained by the framework he seeks to escape through his marriage.

Tesman, in a certain sense, is completely irrelevant to Hedda. The same is true of Løvborg. To Hedda, Løvborg is only relevant insofar as he aspires to combine life and thought—but beyond that, as a person, he matters so little that Hedda is willing to have him sacrifice his life. In killing himself, he will at least admit his failure to live out his idea of a relationship between history and existence—potentially also offering Hedda a faint hope that the beautiful can live on independently of its failing to be realized in his life and work. Unsurprisingly, Hedda mourns the loss of her companion by focusing on herself. Upon receiving the news of Løvborg's suicide, she looks at Brack "with an expression of revulsion [ækelhed]": "Everything I touch seems destined to turn into something mean and low [Å det latterlige og det lave, det lægger sig som en forbandelse ved alt *det*, jeg bare rører ved]" (OI VII 263; HIS IX 194, trans. modified).

After Løvborg's death, nothing is left for Hedda except simply holding out. The situation gets worse when Brack reminds Hedda that, by giving Løvborg one of her dueling pistols, she might be in legal trouble.

---

[28] Yet there are clear parallels between Nora and Hedda Gabler. Neither of them finds an equal in their male companion. Moreover, Nora and Hedda are both being pressured by pragmatic and cynical men (Krogstad and Brack), and their respective demises are accompanied by musical moves, be it in the form of Nora's tarantella or Hedda's wild piano playing just before her suicide.

[29] It is worth noting how Ibsen has many of his male characters invest in the home sphere. His lead women, by contrast, often feel constrained by the (family) home.

BRACK. [. . .] you will be obliged to tell the court why you gave Ejlert Løvborg
the pistol. And what inference will be drawn from the fact that you did
give it to him?

HEDDA [*lowers her head*]. That's true. I didn't think of that.

BRACK. Well, fortunately there is nothing to fear as long as I keep silence.

HEDDA [*looks up at him*]. And so I am in your power, Mr. Brack. From now
on I am at your mercy.

BRACK [*whispers more softly*]. Dearest Hedda . . . believe me . . . I shall not
abuse the position.

HEDDA. In your power, all the same. Subject to your will and your demands.
No longer free! [*She gets up violently.*] No! That's a thought that I'll never
endure! Never. (OI VII 266; HIS IX 199–200)

To her audience, Hedda's freedom had already seemed limited, caught, as she
was, in a situation she cannot get out of. Realizing that her future is now in
Brack's hands, she has lost the little freedom she had left (her hope of future
freedom). Her father's pistols, introduced early on in the play, grant a viable
exit for Hedda.[30] Yet that, too, is no real exit: She can prove her freedom by
killing herself, but then she also kills her potential for freedom. Hedda's world
is increasingly claustrophobic. If Løvborg had made unwanted advances on
her younger self (his desire is still evident), both the Tesmans and Brack will
take what they want and do so regardless of the price that Hedda ends up
paying.[31] Her pregnancy—the possibility of future Tesmans!—is part of her
predicament.

In the absence of a connection between history and life, in the absence of
freedom, what remains, for Hedda, is mere theater. She has already tried to
break out of her boredom by taking on the role as director of her own domestic
drama. She makes the other characters puppets in her productions, often
taking the form of communication games (as in her condescending mockery
of Aunt Julle's new hat), or her many stagings of double conversations in
which she, shamelessly involving her guests (mostly of the opposite sex),
addresses Jørgen and Julle at a level that they are bound to miss. In this way,
she theatrically displays—to herself and to her world—the utter loneliness

---

[30] For an analysis of Hedda's pistols, see Susan L. Feagin, "Where Hedda Dies: The Significance of
Place," in Gjesdal (ed.), *Ibsen's Hedda Gabler: Philosophical Perspectives*, 48–71.

[31] This point is well made in Frode Helland, "The Scars of Modern Life: *Hedda Gabler* in Adorno's
Prism," in *Ibsen's Hedda Gabler: Philosophical Perspectives*, 92–112.

of her future life as Mrs. Tesman.[32] Whereas Nietzsche, in his early days, had dreamed of the rebirth of tragedy as a broad, cultural phenomenon, Hedda has nothing beyond her role as the dramaturge of her living room. Furniture, flowers, people are all reduced to props in her play. With Brack's advances, she has lost even this. She is now a marionette in his play.

In classical Greek tragedy, the protagonists shape their actions in the face of a worthy antagonist. Antigone, for example, is given stage presence through her confrontation with Creon (this, indeed, had been Hegel's point: only in the two of them being equally justified in their point of view is there a genuine tragic conflict[33]). In Ibsen's work, the structure of Greek tragedy, as we saw in Chapter 6, is thoroughly shattered with *Ghosts*. The same applies to *Hedda Gabler*. Hedda, as it were, is a character searching for someone who can give her room to act. In Løvborg, she *almost* finds a worthy counterpart.[34] But when Løvborg gives himself away to working on his magnum opus with the rather plain Mrs. Elvsted and, subsequently, to his excessive drinking, Hedda realizes that he can only prove himself the very moment he is prepared to make it clear that an unfree life, a life of addiction and in dependency of Mrs. Elvsted as an externalized super ego, is not worth living.

When Løvborg shoots himself, however, it is without grandeur and beauty (OI VII 265–266; HIS IX 193). The act that was meant to prove his freedom— in Hedda's words, it would be a liberation "to know that an act of spontaneous courage [friviligt modigt] is yet possible in this world. An act that has something of unconditional beauty [Noget, som der falder et skjær av uvilkårlig skønhed over]" (OI VII 262; HIS IX 190)—ends up as a pathetic gesture.

Once Hedda's hope for freedom and beauty is gone, her world shatters rapidly. She realizes that there is not, and cannot be, an antagonist for her. There is no space for acting and no equal to act against. Under such circumstances, freedom for her is an illusion. Ensconced in the Tesman villa and pregnant with a future Tesman, life for Hedda becomes unbearable—not simply

---

[32] Significantly, only Løvborg, half teasingly, calls her that (e.g., OI VII 227–228; HIS IX 119–120). He also reprimands her for having given herself away to somebody as small-minded as Jørgen Tesman. Hence, while Tesman is visibly impressed by Løvborg's work ("Jeg sad og misunte Ejlert, at han havde kunnet skrive sådant noget. Tænk det, Hedda!" OI VII 236; HIS IX 138), Løvborg, for his part, has nothing good to say about Tesman.

[33] See also Joshua Billings's discussion in *Genealogy of the Tragic: Greek Tragedy and German Philosophy* (Princeton: Princeton University Press, 2014), 161–189.

[34] Judge Brack, too, is sometimes brought in as being, for all his cynicism, Hedda's true antagonist. His motives, though, are often base and it is an unclear question, to say the least, if he recognizes Hedda's longings. Løvborg, who does recognize her longings, had also made advances on Hedda (which, in effect, means that she is or has been an object of desire for all the male characters in the play).

because she has lost Løvborg, but because she has lost her last existential outlet. Her response is desperate and has reminded Ibsen's audiences of Nora's tarantella dance.[35] In Ibsen's directions:

> HEDDA *goes into the inner room and pulls the curtains together behind her. A short pause. Suddenly she is heard to play a wild dance tune on the piano.* (OI VII 267; HIS IX 201)

Her companions ask her to tone it down. She ought to behave, she ought to think of the dead, Tesman's Aunt Rina and Ejlert Løvborg. Hedda's response is swift: "I shall be silent in the future," she says, as she, again, draws the curtains to her room (OI VII 267; HIS IX 202). Upon asking, from within the closed curtains, how she will be able to survive the evenings now that Tesman will work with Mrs. Elvsted on the reconstruction of Løvborg's manuscript, she is told that Brack will keep her company. He, in turn, assures her that he "will gladly come every single evening" and that they will "have a fine time out here together" (OI VII 267; HIS IX 202). Soon after, a shot is heard. Hedda has dared what Løvborg did not. She has shot herself in the temple. As the play ends, Hedda's suicide is followed, first by Tesman's ever present "Think of that!" and then, finally, by Brack's cringe-inducing closing line, "but, good God Almighty . . . people don't do such things!" (OI VII 268; HIS IX 203).

Brack's final words shed an eerie light on Hedda's condescending and ironic insistence on manners earlier in the play. As Hedda responds to Mrs. Elvsted's story of a woman pointing a gun at Ejlert Løvborg, knowing far too well the woman is herself, she distances herself from the action in a way that forges a bond with the knowing audience (but not with Mrs. Elvsted): "this kind of behavior is unknown around here" (OI VII 195; HIS IX 56, trans. modified).[36] Further, Brack's line is anticipated when Hedda tells him that she would rather die than lie about how Løvborg got her gun (the gun she gave him to kill himself "beautifully," only to be told by the Judge that "people say such things. But they don't *do* them" (OI VII 266; HIS IX 198, trans. modified)). Obviously, Hedda, having the courage to do what Løvborg could not, does actually *do* the undoable: she shoots herself "in beauty."

---

[35] Moi offers a particularly apt analysis of this part of *A Doll's House* in *Henrik Ibsen and the Birth of Modernism*, 236–242.

[36] Again, Ibsen indicates the repressive authority of a faceless third-person plural: the they (*man*, in Ibsen's original).

Yet, as Ingmar Bergman emphasized, in his production at the Residenztheater in Munich, Hedda's gesture is futile. She not only fails to stage her life in the Tesman villa, but she also, in Bergman's rendering, fails successfully to stage her death. Bergman presents Hedda's misery in the most brutal of ways. Despite her thirst for beauty, she ends her life with her back mercilessly exposed to the audience (Ibsen, by contrast, has her shoot herself in the back room), and with Brack lifting her head up by her hair, so as, in a final act of humiliation, to matter-of-factly conclude that she truly did finish off her life.[37]

From the point of view of the Hedda character, the two historians—one fails to see that history has meaning beyond narrow academic circles, the other fails properly to realize himself and live by his ideals—constitute a theatrical foil. Hedda struggles to overcome the emptiness of a life that took a turn rather different from what she, musing with Løvborg on the couch of her father's study, must have envisioned. She, as it were, lives at the end of history. Hedda's longings are not for this or that kind of history (be it of the antiquarian, monumental, or critical kind), but for a world in which great acts, acts of a historical proportion, can make a difference. At one point, she toys with the idea of Tesman as a politician, though her enthusiasm quickly gives way to contempt. Hedda, in other words, suffers from the kind of divide that Nietzsche, in both *The Birth of Tragedy* and *Untimely Meditations*, takes to be a symptom of a life that is cut off from its past, and, by the same token, cut off from action. A quote from *Untimely Meditations* makes this point clear:

[M]odern man describes with a curious pride . . . his uniquely characteristic inwardness. It is then said that one possesses content and only form is lacking; but such an antithesis is quite improper when applied to living things. This is precisely why our modern culture is not a living thing: it is not a real culture at all but only a kind of knowledge of culture; it has an idea of and feeling for culture but no true cultural achievement emerges from them. (UM 78; KSA I 272–73)

For Nietzsche, this loss of life takes place without us even noticing. He continues:

---

[37] For a discussion of this point, see Marker and Marker, *Ibsen's Lively Art*, 191.

[This inwardness] carries with it a celebrated danger: the content itself, of which it is assumed that it cannot be seen from without, may occasionally evaporate; from without, however, neither its former presence nor its disappearance will be apparent at all. (UM 81; KSA I 276)

However, unlike the Nietzschean philosopher, Hedda, as Ibsen's character, manages to create a new tragedy, a tragedy for the Nineteenth Century.

The Drama of Untimeliness

Acknowledging that history in the old, inspiring sense (as infused with values and visions) is no longer available, and that it is now impossible for her to express her inner turmoil, Hedda turns the loss of historical context into a tragedy on its own terms. That is, where Nietzsche claims that the cultural preconditions for tragedy have dried out, Ibsen, with *Hedda Gabler*, realizes the potential of a new kind of tragic drama.

With its unapologetic modern sensitivity, *Hedda Gabler* is, to be sure, far from the romantic-mythological aspirations of the young, Wagnerian Nietzsche.[38] Yet, within a larger European context, it is a drama that eminently communicates with Nietzsche's works from the early 1870s—that draws on and transcends it—and, in so doing, indicates the theatrical depth of Nietzsche's legacy *and* the philosophical depth of Ibsen's drama.

Although Nietzsche keeps referring to artists and the performative arts, he does not write systematically about tragedy after *The Birth of Tragedy*. While it has been argued that Nietzsche's later work develops the idea of an artistic life, a life in literature and style, as Alexander Nehamas puts it,[39] I have suggested that the outspoken interest in tragedy, right from the beginning, is paired with more comprehensive reflections on history, culture, and the conditions for a fulfilled human existence. In *Untimely Meditations*, Nietzsche, speaking as a classicist-philosopher, admits that he does not know what meaning classical studies would have for our time "if they were not untimely—that is to say, acting counter to our time and thereby acting on our

---

[38] Music, though, is not absent in the play. For the musical dimensions of *Emperor and Galilean*, HIS VI/B offers note sheets throughout. There are also Edvard Grieg's commissioned music to *Peer Gynt* and the short, but significant stints of dancing and piano playing in, respectively, *A Doll's House* and *Hedda Gabler*. Also, the early plays have a musical dimension.

[39] Nehamas, *Nietzsche: Life as Literature*.

time and, let us hope, for the benefit of a time to come" (UM 60; KSA I 247). Similarly, Ibsen, with *Hedda Gabler*, writes a tragedy of his time, but one that, in its fundamental "untimeliness," points to poetic and artistic developments that go beyond it. As dramaturge and tragic heroine, Hedda displays her displacement in the Nineteenth Century but also, in an equally fundamental way, anticipates the modernist sentiments of drama in the century to come.[40]

Ibsen, in this period, sums up his credo in proto-existentialist terms: "Our whole being is nothing but a fight against the dark forces within ourselves."[41] It is as if his characters constitute a proto-modernist gallery of individuals struggling to find their footing in life—a wry, realist parade of characters facing aporetic imperatives that are all the same personal and historical.

In his early work, Nietzsche dreamt of a rebirth of the spirit of Greek tragedy, with its forceful Dionysiac chorus, in nineteenth-century musical drama. In *Hedda Gabler*, the chorus—if we want to use this term in a Nietzschean sense—is shrunk to Hedda's lonely hysterical piano playing just before her suicide. In the closing scene that takes place in the "inner room," sealed off from the audience's view, Hedda *"is heard to play a wild dance tune on the piano"* (OI VII 267; HIS IX 201). Løvborg is dead and Mrs. Elvsted is now a regular in Hedda's own house. Hedda's universe rapidly shrinks until nothing is left but a pervasive claustrophobia. This is the moment at which Hedda Gabler, the General's daughter, can no longer take it. All that is left is her acting out of the final, musical crescendo. This part of the play remained unchanged from the draft to the final version.

Three years after Ibsen's death, Munch painted Ibsen's portrait and placed him between Nietzsche and Socrates (see the Introduction). A few years before the publication of *Hedda Gabler*, Ibsen himself had invited such a presentation when calling for "a synthesis of poetry, philosophy, and religion in a new category and force of life [livsmagt] that we living still cannot conceive."[42] Munch had also been hired to make a number of sketches for

---

[40] The Nietzschean resonances extend to the period after the publication of *Hedda Gabler*. Once we expand our scope from a narrow focus on *The Birth of Tragedy* to a broader interest in Nietzsche's work, it becomes clear how a drama such as *The Master Builder* brings to mind the idea of the architect of the future, whose vision does not leave him dizzy (Nietzsche even speaks of the architect, *Baumeister*, of the future, UM 94; KSA I 294). In *On the Uses and Disadvantages of History for Life*, Nietzsche writes as follows: "He who cannot sink down on the threshold of the moment and forget all the past, who cannot stand balanced like a goddess of victory without growing dizzy and afraid, will never know what happiness is" (UM 62; KSA I 250). Similar resonances—addressing, mostly, the role of art, the question of value, and the challenges of human individuality and existence—can be found in Ibsen's work all the way to *When We Dead Awaken*. For a discussion of *The Master Builder* and Nietzsche, see Frode Helland, "Ibsen and Nietzsche: *The Master Builder*," *Ibsen Studies*, vol. 9, no. 1 (2009): 50–75.

[41] Meyer, *Henrik Ibsen*, vol. III, 146.

[42] See http://ibsen.uio.no/SAK_P18870924Sto_Aftonbl.xhtml (Accessed June 2019).

Hermann Bahr, Max Reinhardt's collaborator in Berlin, and his production of *Hedda Gabler*. In a particularly striking sketch, he has Hedda in a powerful, yet utterly vulnerable pose (Refer Color Plate 8). She appears to be in charge and, at the same time, completely without control. Her tidy dress is giving her protection, yet also exposing her isolation. It is perhaps this sentiment that would later lead Adorno to see Hedda as an emblematic victim of the petite bourgeoisie.[43]

The year of *Hedda Gabler*'s completion was also the year *The Vikings at Helgeland* would premier in Munich.[44] We saw, in Chapter 1, that readers of Ibsen's work have pointed out parallels between Hedda and Hjørdis from *The Vikings at Helgeland*. Like Hjørdis, Hedda is proud and uncompromising and she is struggling to inhabit a world in which old values are no longer entertained and her identity is disintegrating. Like Hjørdis, Hedda faces a male companion whose death offers no redemption, and like her, Hedda's death appears to leave no mark. The world moves on; new worldviews take over. Yet the poet is left to bring testimony.

In Ibsen's time, though, Hedda was not an appreciated character. Edmund Gosse, Ibsen's translator, wrote an early review of the play. He values the character of Mrs. Elvsted, whose life is dedicated to supporting first Løvborg, then Tesman in his reconstruction of the manuscript that Hedda has burned. Hedda, by contrast, is viewed as a monstrous woman. She has no morality—at least not a conventional morality of the kind that can easily be accepted. Her selfishness is nothing short of a perversion. As Gosse has it: she is guilty of "indifferentism and morbid selfishness, all claws and thirst for blood under the delicate velvet of her beauty."[45]

Gosse's review captures the spirit of the reception in Ibsen's time. For, as the work premiered in and outside of Norway, reviewers got caught up in discussions of Hedda's supposed lack of morality from the beginning to the end of the play. Less attention was paid to her sense of inhabiting a world in which morality has become questionable and the shared backdrop of human values, in terms of which morality seemed meaningful, has ceased to exist.[46]

---

[43] Theodor W. Adorno, *Minima Moralia: Reflections from Damaged Life*, trans. E. F. N. Jephcott (London: Verso, 2010), 93–94; *Minima Moralia. Reflexionen aus dem beschädigten Leben, Gesammelte Schriften*, vol. IV (Frankfurt am Main: Suhrkamp, 1980), 103–105.

[44] See Koht, *Henrik Ibsen*, vol. II, 239.

[45] See http://ibsen.nb.no/id/102023.0 (Accessed June 2019).

[46] Christopher Innes (ed.), *Henrik Ibsen's Hedda Gabler: A Sourcebook* (London: Routledge, 2003) offers helpful material on the reception.

Like so many of Ibsen's female protagonists, Hedda realizes that beautiful ideals can no longer be taken for granted. To conceive of beauty in a world that can no longer sustain it is but a false aesthetic consciousness. However, what Hedda craves is not beyond this world. It is not the beauty of elevated ideals, but one that, in establishing meaningful connections with history, gives substance and shape to the everyday fabric of thought and interaction. Here she resembles Hjørdis, Nora, and Helene Alving. Ibsen's female characters do not long for the impossible. They long for a world that they can meaningfully inhabit and call theirs—a world that is, in this sense, both historical and new. Hjørdis, Nora, Helene, and Hedda are not utopian dreamers. They stand out, rather, by virtue of their care for this world and for a future that both continues and breaks with the tradition. Ibsen's tragic characters are profoundly earnest; they do, in an important sense, take their lives, their worlds, and their historicity *seriously*.[47]

If this, as the reviewers pointed out, is nihilism, then it is one that escapes not only the lethargy of Nietzsche's passive nihilist, but also the optimism and fanfare of his world-creating counterpart.[48] Ibsen, in this period, presents himself as a pessimist.[49] He does not, he says, "believe in the eternal life of human ideals." Ibsen adds, though, that this leaves room for an optimism about the "fertility of [human] ideals and their ability to develop."[50] From this point of view, Ibsen's drama, like Nietzsche's philosophy, pleads for an affirmation of life—an affirmation that, as realized by the Oswald character (see Chapter 6), can only come through acceptance of human finitude, thus also of historical existence. For Ibsen, there is beauty in such an acceptance: From his early drama until the very late plays, he explores the weight of historical existence while, at the same time, creating new forms of art and history.

---

[47] We can, in this context, think back to Nietzsche's argument from *The Birth of Tragedy* that only as art is life justified.

[48] Georg Brandes distinguishes between two different kinds of pessimism. Ibsen's pessimism, he claims, is not of the sentimental and longing kind, but more related to moral indignation: he does not complain, but instead he "accuses." Brandes, *Ibsen*, 1.

[49] Ibsen's drama, in this way, is part of a larger nineteenth-century interest in the phenomenon of *Weltschmerz*. For a study of pessimism and *Weltschmerz* (albeit one that does not fully address Nietzsche's contribution), see Frederick C. Beiser, *Weltschmerz: Pessimism in German Philosophy, 1860–1900* (Oxford: Oxford University Press, 2016).

[50] http://ibsen.uio.no/SAK_P18870924Sto_Aftonbl.xhtml (Accessed June 2019), my trans.

Concluding Remarks

After *Hedda Gabler*, Ibsen wrote four more plays: *The Master Builder, Little Eyolf, John Gabriel Borkman*, and *When We Dead Awaken*. With its darker tone and dense, image-laden prose, his late work has been described as melancholy. In each of these late plays, the topic of the past, of individual and collective history, features centrally. At least two of the late plays—three, if we include *The Master Builder*—revolve around intellectuals and artists whose creativity is both sourced from and limited by a past they fail to live up to. Ibsen also returns to his early historical drama.

Although Ibsen is not a philosopher, he explores, through dramatic means, the promises, boundaries, and internal contradictions of the ideas and worldviews that dominate his time. By moving from theory (widely conceived) to a staging of lives lived and concrete challenges encountered by the individual dramatic characters, Ibsen offers a form in which thoughts are embodied and presented as options with real-life consequences and costs. With its multifarious characters and the interactions between them, his drama presents an active and ongoing exploration of existential-philosophical ideas. One might say that his drama is Socratic in that it raises questions without seeking to answer them by way of a final conclusion. Yet from beginning to end, Ibsen's drama brings philosophy to bear on what matters most: the effort—sometimes hopeless, sometimes terrifying, but never plain dull—to find meaning. In this way, Ibsen surely deserves the position between Nietzsche and Socrates, between ancient and modern philosophy, that Munch had assigned him in *The Geniuses*.

As a playwright, Ibsen found himself within a culture that, in his view, seemed in urgent need of attention. In his work, there is a continuity between the quest for historical meaning and individual existence. Historical meaning, moreover, is not given once and for all. It is not an object, but a pursuit—fragile, contingent, and in constant need of care and attention. Sometimes we manage to live meaningfully with our history. At other times, we suffer from a disconnect, a sense that history has ceased to offer

The Drama of History. Kristin Gjesdal, Oxford University Press (2021). © Oxford University Press.
DOI: 10.1093/oso/9780190070762.001.0001.

a background against which lives can be meaningfully lived. This is true of Ibsen's characters from Hjørdis to Hedda Gabler. In Ibsen's contemporary drama, we also encounter the formation of the bourgeoisie, which, in a certain sense, understands itself as being above or beyond history. Yet in Ibsen's play, history always catches up and breaks through the sheen of ahistorical truths and values.

Ibsen was not alone in exploring this aspect of human history. Nor is he alone in realizing the dramatic power of philosophy. As I have sought to show, Ibsen comes of age and develops as an artist in a period in which stage-art, criticism, and drama are infused with a philosophical dimension and, likewise, reflections on drama and theater had, for a century or more, featured prominently in philosophical thought. At the center of this interaction, I have argued, stand the topics of history and human historicity. This had been true since Lessing and the beginning of modern philosophy of theater, and it was true of the artistic-intellectual environment a century later. In this context, Hegel and Nietzsche are important names—*both* as far as their works would influence Scandinavian culture, and drama in particular, *and* in the sense that they, even among their nineteenth-century peers, are philosophers whose works explore, with depth and profundity, the ethical, artistic, and existential dimensions of history.

As part of this culture, it cannot surprise us that Ibsen, a playwright situated in this milieu, would seek to place history on stage. In an extraordinarily perceptive manner, Ibsen's work dissects and analyzes the challenge involved in existing historically: not simply to be, as we all are, in history, but to see that, if it is to be meaningful at all, history must be appropriated and made our own. Taking a wide range of dramatic forms, history and historical existence remain front and center in Ibsen's work and connects his drama to the kind of concerns that philosophers, at the time, would explore in discursive form.

In my engagement with Ibsen's drama, I have not wanted to trace Ibsen's allusions or references to philosophical ideas (though they certainly exist!). I have wanted, instead, to show how he uses the dramatic form to wrestle with and explore philosophical ideas as they were generated and given credence within the cultural context of which he was a part. In nineteenth-century culture, philosophy was not confined to narrow academic quarters, but was a central part of a broader, cultural discourse. It is as part of such a broader discourse that philosophy came to influence the writings of Ibsen and his peers. Likewise does Ibsen aspire to a position as a playwright whose engagement with history, life, and art matters beyond the stage.[1]

With surgical precision, Ibsen analyzes not just the ways in which individuals fail to free themselves from their past, but also the costs of seeking to cut loose from the wider context of one's history and culture. He stages the despair and the pain with which modern individuals grapple with the threat of meaninglessness. And he gives us a panoply of characters whose lives and daily struggles bear witness to times changing and the burden of coming to terms with the past. Ibsen's emphasis on history is, in my view, part of his larger turn against aestheticism. Here he joins forces with the *Sturm und Drang* philosophers, Hegel, and Nietzsche. The same applies to his merging of history with an interest in what distinguishes modern drama and the sense that the latter cannot be developed without an understanding of the former. Ibsen's engagement with such ideas—his drawing on and borrowing from a larger nineteenth-century intellectual context—concretely shows how philosophy, as both Hegel and Nietzsche would insist, does not thrive in a separate sphere of abstract ideas and concepts, but develops as a response to and part of a larger cultural-historical world. Needless to say, drama is not the only artform inviting such exchanges. However, drama seems particularly conducive to such exchanges.

It is my hope that this study, while specific in its focus on history and historicity, can exemplify how philosophy and drama not only coexisted but also, with their differences in form and objectives, created a particularly productive synergy. Ibsen's drama philosophizes—and it philosophizes well. Yet, it never aspires to be philosophy. The interaction between philosophy and drama matters because, precisely in pursuing different goals and forms of expression, they can offer mutual sustenance and enhancement. This, I have suggested, is one of the lessons to be learned from Ibsen's staging of the Nineteenth Century. As philosophers, we will be poorer if we leave out the kind of drama art can bring to thought. And, as artists and critics, we will be poorer if we leave out the quest for truth and understanding that philosophy, when generously conceived, can offer.

---

[1] Ibsen's writing on theater is available in *Ibsen on Theater*, ed. Frode Helland and Julie Holledge, trans. May-Brit Akerholt (London: Nick Hern Books, 2019).

Bibliography

Aall, Anathon. "Ibsen og Nietzsche." *Samtiden*, vol. 17, no. 3 (1906): 147–163.

Aarseth, Asbjørn. "*Peer Gynt* and Hegel's Ideas on Egyptian Art." *Scandinavian Studies*, vol. 4 (2001): 535–546.

Aarseth, Asbjørn. "Vital Romanticism in Ibsen's Late Plays." In *Strindberg, Ibsen and Bergman: Essays on Scandinavian Film and Drama*. Edited by Harry Perridon. Maastricht: Shaker Publishing, 1998, 1–23.

Aarseth, Asbjørn. *Peer Gynt and Ghosts: Text and Performance*. London: Macmillan Education, 1989.

Aarseth, Asbjørn. *Dyret i Mennesket. Et bidrag til tolkning av Henrik Ibsens "Peer Gynt."* Oslo: Universitetsforlaget, 1975.

Abel, Douglas. "Wisdom! Light! Beauty! A Thematic Analysis of Ibsen's *Emperor and Galilean*." *Modern Drama*, vol. 43, no. 1 (2000): 78–86.

Adorno, Theodor W. *Minima Moralia: Reflections from Damaged Life*. Translated by E. F. N Jephcott. London: Verso, 2010.

Adorno, Theodor W. *Aesthetic Theory*. Translated by Robert Hullot-Kentor. Minneapolis: University of Minnesota Press, 1997.

Adorno, Theodor W. *Minima Moralia. Reflexionen aus dem beschädigten Leben. Gesammelte Schriften*. Vol. 4. Frankfurt am Main: Surhkamp, 1980.

Andersen, Hans Christian. *En Comedie i det Grønne. Samlede Skrifter*. Vol. 9. Copenhagen: C. A. Reitzels Forlag, 1978.

Anderson, Andrew Runni. "Ibsen and the Classic World." *The Classical Journal*, vol. 11, no. 4 (1916): 216–225.

Andreas-Salomé, Lou. *Henrik Ibsens Frauen-Gestalten. Psychologische Bilder nach seinen sechs Familiendramen*. Edited by Cornelia Pechota. Taching am See: Medien Edition, Welsch, 2012.

Andreas-Salomé, Lou. *Ibsen's Heroines*. Translated by Siegfried Mandel. Redding, CT: Black Swan Books, 1985.

Andreas-Salomé, Lou. *Henrik Ibsens Kvindeskikkelser*. Translated by Hulda Garborg. Kristiania: Alb. Cammermeyer forlag, 1893.

Anker, Øyvind. "Ibsen og den skandinaviske Forening i Roma." *Edda*, no. 56 (1956): 161–178.

Aristotle. *Poetics*. Translated by Gerald F. Else. Ann Arbor: University of Michigan Press, 1970.

Arvin, Neil Cole. *Eugène Scribe and the French Theater, 1815–1860*. Cambridge, MA: Harvard University Press, 1924.

Asbjørnsen, Peter Christen. *Norske Huldreeventyr og Folkesagn*. 2 vols. Christiania: Fabritius forlag, 1845–1877.

Barish, Jonas. *The Antitheatrical Prejudice*. Berkeley: University of California Press, 1981.

Bauer, Nancy. *Simone de Beauvoir, Philosophy, and Feminism*. New York: Columbia University Press, 2001.

Beerling, Reinier Franciscus. "Hegel und Nietzsche." *Hegel-Studien*, no. 1 (1961): 229–246.

Beiser, Frederick C. *Weltschmerz: Pessimism in German Philosophy, 1860–1900*. Oxford: Oxford University Press, 2016.

Beiser, Frederick C. *The Romantic Imperative: The Concept of Early German Romanticism*. Cambridge, MA: Harvard University Press, 2003.

Bennett, Tony. *The Birth of the Museum: History, Theory, Politics*. London: Routledge, 1995.

Bernstein, J. M. "Fragment, Fascination, Damaged Life: The Truth about Hedda Gabler." In *The Actuality of Adorno: Critical Essays on Adorno and the Postmodern*. Edited by Max Pensky. Albany, NY: SUNY Press, 1997, 154–183.

Beyer, Harald. *Nietzsche og Norden*. 2 vols. Bergen: Grieg Forlag, 1958–1959.

Beyer, Harald. *Søren Kierkegaard og Norge*. Kristiania: Aschehoug, 1924.

Billings, Joshua. "Nietzsche's Philology of the Present," forthcoming in *New Literary History* 51.3 (2020).

Billings, Joshua. *Genealogy of the Tragic: Greek Tragedy and German Philosophy*. Princeton: Princeton University Press, 2014.

Bjørnson, Bjørnstjerne. *Brev*, første samling: *Gro-Tid. Brev fra årene 1857–1879*. Edited by Halvdan Koht. Kristiania and Kjøbenhavn: Gyldendal, 1912.

Bjørnson, Bjørnstjerne. Commentary in *Dagbladet*, December 22, 1881. http://ibsen. nb.no/id/56318.0 (Accessed July 2019).

Bøgh, Erik. Review in *Dagens Nyheder* (København 24. desember 1879, nr. 348, Tolvte Aargang). http://ibsen.nb.no/id/11234213.0.

Bohrer, Karl Heinz. *Die Kritik der Romantik*. Frankfurt am Main: Suhrkamp, 1989.

Boyce, Kristin. "Philosophy, Theater, and Love: Ibsen's *Hedda Gabler* and Plato's *Symposium*." In Gjesdal (ed.) 2018, 132–152.

Brandes, Edvard. "Review of Ibsen's *A Doll's House*." *Ude og Hjemme*, København (January, 4. 1880), no. 118, Tredie Aargang: 148–153. http://ibsen.nb.no/id/11193496.0. (Accessed June 2019).

Brandes, Georg Morris Cohen. *Aristokratisk radikalisme. Fr. Nietzsche. Tre Essays*. By Georg Brandes og Harald Høffding. Aarhus: Akademisk boghandel, 1972.

Brandes, Georg Morris Cohen. *Main Currents in Nineteenth Century Literature*. Translator not listed. London: Heinemann, 1923.

Brandes, Georg Morris Cohen. *Adam Oehlenschläger: Aladdin. Samlede skrifter*, vol. 1–2. København: Gyldendalske Boghandel, 1919.

Brandes, Georg Morris Cohen. *François de Voltaire*. 2 vols. Kjøbenhavn: Gyldendal, 1916–1917.

Brandes, Georg Morris Cohen. *Henrik Ibsen*. Kjøbenhavn: Gyldendalske Boghandel, 1916.

Brandes, Georg Morris Cohen. *Nietzsche*. Translated by A. G. Chater. New York: Macmillan Company, 1915.

Brandes, Georg Morris Cohen. *William Shakespeare: A Critical Study*. Translated by William Archer et al. London: William Heinemann, 1898.

Brandes, Georg Morris Cohen. *William Shakespeare*. Kjøbenhavn: Gyldendal, 1895–1896.

Brandes, Georg Morris Cohen. *Æsthetiske Studier*. 2nd ed. Kjøbenhavn: Gyldendal, 1888.

Brandes, Georg Morris Cohen. *Hovedstrømninger i det 19de Århundredes Litteratur*. Kjøbenhavn: Gyldendal, 1872.

Breazeale, Daniel. "The Hegel-Nietzsche Problem." *Nietzsche-Studien*, no. 4 (1975): 146–164.

Brennan, Katie. "Nietzsche's *Hamlet* Puzzle: Life Affirmation in *The Birth of Tragedy*." In *The Routledge Companion to Shakespeare and Philosophy*. Edited by Craig Bourne and Emily Caddick Bourne. London: Routledge, 2019, 398–408.

Brennan, Katie. "Nietzsche's Shakespeare: Musicality and Historicity in *The Birth of Tragedy*." *Memoria di Shakespeare*, vol. 1 (2014): 109–128.

Buck-Morss, Susan. *Hegel, Haiti, and Universal History*. Pittsburgh: University of Pittsburgh Press, 2009.

Bull, Francis. "The Influence of Shakespeare on Wergeland, Ibsen and Bjørnson." *The Norseman*, no. 15 (1957): 88–95.

Bull, Francis. "Bjørnson kontra Nietzsche." *Samtiden*. Oslo: Aschehoug, 1947: 160–169.

Calder, William M., III. "The Riddle of Wilamowitz's *Phaidrabild*." *Greek, Roman, and Byzantine Studies*, vol. 20 (1979): 219–236.

Carlson, Marvin. *Voltaire and the Theater of the Eighteenth Century*. London: Greenwood Press, 1998.

Cavell, Stanley. *Conditions Handsome and Unhandsome: The Constitution of Emersonian Perfectionism*. Chicago: University of Chicago Press, 1990.

Church, Jeffrey. *Nietzsche's Culture of Humanity: Beyond Aristocracy and Democracy in the Early Period*. Cambridge: Cambridge University Press, 2015.

Collin, Josef. *Henrik Ibsen. Sein Werk, seine Weltanschauung, sein Leben*. Heidelberg: Carl Winters Universitätsbuchhandlung, 1910.

de Sousa, Elisabete M. "Eugène Scribe: The Unfortunate Authorship of a Successful Author." In *Kierkegaard and the Renaissance and Modern Traditions*. Vol. 3: *Literature, Drama, and Music*. Edited by Jon Stewart. Farnham: Ashgate, 2009, 169–185.

Del Caro, Adrian. "Reception and Impact: The First Decade of Nietzsche in Germany." *Orbis Litterarum*, vol. 37 (1982): 32–46.

Diderot, Denis. *Herren af Diderot's Theatralske Verker, tilligemed en Samtale over den dramatiske Digtekunst*. Translated by Knud Lyne Rahbek. Kjøbenhavn: Johan Rudolf Thiele, 1779.

Dilthey, Katharina. "Eine Erinnerung an Henrik Ibsen." *Westermanns illustrierte deutsche Monatshefte*, December 1922: 362–364.

Dilthey, Wilhelm. *Gesammelte Schriften*. 26 vols. Göttingen: Vandenhoeck and Ruprecht, 1914–2005.

Dilthey, Wilhelm. *Poetry and Experience. Selected Works*. Vol. 5. Edited by Rudolf A. Makkreel and Frithjof Rodi. Various translators. Princeton: Princeton University Press, 1985.

Dingstad, Ståle. *Den smilende Ibsen. Henrik Ibsens forfatterskap—stykkevis og delt*. Oslo: Centre for Ibsen Studies, 2013.

Dohm, Hedwig. "Nietzsche and Women." Translated by Anna Ezekiel. In *Women Philosophers in the Long Nineteenth Century: The German Tradition*. Edited by Dalia Nassar and Kristin Gjesdal. Oxford: Oxford University Press, forthcoming.

Dohm, Hedwig. "Nietzsche und die Frauen." *Ausgewählte Texte*. Edited by Nikola Müller and Isabel Rohner. Berlin: Trafo, 2006, 124–136.

Dohm, Hedwig. *Die Antifeministen. Ein Buch der Verteidigung*. Berlin: Ferd. Dümmler, 1902.

Dukore, Bernard F. "Karl Marx's Youngest Daughter and *A Doll's House*." *Theatre Journal*, vol. 42, no. 3 (1990): 308–321.

Dukore, Bernard F. *Money and Politics in Ibsen, Shaw, and Brecht*. Columbia: University of Missouri Press, 1980.

Dvergsdal, Alvhild. "To be Oneself: Satan's Ruse. Critical Reflections on Self-Realization in Henrik Ibsen's *Peer Gynt*." *Ibsen Studies*, vol. 3, no. 1 (2003): 32–53.

Eaton, J. W. *The German Influence in Danish Literature in the Eighteenth Century: The German Circle in Copenhagen 1750–1770*. Cambridge: Cambridge University Press, 1922.

Emden, Christian J. *Friedrich Nietzsche and the Politics of History*. Cambridge: Cambridge University Press, 2008.

Englert, Uwe. *Magus und Rechenmeister. Henrik Ibsens Werk auf den Bühnen des Dritten Reiches*. Tübingen: Franke Verlag, 2007.

Erichsen, Valborg. "Søren Kierkegaards betydning for norsk aandsliv." *Edda*, vol. 19 (1923): 252–269.

Ewbank, Inga-Stina. "Ibsen and Shakespeare: Reading the Silence." In *Ibsen at the Centre for Advanced Study*. Edited by Vigdis Ystad. Oslo: Scandinavian University Press, 1997, 85–104.

Ewbank, Inga-Stina. "Ibsen's Language: Literary Text and Theatrical Context." *The Yearbook for English Studies*, vol. 9 (1979): 102–115.

Faaland, Josef. *Henrik Ibsen og antikken*. Oslo: Grundt Tanum, 1943.

Farfan, Penny. *Women, Modernism, and Performance*. Cambridge: Cambridge University Press, 2004.

Feagin, Susan L. "Where Hedda Dies: The Significance of Place." In Gjesdal (ed.) 2018, 48–71.

Fell, Jill. *Alfred Jarry*. London: Reaktion Books, 2010.

Ferguson, Robert. *Henrik Ibsen: A New Biography*. New York: Dorset Press, 1996.

Fergusson, Francis. *The Idea of a Theater*. Princeton: Princeton University Press, 1968.

Figueiredo, Ivo de. *Henrik Ibsen. Masken*. Oslo: Aschehoug, 2007.

Figueiredo, Ivo de. *Henrik Ibsen. Mennesket*. Oslo: Aschehoug, 2006.

Fischer-Lichte, Erika. "Ibsen's *Ghosts*—A Play for All Theatre Concepts?" *Ibsen-Studies*, vol. 7, no. 1 (2007): 61–83.

Flaubert, Gustave. *Madame Bovary*. Translated by Eleanor Marx-Aveling. London: Wordsworth Editions, 1987.

Forst, Rainer. "The Injustice of Justice: Normative Dialectics According to Ibsen, Cavell and Adorno." *Graduate Faculty Philosophy Journal*, vol. 28, no. 2 (2007): 39–51.

Forster, Michael N. "Hegel's Dialectical Method." In *The Cambridge Companion to Hegel*. Edited by Frederick C. Beiser. Cambridge: Cambridge University Press, 1993, 130–170.

Frank, Manfred. *Unendliche Annäherung*. Frankfurt am Main: Suhrkamp Verlag, 1997.

Frenzel, Herbert A. *Geschichte des Theaters. Daten und Dokumente 1470–1840*. München: Deutscher Taschenbuch Verlag, 1979.

Frazer, Michael L. *The Enlightenment of Sympathy: Justice and the Moral Sentiments in the Eighteenth Century and Today*. Oxford: Oxford University Press, 2010.

Freud, Sigmund. "Some Character-Types Met with in Psycho-Analytic Work." In *The Penguin Freud Library*. Vol. 14: *Art and Literature*. Translated by James Strachey. London: Penguin, 1985, 308–316.

Freytag, Gustav. *Die Technik des Dramas*. Leipzig: Hirzel, 1886.

Fulsås, Narve. *Historie og nasjon. Ernst Sars og striden om norsk kultur*. Oslo: Universitets-forlaget, 1999.

Fulsås, Narve, and Gudrun Kühne-Bertram. "Ibsen and Dilthey: Evidence of a Forgotten Acquaintance." *Ibsen Studies*, vol. 9, no. 1 (2009): 3–18.

Fulsås, Narve, and Tore Rem. *Ibsen, Scandinavia and the Making of a World Drama*. Cambridge: Cambridge University Press, 2018.

Gadamer, Hans-Georg. *Plato's Dialectical Ethics: Phenomenological Interpretations Relating to the Philebus*. Translated by Robert M. Wallace. New Haven: Yale University Press, 1991.

Gadamer, Hans-Georg. *Gesammelte Werke*. Tübingen: J. C. B Mohr (Paul Siebeck), 1985.

Garborg, Arne. Review in *Dagbladet*, December 14, 1881, http://ibsen.nb.no/id/446.0 (Accessed June 2019).

Garborg, Hulda. *Rosseau og hans tanker i nutiden*. Kristiania: Gyldendal, 1909.

Gatland, Jan Olav. *Repertoaret ved det Norske Theater 1850–1863*. Bergen: Universitetsbiblioteket i Bergen, 2000.

Gjervan, Ellen Karoline. "Ibsen Staging Ibsen: Henrik Ibsen's Culturally Embedded Staging Practice in Bergen." *Ibsen Studies*, vol. 11, no. 2 (2011): 117–144.

Gjesdal, Kristin. "A Task Most Pressing: Dilthey's Philosophy of the Novel and His Rewriting of Modern Aesthetics." In *Interpreting Dilthey: Critical Essays*. Edited by Eric S. Nelson. Cambridge: Cambridge University Press, 2019, 200–217.

Gjesdal, Kristin (ed.). *Ibsen's Hedda Gabler: Philosophical Perspectives*. Oxford: Oxford University Press, 2018.

Gjesdal, Kristin. "Interpreting Hamlet: The Early German Reception." In *Shakespeare's Hamlet: Philosophical Perspectives*. Edited by Tzachi Zamir. Oxford: Oxford University Press, 2018, 247–273.

Gjesdal, Kristin. *Herder's Hermeneutics: History, Poetry, Enlightenment*. Cambridge: Cambridge University Press, 2017.

Gjesdal, Kristin. "The Theatre of Thought: A.W. Schlegel on Modern Drama and Romantic Criticism." In *The Philosophy of Theatre, Drama and Acting*. Edited by Tom Stern. London: Rowman and Littlefield, 2017, 43–65.

Gjesdal, Kristin. "Bildung." In *The Oxford Handbook of German Philosophy in the Nineteenth Century*. Edited by Michael N. Forster and Kristin Gjesdal. Oxford: Oxford University Press, 2016, 695–719.

Gjesdal, Kristin. "Shakespeare's Hermeneutic Legacy: Herder on Modern Drama and the Challenge of Cultural Prejudice." *Shakespeare Quarterly*, vol. 64, no. 1 (2013): 60–69.

Gjesdal, Kristin. "Self-Knowledge and Aesthetic Consciousness in Ibsen and Hegel." In *Ibsen and the Modern Self, Acta Ibseniana VII*. Edited by Kwok-kan Tam, Terry Siu-han Yip, and Frode Helland. Hong Kong: Open University of Hong Kong Press, 2010, 1–17.

Gjesdal, Kristin. "Ibsen and Hegel on Egypt and the Beginning of Great Art." *Bulletin of the Hegel Society of Great Britain*, vol. 28, no. 55/56 (2007): 67–86.

Gjesdal, Kristin. Reading Shakespeare, Reading Modernity." *Angelaki*, vol. 9, no. 3 (2004): 17–31.

Gosse, Edmund, "A Norwegian Drama." In *Ibsen: The Critical Heritage*. Edited by Michael Egan. London: Routledge, 1972, 45–50.

Grene, Nicholas. *Home on The Stage: Domestic Spaces in Modern Drama*. Cambridge: Cambridge University Press, 2014.

Grossman, Manuel L. "Alfred Jarry and the Theater of His Time." *Modern Drama*, vol. 13, no. 1 (1970): 10–21.

Guleng, Mai Britt. "Lorentz Dietrichson and the Making of Norwegian Art History." In *Towards a Science of Art History: J. J. Tikkanen and Art Historical Scholarship in Europe*. Edited by Johanna Vakkari. *Studies in Art History*, no. 38, Helsinki, 2009: 59–70.

Guleng, Mai Britt, Jon-Ove Steihaug, and Ingebjørg Ydstie (eds.). *Munch 1863–1944*. Milan: Skira Editore, 2013.

Güthenke, Constanze. *Studying Antiquity in Nineteenth-Century Germany: Classical Scholarship and the Language of Attachment, 1790–1920*. Cambridge: Cambridge University Press, 2020.

Haakonsen, Daniel. *Henrik Ibsen. Mennesket og kunstneren*. Oslo: Aschehoug, 2003.

Halliwell, Stephen. *Aristotle's Poetics*. Chicago: University of Chicago Press, 1998.

Hamann, Johann Georg. *Writings on Philosophy and Language*. Edited and translated by Kenneth Haynes. Cambridge: Cambridge University Press, 2009.

Han-Pile, Béatrice. "Nietzsche's Metaphysics in the *Birth of Tragedy*." *The European Journal of Philosophy*, vol. 14, no. 3 (2006): 373–403.

Hansen, Peter. Review in *Illustreret Tidende* i København, January 8, 1882. See http://ibsen.nb.no/id/400.0 (Accessed July 2019).

Hansen, Thomas Fauth. "The Expression of Infinity: Reflections on Heiberg's View of Contemporary Culture." In Stewart (ed.) 2008, 449–471.

Hansson, Ola. *Friedrich Nietzsche. Hans Personlighed og hans system*. Translated by Arne Garborg. Christiania: Alb. Cammeyers forlag, 1890.

Hanstein, Adalbert von. *Ibsen als Idealist. Vorträge über Henrik Ibsens Dramen*. Leipzig: G. Freund Verlag, 1897.

Haugen, Einar Ingvald. *Ibsen's Drama: Author to Audience*. Minneapolis: University of Minnesota Press, 1979.

Hegel, G. W. F. *Introduction to the Lectures on the History of Philosophy*. Translated by T. M. Knox and A. V. Miller. Oxford: Clarendon Press, 1995.

Hegel, G. W. F. *Elements of the Philosophy of Right*. Edited by Allen W. Wood. Translated by H. B. Nisbet. Cambridge: Cambridge University Press, 1991.

Hegel, G. W. F. *Lectures on the History of Philosophy*. 3 vols. Translated by E. S. Haldane and Frances H. Simson. Lincoln: University of Nebraska Press, 1990.

Hegel, G. W. F. *Lectures on the Philosophy of Religion: The Lectures of 1827*. Edited by Peter C. Hodgson. Translated by R. F. Brown, P. C. Hodgson, and J. M. Stewart. Berkeley: University of California Press, 1988.

Hegel, G. W. F. *Vorlesungen über die Philosophie der Religion*. Edited by Walter Jaeschke. Vols. 3–5 of *Vorlesungen. Ausgewählte Nachschriften und Manuskripte*. Hamburg: Felix Meiner, 1985.

Hegel, G. W. F. *Phenomenology of Spirit*. Translated by A. V. Miller. Oxford: Oxford University Press, 1981.

Hegel, G. W. F. *The Difference between Fichte's and Schelling's System of Philosophy*. Translated by Walter Cerf and H. S. Harris. Albany, NY: SUNY Press, 1977.

Hegel, G. W. F. *Aesthetics: Lectures on Fine Art*. 2 vols. Translated by T. M. Knox. Oxford: Clarendon Press, 1975.

Hegel, G. W. F. *Early Theological Writings*. Translated by T. M. Knox. Philadelphia: University of Pennsylvania Press, 1975.

Hegel, G. W. F. *Werke in 20 Bänden*. Edited by Eva Moldenhauer and Karl Markus Michel. Frankfurt am Main: Suhrkamp Verlag, 1970.

Hegel, G. W. F. *Einleitung in die Geschichte der Philosophie*. Edited by Johannes Hoffmeister. Hamburg: Felix Meiner, 1940.

Hegel, G. W. F. *Hegels theologische Jugendschriften*. Ed. Hermann Nohl. Tübingen: J. C. B. Mohr, 1907.

Heiberg, Johan Ludvig. *Heiberg's On the Significance of Philosophy for the Present Age and Other Texts*. Edited and translated by Jon Stewart. Copenhagen: C. A. Reitzel, 2006.

Heiberg, Johan Ludvig. *Prosaiske Skrifter*. 11 vols. Kjøbenhavn: C.A. Reitzel, 1861–1862.

Helland, Frode. "The Scars of Modern Life: *Hedda Gabler* in Adorno's Prism." Gjesdal (ed.) 2018, 92–112.

Helland, Frode. *Ibsen in Practice: Relational Readings of Performance, Cultural Encounters and Power*. London: Bloomsbury Methuen Drama, 2015.

Helland, Frode. "Empire and Culture in Ibsen: Some Notes on the Dangers and Ambiguities of Interculturalism." *Ibsen Studies*, vol. 9, no. 2 (2009): 136–159.

Helland, Frode. "Ibsen and Nietzsche: *The Master Builder*." *Ibsen Studies*, vol. 9, no. 1 (2009): 50–75.

Helland, Frode. "Henrik Ibsen og det politiske: *Et dukkehjem*." *Lesing og eksistens. Festskrift til Otto Hageberg på 70-årsdagen*. Edited by Per Thomas Andersen. Oslo: Gyldendal, 2006, 134–150.

Helland, Frode. *Melankoliens spill. En studie i Henrik Ibsens siste dramaer*. Oslo: Universitetsforlaget, 2000.

Helland, Frode, and Julie Holledge (eds.). *Ibsen on Theater*. Translated by May-Brit Akerholt. London: Nick Hern Books, 2019.

Hemmer, Bjørn. *Ibsen og Bjørnson. Essays og analyser*. Oslo: Aschehoug, 1978.

Herder, Johann Gottfried. *Shakespeare*. Translated by Gregory Moore. Princeton: Princeton University Press, 2008.

Herder, Johann Gottfried. *Selected Writings on Aesthetics*. Edited and translated by Gregory Moore. Princeton: Princeton University Press, 2006.

Herder, Johann Gottfried. *Selected Early Works 1764–1767*. Edited by Ernest A. Menze and Karl Menges. Translated by Ernest A. Menze with Michael Palma. University Park: Pennsylvania State University Press, 1992.

Herder, Johann Gottfried. *Werke in zehn Bänden*. Edited by Martin Bollacher et al. Frankfurt am Main: Deutscher Klassiker Verlag, 1989.

Hettner, Hermann. *Das moderne Drama. Aesthetische Untersuchungen*. Braunschweig: F. Vieweg, 1852.

Hirt, Aloys. *Die Geschichte der Baukunst bei den Alten*. Vol. 1. Berlin: G. Reimer, 1821.

Høffding, Harald. "Demokratisk radikalisme." In *Fr. Nietzsche. Tre Essays*. Edited by Georg Brandes and Harald Høffding. Aarhus: Akademisk Boghandel, 1972.

Holledge, Julie. "Pastor Hansen's Confirmation Class: Religion, Freedom, and the Female Body in *Et Dukkehjem*." *Ibsen Studies*, vol. 1, no. 10 (2010): 3–16.

Hollinrake, Roger. *Nietzsche, Wagner, and the Philosophy of Pessimism*. London: Georg Allen and Unwin Ltd., 1982.

Houlgate, Stephen. "Hegel's Theory of Tragedy." In *Hegel and the Arts*. Edited by Stephen Houlgate. Evanston: Northwestern University Press, 2007, 146–179.

Houlgate, Stephen. *Hegel, Nietzsche and the Criticism of Metaphysics*. Cambridge: Cambridge University Press, 1986.

Höyng, Peter. "Lessing's Drama Theory: Discursive Writings on Drama, Performance, and Theater." In *A Companion to the Works of Gotthold Ephraim Lessing*. Edited by Barbara Fischer and Thomas C. Fox. Rochester: Camden House, 2005, 211–229.

Huddleston, Andrew. *Nietzsche on the Decadence and Flourishing of Culture*. Oxford: Oxford University Press, 2019.

Hutchings, Kimberly, and Tuija Pulkkinen (eds.). *Hegel's Philosophy and Feminist Thought: Beyond Antigone?* New York: Palgrave Macmillan, 2010.

Hvattum, Mari. *Gottfried Semper and the Problem of Historicism*. Cambridge: Cambridge University Press, 2004.

Ibsen, Henrik. *A Doll's House and Other Plays. With Pillars of the Community, Ghosts and An Enemy of the People*. Translated by Deborah Dawkin and Erik Skuggevik. London: Penguin, 2016.

Ibsen, Henrik. *Henrik Ibsens Skrifter*. 16 vols. Edited by Vigdis Ystad et al. Oslo: Aschehoug forlag, 2008–2010.

Ibsen, Henrik. *Peer Gynt: A Dramatic Poem*. Translated by John Northam. Oslo: Scandinavian University Press, 1993.

Ibsen, Henrik. *Four Major Plays*. Translated by James McFarlane and Jens Arup. Oxford: Oxford University Press, 1981.

Ibsen, Henrik. *The Pillars of Society. Plays*. Vol. 4. Translated by Michael Meyer. London: Methuen, 1980.

Ibsen, Henrik. *The Oxford Ibsen*. 8 vols. Edited and translated by James Walter McFarlane. Oxford: Oxford University Press, 1961.

Ibsen, Henrik. *Hundreårsutgaven*. 21 vols. Edited by Francis Bull, Halvdan Koht, and Didrik Arup Seip. Oslo: Gyldendal forlag, 1928–1957.

Ibsen, Henrik. *The Collected Works of Henrik Ibsen*. 13 vols. Edited by William Archer. New York: Charles Scribner's Sons, 1914.

Ibsen, Henrik. *Nora oder ein Puppenheim*. Translated by Wilhelm Lange. Leipzig: Reclam, 1879.

Innes, Christopher (ed.). *Henrik Ibsen's Hedda Gabler: A Sourcebook*. London: Routledge, 2003.

Janss, Christian. "When Nora Stayed: More Light on the German Ending." *Ibsen Studies*, vol. 17, no. 1 (2017): 3–27.

Jensen, Anthony K. *Nietzsche's Philosophy of History*. Cambridge: Cambridge University Press, 2013.

Johnston, Brian. *The Ibsen Cycle: The Design of the Plays from Pillars of Society to When We Dead Awaken*. University Park: Pennsylvania State University Press, 1992.

Johnston, Brian. *To the Third Empire: Ibsen's Early Drama*. Minneapolis: University of Minnesota Press, 1980.

Kaplan, Merrill. "Hedda and Hjørdis: Saga and Scandal in *Hedda Gabler* and *The Vikings at Helgeland*." *Ibsen Studies*, vol. 4, no. 1 (2006): 18–29.

Kaufman, Michael W. "Nietzsche, Georg Brandes, and Ibsen's *Master Builder*." *Comparative Drama*, vol. 6 (1972): 169–186.

Keyser, Rudolf. *Den norske kirkes historie under katholicismen*. https://babel.hathitrust. org/cgi/pt?id=wu.89097230825;view=1up;seq=1142 (Accessed June 2019).

Kittang, Atle. *Ibsens heroisme. Frå Brand til Når vi døde vågner*. Oslo: Gyldendal, 2002.

Koht, Halvdan. "Shakespeare and Ibsen." In *Ibsen: A Collection of Critical Essays*. Edited by Rolf Fjelde. Englewood Cliffs, NJ: Prentice-Hall Inc., 1965, 41–52.

Koht, Halvdan. *Henrik Ibsen. Eit diktarliv*. 2nd. ed. 2 vols. Oslo: Aschehoug, 1954.

Koht, Halvdan. *The Life of Ibsen*. 2 vols. Translated by Ruth Lima McMahon and Hanna Astrup Larsen. New York: W. W. Norton, 1931.

Koppang, Ole. *Hegelianismen i Norge*. Oslo: Aschehoug, 1943.

Kornhaber, David. *The Birth of Theater from the Spirit of Philosophy: Nietzsche and the Modern Drama*. Evanston: Northwestern University Press, 2016.

LaMothe, Kimerer L. *Nietzsche's Dancers: Isadora Duncan, Martha Graham, and the Revaluation of Christian Values*. London: Palgrave Macmillan, 2006.

Lampert, Jay. "Hegel and Ancient Egypt: History and Becoming." *International Philosophical Quarterly*, vol. 35, no. 1 (1995): 43–58.

Large, Duncan. "Nietzsche's Shakespearean Figures." In *Why Nietzsche Still? Reflections on Drama, Culture, and Politics*. Edited by Alan D. Schrift. Berkeley: University of California Press, 2000, 45–66.

Lathe, Carla. "Edvard Munch's Dramatic Images 1892–1909." *Journal of the Warburg and Courtauld Institutes*, vol. 46 (1983): 191–206.

Lessing, Gotthold Ephraim. *Hamburg Dramaturgy*. Translated by Helen Zimmern. New York: Dover, 1962.

Lindén, Arne. "Peer Gynt i Egypten." *Edda*, vol. 40 (1940): 237–265.

Lisi, Leonardo F. *Marginal Modernity: The Aesthetics of Dependency from Kierkegaard to Joyce*. New York: Fordham University Press, 2013.

Lisi, Leonardo F. "The Art of Doubt: Form, Genre, History in *Miss Julie*." In *The International Strindberg: New Critical Essays*. Edited by Anna Westerståhl Stenport. Evanston: Northwestern University Press, 2012, 249–276.

Lisi, Leonardo F. "Endelighedens æstetik: Modernismens problematik hos Kierkegaard og Ibsen." In *Kierkegaard, Ibsen og det moderne*. Edited by Vigdis Ystad et al. Oslo: Universitetsforlaget, 2010, 99–116.

Lynner, Ferdinand G. *Hærmænene paa Helgeland. Henrik Ibsens forhold til kilderne i den norrøne literatur*. Kristiania: Malling, 1909.

Mack, Michael. *Spinoza and the Specters of Modernity*. New York: Continuum, 2010.

Marchand, Suzanne L. *German Orientalism in the Age of Empire: Religion, Race, and Scholarship*. Cambridge: Cambridge University Press, 2009.

Marker, Frederick J., and Lise-Lone Marker. *Ibsen's Lively Art: A Performance Study of the Major Plays*. Cambridge: Cambridge University Press, 1989.

Matos, Timothy Carlos. "Choleric Fictions: Epidemiology, Medical Authority, and *An Enemy of the People*." *Modern Drama*, vol. 51, no. 3 (2008): 353–368.

McDowell, John. "The Apperceptive I and the Empirical Self: Towards a Heterodox Reading of 'Lordship and Bondage' in Hegel's *Phenomenology*." In *Hegel: New Directions*. Edited by Katerina Deligiorgi. Chesheim, Bucks: Acumen, 2006, 33–48.

Meyer, Michael. *Ibsen: A Biography*. Harmondsworth: Penguin, 1985.

Meyer, Ursula I. (ed.). *Die Welt der Philosophin*. 3 vols. *Aufklärung und revolutionärer Aufbruch*. Aachen: ein-FACH Verlag, 1997.

Midbøe, Hans. *Max Reinhardts iscenesettelse av Ibsens Gespenster i Kammerspiele des deutschen Theaters Berlin 1906—Dekor Edvard Munch*. Det Kgl. norske videnskapers selbskaps skrifter 1969, nr. 4. Trondheim: F. Brun, 1969.

Mikus, Birgit. *The Political Woman in Print: German Women's Writing 1845–1919*. Oxford: Peter Lang, 2014.

Mill, John Stuart. *Utilitarianism*. Edited by George Sher. London: Hackett, 2002.

Moi, Toril. *Henrik Ibsen and the Birth of Modernism: Art, Theater, Philosophy*. Oxford: Oxford University Press, 2006.

Moland, Lydia. *Hegel's Aesthetics: The Art of Idealism*. Oxford: Oxford University Press, 2019.

Monrad, Marcus Jacob. *Æsthetik. Det Skjønne og dets Forekomst i Natur og Kunst*. 3 vols. Christiania: Cammermeyer, 1889–1890.

Monrad, Marcus Jacob. Monrad i *Morgenbladet* i Kristiania January 15, 1882 [No. 14A, 64de Aarg.], http://ibsen.nb.no/id/11192753.0 (Accessed June 2019).

Monrad, Marcus Jacob. *Tankeretninger i den nyere Tid. Et kritisk Rundskue.* Oslo: Aschehoug, 1874.

Monrad, Marcus Jacob. "Review of *The Pretenders.*" *Morgenbladet* (January 16, 21, 24, 1864). http://ibsen.nb.no/id/11178069 (Accessed October 2019).

Monrad, Marcus Jacob. *Tolv Forelæsninger om det Skjønne.* Christiania: Det Norske Studentersamfunds forlag, 1859.

Moretti, Franco. *The Bourgeois: Between History and Literature.* London: Verso, 2013.

Mortensen, Finn Hauberg. "Heiberg and the Theater: In Oehlenschläger's Limelight." *The Heibergs and the Theater: Between Vaudeville, Romantic Comedy and National Drama.* Edited by Jon Stewart. Copenhagen: Museum Tusculanum Press, 2012, 17–42.

Munch, Edvard. *Munch med egne ord.* Edited by Poul Erik Tøjner. Oslo: Press, 2003.

Muthu, Sankar. *Enlightenment against Empire.* Princeton: Princeton University Press, 2003.

Nagy, András. "Either Hegel or Dialectics: Johan Ludvig Heiberg, '*Homme de théâtre.*'" In *Johan Ludvig Heiberg: Philosopher, Littérateur, Dramaturge, and Political Thinker.* Edited by Jon Stewart. Copenhagen: Museum Tusculanum Press, 2008, 357–395.

Naugrette, Catherine. "Patrice Chéreau's *Peer Gynt*: A Renewed Reception of Ibsen's Theater in France." In *Global Ibsen: Performing Multiple Modernities.* Edited by Erika Fischer-Lichte, Barbara Gronau, and Christel Weiler. London: Routledge, 2011, 166–175.

Nehamas, Alexander. *Nietzsche: Life as Literature.* Cambridge, MA: Harvard University Press, 1985.

Nietzsche, Friedrich. *Ecce Homo. The Anti-Christ, Ecce Homo, Twilight of the Idols, and Other Writings.* Edited by Aaron Ridley and Judith Norman. Translated by Judith Norman. Cambridge: Cambridge University Press, 2005.

Nietzsche, Friedrich. *The Gay Science.* Edited by Bernard Williams. Translated by Josefine Nauckhoff. Cambridge: Cambridge University Press, 2001.

Nietzsche, Friedrich. *The Birth of Tragedy and Other Writings.* Edited by Raymond Geuss and Ronald Speirs. Translated by Ronald Speirs. Cambridge: Cambridge University Press, 1999.

Nietzsche, Friedrich. *Untimely Meditations.* Edited by Daniel Breazeale. Translated by R. J. Hollingdale. Cambridge: Cambridge University Press, 1999.

Nietzsche, Friedrich. *On the Genealogy of Morality.* Translated by Maudemarie Clark and Alan J. Swensen. Indianapolis: Hackett Publishing, 1998.

Nietzsche, Friedrich. *Human, All Too Human: A Book for Free Spirits.* Translated by R. J. Hollingdale. Cambridge: Cambridge University Press, 1996.

Nisbet, H. B. *Gotthold Ephraim Lessing: His Life, Works, and Thought.* Oxford: Oxford University Press, 2013.

Nordhagen, Per Jonas. *Henrik Ibsen i Roma, 1864–1868.* Oslo: Cappelen Forlag, 1981.

Noreng, Harald. "En folkefiende—helt eller klovn?" In *Ibsen på festspillscenen.* Edited by Harald Noreng. Bergen: J.W. Eide Forlag, 1969, 15–27.

Oehlenschläger, Adam. *Aladdin eller den forunderlige Lampe.* København: Det nordiske Forlag, 1898.

Ording, Fredrik. *Henrik Ibsens vennekreds Det lærde Holland. Et kapitel av norsk kulturliv.* Den norske Historiske Forening. Grøndahl & Søns Boktrykkeri. Oslo 1927.

Ørjasæter, Kristin. "Mother, Wife, and Role Model: A Contextual Perspective on Feminism in *A Doll's House.*" *Ibsen Studies,* vol. 5, no. 1 (2005): 19–47.

Owesen, Ingeborg Winderen. "Edvard Munch: Between Gender, Love, and Women's Rights." In *Edvard Munch 1863–1944*. Edited by Mai Britt Guleng, Jon-Ove Steihaug, and Ingebjørg Ydstie. Milan: Skira Editore, 2013, 296–305.

Owesen, Ingeborg Winderen. "Friedrich Nietzsches innflytelse og betydning for Edvard Munch." *Agora*, no. 3–4 (1995): 94–111.

Oxfeldt, Elisabeth. *Nordic Orientalism: Paris and the Cosmopolitan Imagination 1800–1900*. Copenhagen: Museum Tusculanum Press, 2005.

Pascal, Roy (ed.). *Shakespeare in Germany 1740–1815*. New York: Octagon Books, 1971.

Pasche, Wolfgang. *Skandinavische Dramatik in Deutschland. Bjørnstjerne Bjørnson, Henrik Ibsen, August Strindberg auf der deutschen Bühne 1867–1932*. Basel: Helbing & Lichtenhahn Verlag, 1979.

Paulin, Roger. *The Critical Reception of Shakespeare in Germany 1682–1914: Native Literature and Foreign Genius*. Hildesheim: Georg Olms, 2003.

Pearce, John C. "Hegelian Ideas in Three Tragedies by Ibsen." *Scandinavian Studies*, vol. 34, no. 4 (1962): 245–257.

Pinkard, Terry. *Hegel: A Biography*. Cambridge: Cambridge University Press, 2000.

Pinkard, Terry. *Hegel's Phenomenology: The Sociality of Reason*. Cambridge: Cambridge University Press, 1996.

Pippin, Robert B. *Hegel on Self-Consciousness: Desire and Death in the Phenomenology of Spirit*. Princeton: Princeton University Press, 2014.

Pippin, Robert B. *Idealism as Modernism: Hegelian Variations*. Cambridge: Cambridge University Press, 1997.

Pöggeler, Otto. *Hegels Kritik der Romantik*. Bonn: Friedrich Wilhelms Universität, 1965.

Puchner, Martin. *The Drama of Ideas: Platonic Provocations in Theater and Philosophy*. Oxford: Oxford University Press, 2010.

Rahbek, Knud Lyne. *Om Ludvig Holberg som lystspildigter og om hans lystspil*. 3 vols. Kjøbenhavn: Brødrene Thiele, 1815–1817.

Rees, Ellen. "Tropological Turns in *Peer Gynt*." *Ibsen Studies*, vol. 2, no. 8 (2008): 150–172.

Reginster, Bernard. *The Affirmation of Life: Nietzsche on Overcoming Nihilism*. Cambridge, MA: Harvard University Press, 2009.

Reich, Hauke (ed.). *Rezensionen und Reaktionen zu Nietzsches Werken 1872–1889*. Berlin: Walter de Gruyter, 2013.

Rhodes, Norman. *Ibsen and the Greeks*. Lewisburg: Bucknell University Press, 1995.

Ridley, Aaron. *Nietzsche on Art*. London: Routledge, 2007.

Robertson, John G. *Lessing's Dramatic Theory. Being an Introduction to and Commentary on His Hamburgische Dramaturgie*. New York: Benjamin Blom, 1965.

Robins, Elizabeth. *Ibsen and the Actress*. London: Woolf, 1928.

Rønning, Helge. *Den umulige friheten. Henrik Ibsen og moderniteten*. Oslo: Gyldendal, 2006.

Rottem, Øystein. "'Den antike tragedie, gjenopstaaet paa moderne jord': et notat om skjebnesynet i Henrik Ibsens *Gengangere*." *Edda*, vol. 91, no. 4 (1991): 345–358.

Röttges, Heinz. *Nietzsche und die Dialektik der Aufklärung*. Berlin: de Gruyter, 1972.

Rush, Fred. *Irony and Idealism: Rereading Schlegel, Hegel, and Kierkegaard*. Oxford: Oxford University Press, 2016.

Rutter, Benjamin. *Hegel on the Modern Arts*. Cambridge: Cambridge University Press, 2010.

Ruud, Martin B. *An Essay toward a History of Shakespeare in Denmark. Studies in Language and Literature*, no. 8, Minneapolis: University of Minnesota, 1920.

Sæther, Astrid. *Suzannah. Fru Ibsen.* Oslo: Gyldendal, 2008.

Sage, Steven F. *Ibsen and Hitler: The Playwright, the Plagiarist, and the Plot for the Third Reich.* New York: Carroll & Graf Publishers, 2006.

Said, Edward W. *Orientalism: Western Conceptions of the Orient.* London: Vintage Books, 1979.

Sandberg, Mark B. *Ibsen's Houses: Architectural Metaphor and the Modern Uncanny.* Cambridge: Cambridge University Press, 2015.

Schacht, Richard. "A Nietzschean Education: Zarathustra/*Zarathustra* as Educator." In *Philosophers on Education: New Historical Perspectives.* Edited by Amélie Oksenberg Rorty. London: Routledge, 1998, 318–333.

Scheffauer, Herman. "A Correspondence between Nietzsche and Strindberg." *The North American Review*, vol. 198 (1913): 197–205.

Schlegel, August Wilhelm. *Lectures on Dramatic Art and Literature.* Translated by John Black. London: Baldwin, Cradock, and Joy, 1815, http://www.gutenberg.org/ebooks/7148 (Accessed June 2019).

Schlegel, August Wilhelm. *Sämtliche Werke.* 16 vols. Edited by Edouard Böcking. Hildesheim: Olms, 1972.

Schmiesing, Ann. *Norway's Christiania Theatre, 1827–1867: From Danish Showhouse to National Stage.* Madison: Fairleigh Dickinson University Press, 2006.

Schneider, Anatol. *Nietzscheanismus. Zur Geschichte eines Begriffs.* Würzburg: Königshausen und Neumann, 1997.

Schneider, Helmut. "Hegel und die ägyptischen Götter. Ein Exzerpt." *Hegel-Studien*, vol. 16 (1981): 56–68.

Shapiro, Bruce G. *Divine Madness and the Absurd Paradox: Ibsen's Peer Gynt and the Philosophy of Kierkegaard.* Westport, CT: Greenwood Press, 1990.

Shepherd-Barr, Kirsten E. *Theatre and Evolution from Ibsen to Beckett.* New York: Columbia University Press, 2015.

Skram, Amalie. "Mere om '*Gengangere*.'" *Optimistisk læsemaade.* Oslo: Gyldendal 1987, 69–76.

Skram, Amalie. "A Reflection on *A Doll's House.*" *Dagbladet.* Translated by Mai-Brit Akerholt (January 19, 1880). http://ibsen.nb.no/id/11186656.0 (Accessed June 2019).

Steiner, George. *The Death of Tragedy.* New York: Knopf, 1961.

Stern, Michael J. *Nietzsche's Ocean, Strindberg's Open Sea.* Berlin: Nordeuropa-Institut der Humboldt-Universität, 2008.

Stern, Robert. *Hegel and the Phenomenology of Spirit.* London: Routledge, 2002.

Stetz, Margaret D. "Mrs. Linde, Feminism, and Women's Work, Then and Now." *Ibsen Studies*, vol. 7, no. 2 (2007): 150–168.

Stewart, Jon (ed.). *The Cultural Crisis of the Danish Golden Age: Heiberg, Martensen, and Kierkegaard.* Copenhagen: Museum Tusculanum Press, 2015.

Stewart, Jon (ed.). *The Heibergs and the Theater: Between Vaudeville, Romantic Comedy and National Drama.* Edited by Jon Stewart. Copenhagen: Museum Tusculanum Press, 2012.

Stewart, Jon (ed.). *Johan Ludvig Heiberg: Philosopher, Littérateur, Dramaturge, and Political Thinker.* Copenhagen: Museum Tusculanum Press, 2008.

Stewart, Jon. *A History of Hegelianism in Golden Age Denmark.* 2 vols. København: C. A. Reitzel's Publishers, 2007.

Stewart, Jon. *Kierkegaard's Relations to Hegel Reconsidered.* Cambridge: Cambridge University Press, 2003.

Straßner, Matthias. *Flöte und Pistole. Anmerkungen zum Verhältnis von Nietzsche und Ibsen*. Würzburg: Königshausen & Neumann, 2003.

Taylor, Charles. *Hegel*. Cambridge: Cambridge University Press, 1975.

Templeton, Joan. *Munch's Ibsen: A Painter's Visions of a Playwright*. Seattle: University of Washington Press, 2008.

Templeton, Joan. "The Doll House Backlash: Criticism, Feminism, and Ibsen." *PMLA*, vol. 104, no. 1 (1989): 28–40.

Templeton, Joan. "Of This Time, of This Place: Mrs. Alving's Ghosts and the Shape of the Tragedy." *PMLA*, vol. 101, no. 1 (1986): 57–68.

Tennant, P. F. D. "Ibsen as a Stage Craftsman." *The Modern Language Review*, vol. 34, no. 4 (1939): 557–568.

Timm, Mikael. *Lusten och Dämonerna. Boken om Bergman*. Stockholm: Norstedts, 2008.

Törnqvist, Egil. *The Serious Game: Ingmar Bergman as Stage Director*. Amsterdam: Amsterdam University Press, 2016.

Trouille, Mary Seidman. *Sexual Politics in the Enlightenment: Women Writers Read Rousseau*. Buffalo, NY: SUNY Press, 1997.

Van Laan, Thomas F. "Ibsen and Nietzsche." *Scandinavian Studies*, vol. 78, no. 3 (2001): 255–302.

Van Laan, Thomas F. "Generic Complexity in Ibsen's *An Enemy of the People*." *Comparative Drama*, vol. 20, no. 2 (1986): 95–114.

Van Laan, Thomas F. "The Ending of A Doll's House and Augier's Maître Guérin." *Comparative Drama*, vol. 17, 4 (1983/84): 297–317.

Vernant, Jean-Pierre, and Pierre Vidal-Naquet. *Myth and Tragedy in Ancient Greece*. Translated by Janet Lloyd. New York: Zone Books, 1988.

Vernant, Jean-Pierre, and Pierre Vidal-Naquet. *Myth et Tragédie en Grèce Ancienne*. Paris: Librairie Francois Maspero, 1972.

Vesterhus, Per. "Hvordan ble Osvald syk?" *Tidsskrift for Den norske Legeforening*, no. 13 (2007): 1814–1816.

Voltaire. *Philosophical Letters: Or, Letters Regarding the English Nation*. Edited by John Leigh. Translated by Prudence L. Steiner. Indianapolis: Hackett, 2007.

Voltaire. *Les Oeuvres complètes de Voltaire*. Geneve: Institut et Musee Voltaire, Geneve and University of Toronto Press, 1969.

Wærp, Lisbeth Pettersen. "Ibsen's Third Empire Reconsidered." In *Ibsens Kaiser und Galiläer. Quellen—Interpretationen—Rezeptionen*. Edited by Richard Faber and Helge Høibraaten. Würzburg: Königshausen & Neumann, 2011, 105–121.

Wærp, Lisbeth Pettersen. *Overgangens figurasjoner. En studie i Henrik Ibsens "Kejser og Galilæer" og "Når vi Døde Vågner."* Dissertation. Tromsø: Det humanistiske fakultet, 2000.

Weinstein, Arnold. *Northern Arts: The Breakthrough of Scandinavian Literature and Art, from Ibsen to Bergman*. Princeton: Princeton University Press, 2008.

Wellek, René. *A History of Modern Criticism, 1750–1950*. 4 vols. London: Jonathan Cape, 1966.

Wilamowitz-Moellendorff, Ulrich von. "Zukunftsphilologie." In Reich (ed.) 2013, 56–77.

Willems, Michèle. "Voltaire." In *Great Shakespeareans*, 18 vols. Edited by Peter Holland and Adrian Poole. Vol. 3. *Voltaire, Goethe, Schlegel, Coleridge*. Edited by Roger Paulin. London: Continuum, 2010, 5–43.

Williams, Simon. *Shakespeare on the German Stage*. 2 vols. Cambridge: Cambridge University Press, 1990.

Wirsing, Claudia. "Dialectics." In *The Oxford Handbook of German Philosophy in the Nineteenth Century*. Edited by Michael N. Forster and Kristin Gjesdal. Oxford: Oxford University Press, 2015, 651–674.

Young, Julian. *Nietzsche's Philosophy of Art*. Cambridge: Cambridge University Press, 1994.

Zangwill, Nick. "Nietzsche on Kant on Beauty and Disinterest." *History of Philosophy Quarterly*, vol. 30 (2013): 75–91.

Zola, Émile. "Naturalism in the Theatre." Translated by Albert Bermel. In *A Sourcebook on Naturalist Theatre*. Edited by Christopher Innes. London: Routledge, 2000 47–52.

Zola, Émile. *Le naturalisme au théâtre: les théories et les exemples*. 2004. http://www.gutenberg.org/files/13866/13866-h/13866-h.htm (Accessed June 2018).

Østerud, Erik. *Det borgerlige subjekt. Ibsen i teorihistorisk belysning*. Oslo: Novus forlag, 1981.

Index